OBJECT RELATIONS IN GESTALT THERAPY

OBJECT RELATIONS IN GESTALT THERAPY

Gilles Delisle

Translated from French by James Everett
with contributions from Michel Dandeneau, Marc-Simon Drouin,
Guilhème Pérodeau, and Dorothy Scicluna

LONDON AND NEW YORK

First published 2013 by
Karnac Books Ltd.

Published 2018 by Routledge
2 Park Square, Milton Park, Abingdon, Oxon OX14 4RN
711 Third Avenue, New York, NY 10017, USA

Routledge is an imprint of the Taylor & Francis Group, an informa business

Copyright © 2013 to Gilles Delisle for the edited collection, and to the individual authors for their contributions.

The rights of the contributors to be identified as the authors of this work have been asserted in accordance with §§ 77 and 78 of the Copyright Design and Patents Act 1988.

All rights reserved. No part of this book may be reprinted or reproduced or utilised in any form or by any electronic, mechanical, or other means, now known or hereafter invented, including photocopying and recording, or in any information storage or retrieval system, without permission in writing from the publishers.

Notice:
Product or corporate names may be trademarks or registered trademarks, and are used only for identification and explanation without intent to infringe.

British Library Cataloguing in Publication Data

A C.I.P. for this book is available from the British Library

ISBN-13: 9781780490359 (pbk)

Typeset by V Publishing Solutions Pvt Ltd., Chennai, India

CONTENTS

ABOUT THE AUTHOR ix

ABOUT THE CONTRIBUTING AUTHORS xi

INTRODUCTION xiii

PART I: HISTORICAL CONSIDERATIONS

CHAPTER ONE
Fifty years of Gestalt therapy 3

CHAPTER TWO
Theorising and knowledge in psychology 11

CHAPTER THREE
Integration in psychotherapy: epistemological and methodological considerations 15

CHAPTER FOUR
A comparative analysis of the Perls, Hefferline, and Goodman theory of Self and Fairbairn's endopsychic structure in terms of Greenberg and Mitchell's (1983) four fundamental problems 27

PART II: PROPOSITIONS FOR AN OBJECT RELATIONAL GESTALT THERAPY

CHAPTER FIVE
Epistemological and methodological preconditions
for a Gestalt therapeutic system   55

CHAPTER SIX
The linear-sequential vision of the Self in Perls, Hefferline,
and Goodman: a critique   61

CHAPTER SEVEN
The Self and object relations: a revision of Perls, Hefferline,
and Goodman   65

CHAPTER EIGHT
Gestalt psychotherapy: from object relations to hermeneutic
dialogue   103

CHAPTER NINE
Neuroscientific perspective of ORGT: neurodynamics
of the Self in therapeutic dialogue   125

CHAPTER TEN
ORGT and evidence-based practice   149
Marc-Simon Drouin

PART III: CASE STUDIES

Introduction to the case studies   165

CHAPTER ELEVEN
Bob   167
Michel Dandeneau

CHAPTER TWELVE
Brian   189
Guilhème Pérodeau

CHAPTER THIRTEEN
Jade   211
Dorothy Scicluna

APPENDIX   241

REFERENCES   245

INDEX   263

ABOUT THE AUTHOR

Gilles Delisle, Ph.D., is a clinical psychologist and associate professor of psychology at the University of Sherbrooke. He is director of clinical training at CIG in Montreal, and a guest trainer at several institutes abroad. He is the director of Neurogestalt, a specialist group in the International Neuropsychoanalysis Society. In 2010 he was appointed President of the State Advisory Council on Psychotherapy and was awarded the Noël-Mailloux Prize by the Quebec College of Psychologists in recognition of lifetime achievement in clinical psychology.

ABOUT THE CONTRIBUTING AUTHORS

Michel Dandeneau, Ph.D. is a clinical psychologist working in private practice in Ottawa, Ontario, Canada since 1991 where he offers individual and couple psychotherapy. He completed a Ph.D. in psychology at the University of Ottawa in 1990 where he was a part-time professor teaching courses in Abnormal Psychology, Human Sexuality, and Couple Therapy. Michel also supervised Master and Doctoral interns in individual and marital psychotherapy at the University of Ottawa and St-Paul's University. He completed his training in ORGT in 2009.

Marc-Simon Drouin, Ph.D. is a clinical psychologist, and full professor of psychology at Université du Québec à Montréal. He is also the director of the university's Centre for psychological services. He is fully trained in ORGT at CIG and is a clinical supervisor at the institute. He has done considerable work in the areas of outcome research in psychotherapy and on the impact of the therapist's own characteristics.

Guilhème Pérodeau, Ph.D. is currently a full professor in the Department of psychology at the University of Québec in Outaouais. She received her Ph.D. in Social Psychology from York University (Toronto, Canada). She did her post-doctoral training at the Douglas Hospital Research Center in Montreal. Dr. Pérodeau's research focuses on psychosocial correlates of the ageing process. As a registered psychologist, she supervises doctoral level trainees at the community mental health and training centre associated with the Department of Psychology at UQO. The psychology clinic provides a comprehensive range of outpatient services to children, family and adults living in the community. She currently holds a part-time private practice in Gatineau (Quebec).

Dorothy Scicluna, Ph.D. is a Clinical Psychologist and Psychotherapist in private practice. She obtained her bachelor's degree in Psychology and French at the University of Malta and immediately pursued with a Doctorate in Clinical Psychology at the University of Padova, Italy. Subsequently, she completed training to post-graduate diploma level in Gestalt Psychotherapy and eventually obtained a Diploma in Supervision. Her approach to psychotherapy and supervision is Integrative. Dorothy is specialized in the field of Eating Disorders. She is also the founder of **The Water Lily Centre** (www.waterlilycentre.com) which provides psychological and psychotherapeutic services for Anorexia Nervosa, Anxiety/OCD, Binge Eating, Bulimia Nervosa, Co-occurring disorders and Trauma Resolution.

INTRODUCTION

Any psychotherapeutic approach necessarily addresses one or several aspects of a disconcertingly complex human reality (Goldfried, 1982b; 1987; Lecomte & Castonguay, 1987; Mahrer, 1989; Norcross & Goldfried, 1992; Rychlak, 1993), and attention to some aspects necessarily implies negligence of others. As any theory evolves, its limits are progressively revealed by continuing contact with clinical reality, and at some point modifications must be made in order to more adequately fit the theory to that reality (Gedo, 1986). Historically, Gestalt therapy did not develop in that way, instead passing orally from one generation of therapists to another (Corbeil, 1992; Miller, 1988; Yontef, 1988). The printed heritage of Gestalt is scanty: in 1992, fifty years after its birth (Perls, 1942), only forty texts had been published in English (Forge, 1995) and of these, over ninety per cent are essentially an introduction to the subject. The theory of the Self (Perls, Hefferline, & Goodman, 1951), cornerstone of Gestalt therapy, has never been substantially revised (Delisle, 1990) in spite of the long-standing opinion of From, its chief exegete, that the theory of the Self was incomplete and needed development (From, 1984). Furthermore, contemporary clinical realities, particularly the thorny problems of personality disorders, have pushed the theory of 1951 to its limits, and challenge Gestalt therapists to more adequately adapt their clinical approaches to contemporary psychopathology. One promising avenue for this adjustment is the psychoanalytic theory of object relations (Bouchard & Derome, 1987; Yontef, 1988).

In spite of its poorly developed literature, Gestalt therapy remains a credible and widespread approach, whose evolution, diverging from its original theoretical positions, has been punctuated by ad hoc conceptual add-ons and insufficiently developed conceptual connections with neighbouring systems (From, 1984; Yontef, 1988b).

At the conceptual and clinical levels then, Gestalt therapists are in need of a systematic revision of their approach, in order to respond more adequately to today's clinical problems. But at the same time, contemporary psychotherapists have become increasingly aware of the importance and the pertinence of the contributions of neuroscience to an understanding of clinical problems, particularly personality disorders. A revision of Gestalt therapy that remains silent on this important discipline cannot be satisfactory.

There are three principal objectives to this book. First, we will propose a revised version of the Perls, Hefferline, and Goodman (1951) theory of the Self, a version more in tune with contemporary aspects of psychopathology. To achieve this revision of Gestalt therapy's theory of the Self, we turn to the psychoanalytic theory of object relations in order to integrate certain pertinent elements of Fairbairn's (1954) theory of object relations. This author is particularly important for our undertaking, because he is perhaps the only psychoanalyst who shares a unitary vision of consciousness with Perls et al. (Bouchard & Derome, 1987; Rubens, 1984; 1994).

Second, this revised theory of the Self will be integrated with a theory of Gestalt object relations psychotherapy. In order to give the reader a necessary historical perspective, we will first present the conceptual approaches of Gestalt, followed by an analysis comparing the Perls, Hefferline, and Goodman (1951) theory of the Self with Fairbairn's (1954) endopsychic structure theory. Following that, we will present a revision of Perls et al. that integrates certain elements of Fairbairn's theory, leading to a theory of Gestalt object relations psychotherapy.

Finally, we will explore the ways in which neuropsychology and the neurosciences can (1) contribute to a richer understanding of the nature of the problems seen in contemporary clinical practice, and (2) orient the therapist in the choice of intervention strategies that adequately take into account the biological reality of those problems. Several authors have recently given attention to possible links between the neurosciences and psychotherapy in general (Cozolino, 2002; Schore, 2003; 2003a): in this book, we will explore these possible links in the specific context of our revised theory of Gestalt psychotherapy.

PART I

HISTORICAL CONSIDERATIONS

CHAPTER ONE

Fifty years of Gestalt therapy

After four editions of his book, Maddi (1989) finally includes Gestalt therapy in his comparative analysis of theories of the personality. Even then, he considers it a recent approach and cites only three references to Perls: (1) *In and Out of the Garbage Pail* (1969), considered by some to be a simple autobiographical essay (Clarckson & Mackewn, 1993; Stoehr, 1994); (2) *Gestalt Therapy Verbatim* (1969); and (3) *Ego, Humor* (sic!) *and Aggression*, which he cites as 1969, although *Ego, Hunger and Aggression* was published in 1942. One can only conclude that the theory of Gestalt therapy is relatively unknown, if a recognized specialist in the field of theories of the personality fails to cite the fundamental 1951 reference (*Gestalt Ttherapy: Excitement and Growth in the Human Personality*) and if other important authors (Drapela, 1987; Hall & Lindszey, 1957; Pervin, 1990) completely ignore the approach.

In spite of its limited visibility, Gestalt therapy has made important contributions to clinical thinking and practice (Bergin & Garfield, 1991). The major contribution of Gestalt is the holistic perspective, the idea that the interrelations between objects and persons are such that no situation can be reduced to the simple sum of its parts. Consequently, Gestalt defends the notion, relatively new at that time (Perls, 1942;

1947; Perls, Hefferline & Goodman, 1951) that the real, here-and-now relationship is as important as transference (Clarckson & MacKewn, 1993, p. 87). For Yontef (1993), psychoanalysis, in recent developments, has clearly integrated many elements borrowed from humanistic psychology and Gestalt therapy, including recognition of the importance of the real relationship. Certain ideas developed by Perls and by Perls et al. have certainly been assimilated, whether consciously or unconsciously, by thinkers in the psychodynamic tradition, sometimes even being announced as their own original discoveries (Burgalières, 1992; Miller, 1988, 1991).

A rapid analysis of the scientific and clinical literature over the last twenty[1] years shows that innovative aspects of Gestalt therapy have been widely applied. As an example of a technical innovation, one can cite the well-known empty-chair technique, whose positive effects on interpersonal and intrapersonal blockages have been well documented (Clarke & Greenberg, 1986; Conoley, Conoley, McConnel & Kimzey, 1983; Goodman & Timko, 1976; Greenberg, 1980; Greenberg & Higgins, 1980; Greenberg, 1983;). The highly effective Gestalt dream analysis techniques have been widely appreciated (Alban & Groman, 1975; Dublin, 1976; Himelstein, 1984), while the "experiments", not to be confused with acting-out (Ginger, 1984), stimulate insight and favour a fuller, more sustained presence on the part of the client (Greenberg & Kahn, 1978). Globally, Gestalt therapy techniques help to counter schizoid withdrawal, narcissistic injury, and regression (Zarcone, 1984). They encourage spontaneity and deeper consciousness of physical sensations and sharpen the here-and-now experience (Ginger, 1984).

Additionally, many researchers and clinicians have applied Gestalt therapy to a diverse set of clinical syndromes such as eating disorders (Meyer, 1991; Pearce, 1988), sexual disorders (Mosher, 1977; 1979a; 1878b), post-traumatic stress (Besyner, 1985; Crump, 1984), speech disorders (Kaplan & Kaplan, 1978), and alcoholism (Buchbinder, 1986). Gestalt therapy has been successful with these disorders, and has been considered by some to be applicable even to the treatment of psychotic disorders, notably allowing schizophrenics to improve their perceptual processes and their hold on reality (Dublin, 1973; Gagnon, 1981; Serok & Zemet, 1983).

In spite of these successful applications, weaknesses in the underlying theoretical structures of Gestalt therapy have been roundly criticized, beginning with charges of conceptual ambiguities (Cadwallader, 1984; Crocker, 1983; Dolliver, 1981; Enns, 1987; Feder, 1978; From, 1984;

Masson, 1989; Peterson, 1977; Saner, 1984) and a lack of clear connections between theory and practice (Miller, 1985; Stoehr, 1992; 1994). These ambiguities, as well as the presence of inherent theoretical flaws, have been considered particularly troublesome in the long-term treatment of serious personality disorders (AQG, 1993; Yontef, 1988). Gestalt therapy has been accused of: (1) neglecting the interpersonal and the intersubjective (Cahalan, 1983; Hycner, 1985; Kovel, 1976; Lewis & Schilling, 1978); (2) underestimating the importance of unconscious processes in pathology (Bouchard, 1990; Bouchard & Derome, 1987; Davidove, 1991; Nevis, 1985); (3) not providing a satisfying conceptual framework for understanding the dynamics of transference and countertransference (Kovel, 1976; Tobin, 1982, 1983, 1985, 1990); and (4) considering cognitive processes as an obstacle to the body's inherent wisdom (Becker, 1982; Kovel, 1976).

Many prominent Gestalt therapists consider that these weaknesses are at least partially attributable to the absence of any theory of psychic development. Adequate treatment of developmental pathways and issues would provide a basis for an integration leading to a coherent global theory (Breshgold, 1989; Breshgold & Zahm, 1992; Polster, 1987; Yontef, 1988).

These criticisms are not all valid, and even to the extent that some may be justifiable, there is nothing in them that is fatally embarrassing for Gestalt theory. Some of them have prompted debate,[2] and while many proselytes of Gestalt continue to defend the theory of 1951 rather than develop it, our approach will be to develop the Gestalt theory of the Self, with a view to using the revised theory to attain a better understanding of the pathogenesis of personality disorders. Several influential American Gestalt therapists (Breshgold & Zahm, 1992; Tobin, 1982, 1990; Wheeler, 1991; Yontef, 1988) have called for this kind of revision, along the lines of making linkages between Gestalt therapy and contemporary psychoanalysis. Canadian Gestalt therapists have also contributed to the discussion: Burgalières (1991) remarking on the similarities between Cashdan's (1988) synthesis of object relations thinking and the classical texts of Gestalt therapy, and Bouchard and Derome (1987), as well as Bouchard (1990), showing the deep affinities between the theory of the Self of Perls, Hefferline, and Goodman and Fairbairn's theory of personality.

Gestalt therapy was created by psychoanalysts just after the Second World War, as a reaction to the rigidity of classical psychoanalysis (Yontef, 1988; 1993, p. 5). But it was not until 1951 that the theory was consolidated by the classical work of Perls, Hefferline, and Goodman, published in two parts: practical and theoretical. The theoretical text, written by Paul Goodman and based on a draft produced by Perls (Clarckson & MacKewn, 1993; L. Perls, 1993; Stoehr, 1994; Wysong & Rosenfeld, 1982), was a social-political critique of American conformity as well as a theory of the Self, this latter being inspired by the Field Theory of Lewin (1935) (Yontef, 1988). This remarkable combination of psychotherapy and socio-political criticism shows the clear influence of Paul Goodman's anarchist and libertarian values. The work is a rare pearl, uniting as it does the personal and the social, the private and the political. But its very range, impressive as it may be, has the effect of diluting the precision of the psychological analyses and of limiting understanding of the dynamics of pathogenesis.

The authors who gave Gestalt therapy its initial impetus (Perls, 1942; Perls, Hefferline & Goodman, 1951) did so essentially by rejecting the Freudian theory of consciousness which holds that psychic life is the product of the actions of various drives, actions which lead to the establishment of a differentiated and conflicted psychic apparatus. Perls et al. attacked the underlying idea of an individual as a closed system and proposed instead a meta-psychology derived from Field Theory, holding that any study of human beings must have, as its starting point, the Field composed of the organism and the environment. In so doing, they, as others (Fairbairn, 1954; Sullivan, 1950a), proposed a radical alternative to the Freudian view of the psyche. The energy of psychic life is not some drive or other, but rather the configuration of the Field itself. This rupture with Freudian thinking extended to other theoretical points. Concerning psychic structures, practically nothing would remain other than terms like "Ego" and "Id" to describe non-reified functional processes activated during cycles of contact. The Self for Gestalt therapists is no longer seen as a fixed institution, simultaneously an archive and an experiential generator, but rather a spatial-temporal "event" that "happens" only when there is an excitation at the contact boundary. For Gestalt therapists, not only the Self but even the Field is unitary, with the consequence that, contrary to common understanding, the distinctions between body, mind, and external world are simply inevitable illusions (Perls, Hefferline & Goodman, 1951, p. 50).

As for dynamic interactions within the Self, in the usual psychoanalytic meaning of the word, for Perls et al. there simply aren't any. If there is no structural differentiation within the psyche, then there cannot be entities participating in intra-psychic conflicts. One might see what could be described as an economic perspective, again in the psychoanalytic meaning of the word, in the contact cycle during which it goes from sensation to mobilization, action, toward a contact that "destroys the Figure", permitting a return to withdrawal, a "state of equilibrium". For most Gestalt therapists, this vision of the individual as a perfectly unified being, both physically and experientially, remains to this day as one of the richest and most convincing ideals of the ultimate goal of the therapeutic enterprise. Here, health is not defined as the simple absence of disease! However the analysis of pathology and its aetiology has been relatively neglected in the elaboration of Gestalt theory (Clarckson & MacKewn, 1993; Delisle, 1991; Yontef, 1988), and consequently today's clinicians lack conceptual tools. For example, From (1984) holds that narcissism can be understood through the concept of confluence—a deficient Self-environment differentiation. For Yontef (1988), a formulation as vague as this is simply useless in the clinical setting, especially in the absence of published supporting evidence.

The theory of the Self put forth by Paul Goodman in 1951 does not adequately explain the loss of unity and continuity which, for Gestalt theory, lies at the heart of all psychopathology. This man of letters, philosopher, and idealistic sociologist, saw the relationship between the human being and the environment in such a way that health is a normal state inherent in the former, and pathology is a deviation induced by the latter.

During the fifty year history of Gestalt therapy, many Gestalt therapists have ventured into the waters of the theoretical analysis of pathology (Clarckson & MacKewn, 1993; Delisle, 1991; Yontef, 1988), and some have specifically reflected upon approaches to deeply pathological manifestations such as narcissistic personalities and borderline personalities (Bouchard, 1990; Bouchard & Derome, 1987; Greenberg, 1989; Staemmler, 1993; Yontef, 1988). All those who have undertaken these ad hoc theoretical analyses recognise that Gestalt therapy in itself does not provide a conceptual framework that can satisfactorily explain these pathologies. Consequently, we feel that it is pertinent to develop dialogue with the object relations theory of W. Ronald D. Fairbairn so that Gestalt therapy can grow beyond being simply a general description of health and the means to improve it, and become a true therapeutic system with a conceptual framework that permits clinicians to understand individual differences and treat patients. These developments could in turn permit a clarification of the structure of the psyche according to Gestalt therapy, opening the door, ultimately, to a Gestalt theory of development. But even before attaining this ultimate goal, the exchange between Gestalt and Fairbairn should rapidly permit better links between theory and clinical practice for today's Gestalt therapist.

Our enterprise is thus an example of the integrative school of thought in psychotherapy, and more specifically of the so-called "unique" integration (Lecomte & Gastonguay, 1987). Although Gestalt therapy itself is historically a product of the integrative interest that continues today to inspire (Bouchard, 1985), Gestalt therapists remain wary of conceptual borrowing and technical eclecticism. Isadore From (1984) roundly condemned a simple-minded eclecticism that linked Gestalt therapy with just about anything, while at the same time implicitly recognizing the incomplete nature of the 1951 theory: "This theory and practice cannot be declared outdated by anyone without proof. Any developments of Gestalt therapy will be corollaries of this theory that needs to be developed" (1984, p. 141, cited by Bouchard & Derome, 1987). But where will these developments come from? For the reasons cited earlier, we find it pertinent to turn toward the theory of Fairbairn.

Product of another intellectual tradition, the theory of W.R.D. Fairbairn, underestimated and neglected during several decades, has returned to the forefront to throw considerable light on the development of personality as a function of early interpersonal relationships (Greenberg & Mitchell, 1983; Grotstein & Rinsley, 1994; Rubens, 1984). Distancing himself from classical psychoanalysis, Fairbairn proposes a radical paradigm shift in affirming that the libido is not essentially the search for pleasure, but instead the search for an object (1943; 1954, p. 31–33), that the Ego is present from birth and has its own energy (1954, p. 9), and that the Ego loses its original unity through processes of splitting and repression as a reaction to frustration.

As Bouchard and Derome (1987) have shown, Fairbairn and Goodman have parallel visions of the evolution of the Self. For both, the Ego/Self is unified at first, but loses this unity in an inevitable, pathological, but ultimately reversible process. In his most radical departure from classical psychoanalysis, Fairbairn holds that far from being the precondition for psychic growth, structural differentiation is a defensive and pathological developmental process (Rubens, 1984; 1994). For both Fairbairn and Goodman, the psyche is unified and has no need to become differentiated in order to develop in a healthy way.

But afterwards, the accent falls in different places: Goodman fixes his attention on the processes implicated in global health, while Fairbairn turns to an explanation of the loss of the early unity of the consciousness, and of the ensuing pathology. Would a simple combination of the two suffice as a revision of the Gestalt theory of the Self leading to a new theory of psychotherapy? As we shall see in the following chapter, it is important to address several fundamental issues when one goes about the business of integrating theories in psychology.

Notes

1. It was only in 1973 that the APA finally recognized GT as an independent entity rather than as a simple extension of Gestalt psychology (Simkin, 1978).
2. For example, the debate opposing Yontef and Tobin in 1982 and 1983 on fundamental questions relating to the theory of the Self and on possible links with Self-psychology.

CHAPTER TWO

Theorising and knowledge in psychology

According to Rennie, Phillips, and Quartaro (1988) there is a growing consensus to the effect that psychology has overestimated methodologically correct research to the detriment of thinking and creativity. As a result, theorising is less respected and known than trivial, busy-work empirical research (Bakan, 1967; Brandt, 1982; Endler, 1984; Gergen, 1982; Secord, 1982). In the same vein, Granger (1994) questions the indiscriminate use of the experimental method in clinical and social psychology, calling instead for an increased use of the potentially richer methods of observation and modelling. It should be pointed out that theorising is in no way easier than research. "(Theorising) demands a considerable effort of concentration, examination, and re-examination. It is the antithesis of casual reflection, lazy reading, and undisciplined speculation" (Gottfredson, 1983). Feyerabend (1975, p. 520) suggests that we all need a good dose of methodological anarchy to help us find new ideas!

What exactly is "theorising"? For Rychlak (1988, p. 250), we are speaking essentially of a series of two or more constructions for which we hypothesise, presume, or perhaps even demonstrate certain interrelationships. In the traditional philosophy of science, theorisation can have two contexts: discovery and justification (Reichenbach, 1953).

In the context of discovery, the ideas belonging to the theory are in a vague, informal state, while in justification, the ideas are more sharply defined and their logical links can be stated in a more explicit and systematic way. At this level, we have formal theory (Heinen, 1985). For the most part, psychological science has concentrated on justification and has considerably neglected discovery (Tzeng & Jackson, 1990, p. 101).

Our enterprise here can be characterised as a functional-deductive epistemology, within a context of discovery. While in the accumulation-induction tradition, theory can only be induced on the basis of an "accumulation" of observed facts, in the functional-deductive tradition, theory is seen essentially as a means of obtaining understanding, and can be in itself a more or less accurate representation of the real world. Theory in the functional-deductive sense has a two-way relationship with observed facts (Tzeng & Jackson, 1990). On the one hand, theory can have scientific pertinence in a heuristic sense, even when the theory is formulated before the accumulation of facts, for the theory can guide workers toward new facts. On the other hand, the elements of the theory must form a logically coherent whole, ultimately permitting empirical verification. As for method, we can consider method as the sum total of the means by which it can be determined if a theoretical construction or proposition can be considered true or false. Method is the vehicle that permits the exercise of verification (Rychlak, 1988, pp. 515–516). There are two formal means to demonstrate truth. The first is demonstration by validation. Here, truth is essentially established by the empirical demonstration, whereby a succession of events is predicted by an hypothesis, and verification of the succession indirectly verifies the hypothesis. The second formal means is procedural, and it is this means that we shall adopt to support our position. This form of demonstration is similar to proof by circumstantial evidence in law, in that one relies on arguments of coherence, plausibility, consistency, face validity, and internal logic (Rychlak, 1993, p. 934). In the absence of the "eyewitnesses" of empirical validation, procedural demonstration allows us to accept a proposition as true, on the grounds that in a globally coherent reality (which no one can question without abandoning science forever), a plausible and internally coherent theory has a clear right to at least provisional acceptance.

Table 1.

Context (Reichenbach, 1953)	Discovery		Justification	
Form (Tzeng & Jackson, 1990)	Functional/ deductive	Summative/ Inductive	Functional/ deductive	Summative/ inductive
Demonstration (Rychlak, 1993)	Demonstration or validation	Demonstration or validation	Demonstration or validation	Demonstration or validation

In conclusion, as we can see in Table 1, our exploration is a theoretical modelling within the context of discovery. We proceed with a functional-deductive epistemology and we aim to establish our positions by means of a procedure based on plausibility, internal consistency, logic, and coherence. As the objective of our enterprise is to integrate certain elements of one theory with the structure of another, we now turn to the specific procedure that we intend to apply to the context of theoretical integration in psychotherapy.

CHAPTER THREE

Integration in psychotherapy: epistemological and methodological considerations

In the first chapter, we saw that several authors had serious reservations about the theoretical foundations of Gestalt therapy. At the end of our review, we shared this critical perception and immediately dissociated ourselves from a defence of the 1951 theory that held that any "limits" found by critics were only a result of a superficial reading of the 1951 work. Monument though it may be, the Perls, Hefferline, and Goodman theory of the Self is not an untouchable museum piece in a glass box (Gagnon, 1993): it needs to be revised and extended (From, 1984, cited by Bouchard & Derome, 1987). Our aim here will be to revise the theory while at the same time respecting its characteristic conceptual structures, to complete it without denaturing it. To this end, we attack the central weakness of the theory, the absence of concepts necessary for an understanding of underlying pathologies, of development, and of individual differences. Gestalt therapy draws its strength from phenomenological roots that have an existential, humanistic colouring. This is the heritage that we must respect.

But then how can we follow the direction suggested by authors like Yontef (1988), Bouchard and Derome (1987), Bouchard (1990), and Wheeler (1991), who call for a dialogue with psychoanalytical object relations theorists coming from an entirely different intellectual and meta-psychological tradition? Here we must proceed with caution and in an orderly fashion, respecting certain essential methodological and epistemological criteria in order to ultimately obtain an acceptable result. It is not enough to simply place two ideas side by side and claim integration: one must take care when the ideas come from quite different visions of human nature.

Generally speaking, there are two ways to envisage the integration of different therapies (Goldfried, 1987). In the first, one seeks to identify elements common to the two approaches, operating on the assumption that these common elements correspond to firm realities that appear in spite of differences in the conceptual language of the two schools. Alternatively, one could seek complementary points, on the assumption that the two therapeutic orientations quite probably stress different aspects of human function and evolution. As a consequence, any intervention that seeks to be completely effective must take this complementary structure into account in order to exploit the wider range of therapeutic tools obtained when both therapeutic approaches are taken together. Even sceptics of eclecticism can agree with the idea that theories can be complementary in this way, and it is quite possible that, in general, theories are fundamentally complementary to each other rather than contradictory (Norcross, 1991). This is in fact the fundamental idea of systems: each orientation has its specific area of expertise and the various orientations can be affiliated in such a way as to reduce their weaknesses and maximise their strengths. Fensterheim (1983), for example, suggests that a therapist can use a psychoanalytical style to formulate hypotheses concerning his or her client's way of organising perceptions and concerning relationships between these perceptions and negative behaviours. But afterwards, a behavioural approach could be more effectively used to change undesired behaviours in a systematic and observable fashion (p. 26). We will be proceeding along the lines of this "complementary" vision of integration.

Apart from a few authors like Dollard and Miller (1950) or Wachtel (1977), it is generally agreed that integration in psychotherapy cannot be achieved by simply attempting to cobble together radically different theories of human nature (Franks, 1984; Franks & Wilson, 1979; Goldfried, 1980; 1982b; Krasner, 1978). For our purposes, then, it is important to repeat that Perls et al. and Fairbairn share essentially the same positive, "ideal" vision of human nature and in their works develop two complementary facets of this vision. Perls et al. (1951) concentrate on optimal human functioning, while the "tragic-realist" vision of Fairbairn (1954) concentrates on a description of inevitable pathologies. And Maddi (1989), in spite of his patchy comprehension of Gestalt theory, correctly describes both Gestalt therapy and the psychoanalysis of object relations as conforming to the same basic model of conflict.

Classical psychoanalysis does not appear to offer the same possibilities for integration as does Fairbairn's approach. According to Rubens (1984, 1994), practically all psychoanalytic theories base their vision of psychic growth on the biological model: growth is a progressive movement through levels of increasing complexity and structural differentiation. This is clearly the case for Freud, for whom growth implies structural differentiation of the Ego from the Id, and the Superego from the Ego.

> This metaphor is manifested in Freud's notion that psychic growth (and health) involves the differentiation of an ego, structurally separate from the id, and later a superego, precipitated out from the ego. It also stands at the root of the generally accepted belief that the self-object differentiation implies structural differentiation within the psyche and the unspoken underlying assumption that the process of self- and object representation is a structural one. (Rubens, 1994, p. 160)

Fairbairn is one of the rare psychoanalytic theorists, if not the only one, for whom healthy development does not imply a necessary psychic differentiation. The goal of differentiation for Fairbairn as well as for Perls et al., is the emergence of a personality that is distinct from the environment and for both these authors, optimal health is attained when conscious unity is maintained.

Enough has been said about the choice of theories that we will seek to integrate. We now turn to discussion of the ways in which we will examine possible conceptual contact points of these theories, to then bring about an integration that will enable us to ultimately formulate a theory of psychotherapy that will be a consistent product of the integrated theories. Unfortunately for our enterprise, integration of theories of psychotherapy is still a young art, and there is as yet no set of clearly established guidelines.

A consensus has been achieved, however, in support of the idea that neither extreme of traditional fragmentation or premature unification will wisely serve the field of psychotherapy or its clients. At present, we are in no position to judge, once and for all, which single theory, single technique, or single unification scheme is best. [...] Meantime, numerous psychotherapists are exploring and working toward integration in the Zeitgeist of informed pluralism. (Norcross & Newman, 1992, pp. 5–6)

Mahrer (1989) proposed a general model for the integration of psychotherapies that presents the flexibility that we consider particularly important. In addition, Mahrer's model recognizes (1) that pertinent theoretical construction can sometimes precede collection of all the relevant data, and (2) there is a necessary two-way "communication" between data and theory, as postulated by the functional-deductive epistemology that we mentioned earlier. In the absence of a tradition of time-tested formulae for the integration of theories, Mahrer appears to us to propose a relatively well-tooled conceptual workshop even though we will be adding other methodological tools as we proceed.

Mahrer begins with a critical distinction between a theory of human nature and a theory of psychotherapy, a distinction made by others as well (Frankl, 1984; Franks, 1984; Franks & Wilson, 1979; Goldfried, 1982b; Jacoby, 1975; Krasner, 1978; Mahrer, 1978a; Messer & Winnokur, 1984). Although there are a good number of theories of human nature, there are few true theories of psychotherapy. To be considered a true therapeutic system, an approach must address three levels of reality: (1) a theory of human nature; (2) a theory of psychotherapy that translates the general principles of this theory into a clinically applicable version of these principles; and (3) a set of operational, specific, and concrete clinical procedures. Our two general theories of the Self, that of Perls et al. (1951) as well as the endopsychic structure theory of Fairbairn, can both be considered theories of human nature.

At this point, a critical pause is in order. We have already shown that these two theories share a fundamental assumption concerning human nature, and that they develop complementary aspects of human functioning (health for Perls et al. and pathology for Fairbairn). How can we go about further judging the coherence, validity, and especially the compatibility of these two theories of human nature? Are there accepted conceptual tools that would allow us to make such judgements on a basis other than arbitrary personal preferences? Mahrer is silent on this point. After a century of psychological literature there is still no accepted theory that commands universal acceptance (Millon & Klerman, 1986; Rychlak, 1993; Tzeng & Jackson, 1990). Does this mean that a blind choice is as good as any? Not quite.

Workers who have wrestled with the compatibility issues surrounding the integration of theories have made contributions at three levels of approach. At the most abstract, general level, Maddi (1989) for instance critically analyses various theories of the personality as a function of their membership in certain axes or conceptual families. At an intermediate, "psychotherapeutic" level, Bugental and Bracke (1992) attempt to enrich the existential-humanistic perspective with contributions from the new psychoanalysis, and take pains to specify the criteria of conceptual importation, in order to preserve the essential characteristics of the existential perspective. Finally, at a more specific level and within the perspective of Gestalt therapy, Yontef (1988) is open to importing elements from the new psychoanalysis into Gestalt thinking, but also proposes a series of criteria to guide this integration while conserving the fundamental Gestalt vision of human nature. We will return below to a discussion of these criteria of integration; for the moment we can draw some general conclusions. At whatever level, from the most general (Maddi) to the most specific (Yontef), by way of an intermediate, psychotherapeutic level (Bugental & Bracke), integration is seen to be possible only when there is a compatibility between theories concerning their fundamental conceptions of human nature. Returning now to our concerns, and with respect to this first criterion of conceptual compatibility, we can say that although they belong historically to two traditionally opposed schools of thought, Gestalt therapy and Fairbairn accept clearly compatible visions of human nature. For instance, there can be no doubt concerning the existential roots of both approaches. Grotstein (1994) has clearly identified the existentialist in Fairbairn, and the influence of Sartre on Paul Goodman has never been questioned (L. Perls, 1993): Goodman himself, speaking of his contribution to the 1951 text, said: "I added a good deal of existenz to Gestalt psychoanalysis" (Stoehr, 1994, p. 105). (Later in his teachings, Goodman distanced himself from Sartre and his "subjective existential individualism", which he condemned as too self-centreed and liable to deviate into neurotic defences (Stoehr, 1994, p. 105)).

Both held that a person has, and is consciously aware of, the power to neutralize or eliminate various influences that could control his behaviour. For Perls et al., this power is that of the Self consciously escaping from disastrous loyalties (1951, p. 244). Fairbairn speaks in terms of infantile dependence developing into mature dependence (1954, p. 34). For Sartre, existence precedes essence, and a human being is a work in progress, the individual being defined by his or her acts. Perls et al. defined the Self as the system of contacts, the contact boundary in action, while for Fairbairn the psyche is a unitary and self-generated centre that has the potential and the drive toward self-expression in the real world of objects, as well as the capacity to experience that world, its own experience in the world, and the interaction between the two (Rubens, 1984, p. 106).

In his classification of formal theories of personality, Maddi (1989) places the Gestalt therapy of Perls et al. in the family he calls "conflictual", the conflict being of an intra-psychic nature. Some of Maddi's remarks concerning Gestalt therapy are puzzling, as when he speaks of the "Gestalt theory of development" although the vast majority of Gestaltists deplore the absence of an adequate theory of development in Gestalt therapy. On the other hand, in interpreting conflict according to Gestalt as a result of interactions among introjects, Maddi can preserve the Gestalt vision of the unitary Self and at the same time facilitate integration with an author like Fairbairn. Again, in speaking in a general way of object relations theories, Maddi sees them as theories of psycho-social conflict. One might reproach Maddi for sloppily classing together theorists as different as Klein, Fairbairn, and Kernberg. However, if we include in "psycho-social" the infant's relations with the real mother, it would seem fair to say that Fairbairn's theory of personality is constructed on the foundation of the conflict between the needs of the young infant and the mother's insufficient responses. Thus for Maddi, speaking generally, the personality theories of Gestalt therapy and Fairbairn have the same foundation: the conflict between the Self and the environment. All the same, it is a bit disconcerting to see how, for Maddi, the expected relations are inversed: instead of seeing a relational theory for Gestalt therapy and an intra-psychic theory for Fairbairn, Maddi presents the opposite relations.

In summary, we can confidently assert that the two theories that we will compare proceed from the same vision of human nature: thus, this critical precondition for theoretical integration has been satisfied. But does this initial compatibility extend to the same causal logic and explanatory conceptual framework. And if not, are these frameworks at least complementary?

In an article proposing a typology of causal frameworks, Rychlak (1993) holds that questions of complementarity in psychology must be discussed with reference to four frameworks of equal stature, each being irreducible to the others, and each capable of application to the explanation of a wide range of behaviours. Beginning with Aristotle's primary causes and applying them to various systems of knowledge Rychlak (1977) arrives at four fundamental and irreducible frameworks: Psysikos, Bios, Socius, and Logos. Physikos comes directly from physical science and is primarily applied to the explanation of physical processes such as gravity. For Physikos, there is no fundamental difference between the behaviour of animate and inanimate objects, both being subject to fields of energy and force. If we insist on distinguishing animate from inanimate, we arrive at Bios. Those who believe that free will has a physiological base, that human consciousness is contained within a biological system, establish their system within the Bios framework. When we think instead in terms of relationships and when, like Gergen (1989) we emphasize exogenous cultural factors rather than endogenous cognitive factors, we move into the Socius framework. Finally, Logos explains behaviour in terms of predicates, personal constructs, and mental operations in the sense of Brentano. Logos is established not in physical structures nor in social experiential structures, but rather in the ever-changing meanings that these take on in the conceptual constructions of human beings.

Unless he is attempting the impossible, anyone advancing a theory of human nature must necessarily opt for one particular fundamental base—an explanatory framework—within which he will develop his theory. In so doing, there is an implicit recognition that no one framework can adequately explain all facets of the subject. According to Rychlak, complementarities are necessary in psychology because these frameworks cannot be further reduced, one to another, than can the particle and wave of quantum physics. On the basis of their explanatory logics, Gestalt therapy proceeds from Bios, while Fairbairn's theory belongs more to Socius. In Gestalt, we have the first sentence of Perls et al. to the effect that

> Experience occurs at the boundary between the organism and its environment, primarily the skin surface and the other organs of sensory and motor response. Experience is the function of this boundary, and psychologically what is real are the "whole" configurations of this functioning, some meaning being achieved, some action completed. (Perls, Hefferline & Goodman, 1951, p. 267)

It might seem, however, that the concept of field that permeates their work is more compatible with Physikos, all the more so that for Perls et al., Bios is a function of the field. And even though these authors, in developing their ideas, come to treat other realities (one might wonder if they don't change frameworks to attribute pathology to Socius), their initial formulation is determinant, and accordingly we will consider that their framework is Physikos-Bios. As we advance in our critical analysis of Perls et al., we will uncover other fundamental elements of their argument that support our interpretation.

In his famous synopsis (1951; 1954; 1963) Fairbairn, after having refuted the Freudian idea that the libido is the search for pleasure (Bios), presents the keystone of his system in these words: "Any theory of ego development that is to be satisfactory must be conceived in terms of relationships with objects, and in particular relationships with objects which have been internalised during early life under the pressure of deprivation and frustration" (1954, p. 162). Thus for Fairbairn, development can be understood only in terms of objects internalised as a result of frustrations with real persons in the environment. We believe then, that Fairbairn places his theory in the irreducible framework of Socius.

These are the considerations that have led us to choose Fairbairn rather than another theorist, and to seek those elements of his theoretical system that could enrich and complete the theory of human nature that will be the foundation of Gestalt practice. These two theories have the same fundamental vision of human nature and see development as a function of conflict, from the perspective of two complementary explanatory frameworks. These first epistemological elements in place, we now turn to methodologies specific to integration in psychotherapy, in order to seek additional guidelines that will help us identify possibilities for integration for these two theoretical approaches.

As we stated earlier, integration in psychotherapy is still too young for it to have tested and accepted methodologies. Nevertheless, some pioneers have suggested an attitude favourable to theoretical integration.

For example, Wachtel (1984) recommends that we adopt an admiring but critical attitude with respect to each approach examined. Furthermore this same author, criticized by Messer and Winnokur (1980) for omitting crucial elements of psychoanalysis in his model of "cyclical psychodynamics", responds by saying that something must be done to improve the efficacy of psychotherapy, even if we do not as yet possess the means to achieve this end (Wachtel, 1984, p. 46).

Mahrer's (1989) model, mentioned earlier, could also guide our attempt at integration. Still recent, there is as yet no critical analysis of this model's feasibility. The author is respected, and in his preface to Mahrer's work, John C. Norcross, editor in chief of the Journal of Integrative and Eclectic Psychotherapy, leaves no doubt of the value of Mahrer's work in his eyes:

> I have met hundreds of people praising the merits of informed pluralism in psychotherapy and have read countless manuscripts advancing superordinate integrative frameworks. These proponents, however, have almost uniformly been oblivious to the underlying critical issue of how to integrate. They have consistently placed the proverbial cart before the proverbial horse. Not Al Mahrer. He strikes at the heart of the matter [...] Not surprisingly, he has provided one of the most enlightening books of psychotherapy integration I have ever read.

Mahrer's model has solid support and, even in the absence of a consensual scientific tradition in the literature, it appears to us to be a justifiable choice. We will be adding additional methodological tools as we proceed, but Mahrer will be our starting point.

Mahrer's model asserts that a theory of psychotherapy is valid only to the extent that it is firmly connected to a theory of human nature that gives it conceptual support and justification. If the theory of human nature at the heart of Gestalt therapy no longer adequately responds to current clinical realities, it is precisely because this theory is incomplete with respect to certain fundamental questions. We feel that the growing gap between the theory of 1951 and current Gestalt practice is not imputable only to the close-mindedness and intellectual negligence of its disciples; this gap is also, and especially, imputable to incoherencies and intrinsic shortcomings that we must try to correct before attempting to harmonise theory and practice. To effect these corrections we have chosen, for reasons given earlier, to analyse the points of similarity and correspondence between the theory of the Self of Perls et al. and the endopsychic structural theory of Fairbairn.

We will be working either from the original texts or from analyses and commentaries published in scientific and professional journals. In other words, we leave aside the oral tradition that has always been the principal means of transmitting the theory of Perls et al. Many have benefited from attending the reading seminars of Isadore From, one of the members of the first group of seven of the New York Institute. The opportunity of reading, in small doses, such a dense text as the theory of the Self, under the direction of a member of the inner circle, is an irreplaceable experience.[1] One penetrates the sense of obscure and difficult passages, one can question, criticise, and obtain answers. But in so going beyond the letter of the text in the context of a seminar, there is a strong temptation to improve, even idolise a work to which one has devoted so much energy to understanding. A difficult passage simply remains obscure to the average reader who does not have access to a living disciple. On the other hand, in oral transmission from disciple to novice, the obscure passages are interpreted in such a way as to receive, sometimes mistakenly, the benefit of the doubt. We feel that Gestalt theory must be defended solely on the basis of its written record; accordingly, we adopt the viewpoint of the serious but solitary reader.

Until now, we have concentrated on justifying our choice of Fairbairn as a source of elements to enrich Gestalt therapy. Now we turn to a consideration of the criteria that will serve to guide the comparative analysis that constitutes the first step in our theorising. In other words, what will be the principal subjects for discussion in the exchange between the two theories? We will opt for a choice that comes from Kuhn.

For Kuhn (1977), adherence to a theory of human nature begins with a metaphysical choice. A scientific community is defined by a common adherence to several complex beliefs and several conceptual commitments that collectively form a disciplinary matrix. Greenberg and Mitchell (1983) follow Kuhn in proposing that models in psychoanalysis are founded on metaphysical commitments with respect to four fundamental problems: (1) the basic unit for analysis; (2) motivation; (3) development; and (4) structure[2]. Authors can be placed in one or another school of thought according to their positions with respect to these questions. Although the position of Greenberg and Mitchell has been criticized for polarising the intra-psychic and the relational (Abend,

1988; Basch, 1987; Civin & Lombardi, 1990; Silverman, 1986), their work is still today a key reference for those interested in the development of thinking in the object relations school of psychoanalysis (Sutherland, 1994).

We think that this parsimonious organisation of elements that characterise a theory of human nature will permit us to adequately examine the positions both of Gestaltists and of Fairbairn, so that we can identify areas that will lend themselves to integration.

So much for the methodological and epistemological considerations worth discussing at this stage of our enterprise. We will develop them further in Part II, when it will be time to put down the bases of a Gestalt theory of object relations, and in Part III, where we will do a critical summary of all that has been said.

Notes

1. The author attended several seminars led by Isadore From, between 1979 and 1981.
2. This analytic grid is not particularly original, being essentially a synthesis of the classical dimensions of a theory of personality, perhaps more economical, if one compares it for example to Hall and Lindsey and their twenty-one criteria.

CHAPTER FOUR

A comparative analysis of the Perls, Hefferline, and Goodman theory of Self and Fairbairn's endopsychic structure in terms of Greenberg and Mitchell's (1983) four fundamental problems

We can now proceed to address each theory with four fundamental problems, beginning with Perls et al. followed by Fairbairn. A discussion follows, in terms of complementary and/or compatible conceptual relations between the theories, as well as possibilities for their integration.

The basic unit of analysis: what is initially present, what is developed later, what constitutes personality?

Perls, Hefferline, and Goodman

Gestalt therapy defines itself as the science and the applied techniques related to figure-ground relationships in the organism-environment field (Perls, Hefferline & Goodman, 1951, p. 36). Gestalt therapy is rooted in certain neo-psychanalytic theories, as well as Buberian existentialism and the dynamic field psychology of Lewin (Bouchard, 1985; Clarckson and MacKewn, 1993; Stoehr, 1994). The two generally recognized canonical texts of Gestalt therapy take marked exception to Freud's individualist psychology, which sees the Self as derived from the action of drives and where the environment has at best a marginal role. For Perls et al. in fact, any research of a biological, psychological, or sociological nature must necessarily begin by positing an interaction between the organism and the environment.

> It makes no sense to speak, for instance, of an animal that breathes without considering air and oxygen as part of its definition, or to speak of eating without mentioning food, or of seeing without light, or locomotion without gravity and supporting ground, or of speech without communicants. There is no single function of any animal that completes itself without objects and environment, whether one thinks of vegetative functions like nourishment and sexuality, or perceptual functions, or motor functions, or feeling, or reasoning. The meaning of anger involves a frustrating obstacle; the meaning of reasoning involves problems of practice. Let us call this interacting of organism and environment in any function the "organism/environment field"; and let us remember that no matter how we theorize about impulses, drives, etc., it is always to such an interacting field that we are referring, and not to an isolated animal. (p. 268)

For Perls et al., a person is inseparable from the field, and "contact between the organism and the environment is the simplest fundamental reality" (p. 1). Gestalt therapy's fundamental unit is thus contact (Bouchard, 1985; Robine, 1991; Yontef, 1993). The clarity of this fundamental unit is a strong point in the Gestalt conceptual structure, which is in turn defined as "the system of contacts at every instant" (p. 9) and again, as existing only where there is activity at the contact boundary. On the other hand, that which derives from the fundamental unit is less clear, as are the constituent parts of the personality according to Gestalt theory. According to Perls et al., the personality is no more than a function of the Self, appearing with language and shaped by object relations during the two first years of life (Bouchard & Derome, 1987). Gestalt therapy holds that manifestations of the Self are a function of the moment of contact. The Id appears during pre-contact, the Ego during the contact itself, and the personality appears only at post-contact. Personality is thought to be a verbal copy of the Self, "the basis on which one would explain one's behaviour, if explanation were to be demanded" (p. 134). This conceptualization of Personality is clearly one of Gestalt therapy's weak points. A strong personality is even thought to be indicative of a system of pre-determined responses, and as such, an indicator of pathology!

> In ideal circumstances the self does not have much personality. [...] Where the self has much personality, we have seen, it is because either it carries with it many unfinished situations, recurring inflexible attitudes, disastrous loyalties; or it has abdicated altogether and feels itself in the attitudes toward itself that it has introjected. (p. 499).

We thus find ourselves in a paradoxical situation with respect to our conceptual framework. On the one hand, the basic unit is clearly defined and forcefully affirmed: contact is the fundamental reality, the conceptual starting point. On the other hand, post-contact sequels are only sketchily developed. How does the individual evolve within and across contact episodes? How do these episodes come to ultimately give the personality its distinctive form?

Contact involves growth through creative adjustment, but there is seemingly no place for a stable sequel of this initial event. And what is worse, it would seem that the accumulation of contact sequels, which should appear in post-contact to enrich the personality, are in fact indicators of pathology. Thus we have one of the more confounding positions of Gestalt therapy: psychological health is marked by strong contacts with no accumulated sequels. In the following sections, we will return to this implicit position of Perls-Goodman.

Fairbairn's position

Fairbairn begins with Klein, but a version of Klein with Freudian drives essentially removed. It is not gratification, but rather the object that is the ultimate goal of libidinal striving. In other words, the object relation is primary, and drives are at the service of this relationship—the pleasure that results from tension reduction is secondary to the relationship, which has priority (Rubens, 1984, p. 430). In fact, Fairbairn considers that the pleasure principle is a deterioration (1954, p. 139), asserting that the object of psychoanalysis is not drives and their vicissitudes, but rather the critical events occurring in the context of the relationship with the mother, without which development is simply impossible (Moore & Fine, 1990). In fact, it is impossible to understand the individual isolated from his natural objects (Greenberg & Mitchell, 1983, p. 177); an attempt to do so would be simply senseless.

Fairbairn summarizes neatly: "From the point of view which I have now come to adopt, psychology may be said to resolve itself into a study of the relationships of the individual to his objects, whilst, in similar terms, psychopathology may be said to resolve itself more specifically into a study of the relationships of the ego to its internalized objects" (1954, p. 60).

Fairbairn replaced the closed systems and Lamarckianism of the nineteenth century with the concepts of open systems (developed in the middle of the twentieth century) in order to understand the development of living organisms, in which the contribution of the environment must always be considered (Sutherland, 1994, p. 17).

For Fairbairn, the basic unit of analysis is the Self in relation to another Self, as well as the nature of the connection between the two. Thus, the Self is to be understood as defined by, and existing in, the relationships that it maintains, that it remembers, that it desires, or that it creates. In Fairbairn's model, the Self's form grows and changes as it accumulates experiences in its relationships, which themselves change over time (Rubens, 1994, p. 153). Fairbairn's Self "seeks" to become the organizing agent of a person who remains conscious of the continuity of his past with his present and the imminent future, having a unique sentiment of himself in relation with others (Sutherland, 1994, p. 20).

Humanist and existentialist though he was (Grotstein, 1994, p. 118), Fairbairn always held that an understanding of personality must take into account its evolution from its biological roots. Those who, like Fairbairn, adopt a contemporary biological perspective, distance themselves from Freud, who constructed his theoretical system along the lines of the scientific thought of his day, notably on the thermodynamic model (Sutherland, 1994, p. 21). Post-Newtonian scientific thinking holds that living organisms are "wholes" greater than the sum of their parts. Their constant interactions with the environment permit transformations at any moment. In spite of these frequent and unpredictable transformations, they preserve their characteristic form by a process of self-regulation. And in spite of its continual renewal, the Self maintains its boundaries by means of self-bounding processes, avoiding dissolution and dislocation of its defining structures (Sutherland, 1994, p. 21).

Humans are social beings who survive not only by adaptation to their environment, but also by its creation (Sutherland, 1994, p. 22).

Discussion

For Perls et al., the basic unit of analysis is contact: for Fairbairn, it is the relationship. If we follow Yontef (1993, p. 274) in defining a relationship as a series of contacts over time, we can immediately see that the two notions are complementary, if not equivalent, the difference residing in the temporal "zoom" factor: the Gestalt therapists focus on the here-and-now micro-perspective, while Fairbairn takes in a wider macro-perspective of the contact. But there is a more important difference. Perls et al. consider the environment in a general way, while Fairbairn stresses the quality of the relationship with the mother.

Fairbairn's language reflects the thinking of the 1930's and 1940's that considered the mother as the only significant environment for the child, but, as we know now, the infant has multiple contacts with the environment from very early on, including several dyadic experiences other than the primary contact with the mother. More recent findings have shown (Zazzo, 1988, in Olivier, 1994) that the newborn needs not only milk, but also contact via all the senses and interactions with others, and also that the very young child is capable of subtle perceptions and rapidly adaptive behaviours—and therefore, of creative adjustments. These findings might seem, at first sight, to confirm certain ideas that Perls et al. could be thought to have anticipated, for instance that the newborn is already a complex organism, in a global relationship with a complex environment, and that theories that the mother-child relationship is the only significant element are oversimplifications based on prejudices present at the time. It remains true, however, that Gestalt therapy terminology, inspired by Field theory, reflects the notion that humans are only so many elements in the environment: this perception diminishes the crucial importance of what is specifically human in the environment.

Globally speaking, the two authors define "psychology" in nearly identical terms as the interaction of the organism with the environment, and both consider psychopathology as the interruption of interaction (Perls et al.) or as a withdrawal from the environment in order to confine interactions to internal objects (Fairbairn).

An integrated Perls et al./Fairbairn theory sees the person as the product of continued interpersonal contact, and therefore as a result of a stabilisation of the elements that constitute adequate contact. Finally, the theory would recognize the capacity of the newborn to establish multiple dyadic relations.

Motivation: what do human beings want, what are the predominant goals underlying human life?

Perls, Hefferline, and Goodman

The person is an organism interacting with the field and "… let us not forget that when we speak of impulses, desires, etc., we are always speaking of this interactive field and not of an isolated animal." (Perls, Hefferline & Goodman, p. 2). Here we have the critical theoretical context outside of which any discussion of motivation in Gestalt therapy theory is a non-starter. Perls et al. do not think of motivation in a sequential structure, in which there is first an intrinsic need and then an environment offering more or less satisfactory possibilities of satisfying that need. The environment is not simply there waiting for the person; it is rather that the person is formed from the environment. From the very beginning, there is a biologically-based adjustment between the organism and the environment, and the fundamental sense of human life is to maintain this adjustment. Any instability in these adjustments is detected by the Self functioning in the "Id" modality. Development's driving force takes the form of the satisfaction of needs that emerge from the Id's functioning—we call this the "completion of contact cycles", or the "completion of figures".

For the Gestaltist, motivation cannot be understood without reference to perception: we perceive the world in terms of our interests. "In the sequence of ground and figure, the emotions take over the motivational force of the urges and appetites; but the motivation, made definite by its objective reference, is thereby stronger" (p. 477).

Gestalt therapy tends to see motivation in dynamic, "process" terms, rather than focusing attention on the particular nature or relative importance of one need or desire as opposed to another. However, in his earliest writings, Perls (1942) criticised Freud for having neglected hunger as the fundamental drive. Perls used the hunger sensation as a metaphor for contact with the environment, even drawing a parallel between physical metabolism and the mental metabolism that is central to Gestalt therapy's theory of human nature. Even earlier, in 1936, he wrote "Oral resistances", which he presented to the International Congress of Psychoanalysis. This text, a precursor of his book *Ego, Hunger, and Aggression*, proposed that the newborn's initial relation to the world is structured by feeding behaviours. It is thought that this interest was awakened and documented essentially by Laura while she nursed Renate, their first child (Clarckson & MacKewn, 1993; L. Perls, 1993). In any case, this emphasis on hunger was largely abandoned in the 1951 text: Perls et al. adopted a more general and fundamental position, concentrating their attention on the dynamics of exchanges at the contact boundary, rather than on their content. Even so, one can sense that the metaphor of growth by alimentary assimilation persists as their preferred illustrative metaphor:

> Now what is selected and assimilated is always novel; the organism persists by assimilating the novel, by change and growth. For instance, food, as Aristotle used to say, is what is "unlike" that can become "like"; and in the process of assimilation the organism is in turned changed. Primarily, contact is the awareness of, and behaviour toward, the assimilable novelty; and the rejection of the unassimilable novelty. (1951, p. 270)

Fairbairn's position

For Fairbairn, motivation theory is at the heart of the conceptual rupture with Freud and Klein (Mitchell, 1994). Although the Freudian notion of "libido" is retained, for Fairbairn this means not pleasure-seeking, but rather object-seeking: the goal is not to discharge energy but rather to establish satisfactory relationships. From the beginning, the infant is turned toward external reality. Contemporary readers of Fairbairn's work seem to have opposing interpretations concerning the nature of motivational forces in his system. Greenberg and Mitchell (1983, p. 154) as well as Rubens (1994, p. 430) find that pleasure, in Fairbairn's work, is a means and not an end. Kernberg (1994, p. 41) rejects the notion that the pleasurable aspects are merely consequences of object relations, attributing this idea to a misinterpretation on the part of Guntrip. For Perls et al., "assimilation" is used in the technical sense of integration with pre-existing biological or psychological structures, and should not be confused with Piaget's use of the term, that is, "a psychological mechanism that modifies external data by a set of actions which, when coordinated, constitute an assimilation schema, a stable, reproducible structure able to incorporate new objects and events" (Vurpillot, 1992).

Fairbairn (1954) contests the Freudian idea that the newborn is motivated by drives anchored in erogenous zones: these zones are instead simply the channels that lead to the object relation. In fact, when pleasure becomes the primary motivation, it is a sign of trouble, a failure in the capacity to establish and maintain rich relationships with others, relationships in which the personality of the other furnishes a more profound satisfaction than using the other for one's own pleasure (Sutherland, 1994, p. 18).

Discussion

Our two theories address "motivation" from different angles, but in complementary ways. For Perls et al., Field dynamics are in the forefront, regardless of the nature of motivation. Since no biological or psychological function can be defined other than as a function of the Field, it becomes meaningless to speculate on the pre-eminence of this or that particular motivation. Does a motivation begin with a fundamental drive that seeks only to use the object to reduce the underlying tension that generates that drive? Or does it rather begin with an object, whose perception creates a desire for contact? If the Self is not a fixed entity, but "sight that sees something" and "touch that touches something" (1951, p. 123), it would seem to follow that the libido is "energy that finds something". These formulations are characteristic of the Physikos component of the Perls et al. position. Does the libido use the object, or does the object create the libido? For Perls et al. the question is badly formulated and unanswerable. Accordingly, there is no substantial discussion of the relative pre-eminence of desires, drives, or needs. Perls et al. propose a process theory, in which specific contents are rarely, if ever, discussed.

Fairbairn, on the other hand, is very specific on motivational contents and on the structural aspects (libidinal and antilibidinal Self) that they produce. For Fairbairn in fact, motivational content is at the very heart of the break from Freudian and Kleinian concepts. Fairbairn emphasises the pre-eminence of relationship over drive. Any understanding or criticism of Fairbairn must begin with recognition of this epistemological (or metaphysical, as Greenberg and Mitchell (1983) would say) foundation.

According to the epistemological perspective that we have adopted, it would be impossible to integrate two theories that postulate contradictory aspects situated at the same conceptual level, for example, pre-eminence of drive as opposed to pre-eminence of the relation. As the differences between Perls et al. and Fairbairn are at different conceptual levels, we can proceed to integrate these two points of view in one conceptual structure. But for that, we must examine the question of the processes that permit contact motivation in the Field to engender a human relationship that, in its meaning and duration, goes beyond immediate experience to contribute to a unique Self.

Development: what are the crucial steps that bring the newborn to adult life?

Perls-Goodman

As we have already noted, although Perls gave cursory attention to questions of development in his 1942 text, this notion has disappeared by 1951. True, one can sense throughout the various Gestalt therapy texts, the recurring presence of the "hunger" metaphor of development, but apart from this there is no explicit treatment of development, as many critics have noted. One can only speculate as to the reason for this surprising omission, since Perls had obviously given the question some thought, and it seems unlikely that an author as rigorous as Goodman would have arbitrarily neglected such an important issue. And in fact, a chapter in 1951 addressed the question of the development of the human species ("Human nature and the anthropology of neurosis"), suggesting that these questions had attracted Goodman's attention. More plausibly, one could suppose that the non-analytical roots of the 1951 theory have something to do with the refusal to present a theory of development, and it is possible that the implicit grounding of the theory in a biological framework made it difficult to elaborate concepts that would contribute to the understanding of the neglected area of individual differences, as pointed out by Maddi (1989).

Fairbairn's position

Fairbairn gives detailed attention to development, and especially the development of pathology (Friedman, 1975; Robbins, 1980, 1996; Greenberg & Mitchell, 1983; Grotstein, 1991, 1994), although the transition from infantile dependency to maturity has been considered the weak point in his treatment of the subject (Sutherland, 1994, p. 20).

Familiar with the work of Klein on the developmental role of the object, and with Freud's notion of the Superego as the internalization of parental objects, Fairbairn went on to propose a theory of development based on object relations. As Bouchard (1990) aptly points out, Fairbairn considers real relationships to be more important than fantasised relationships for development.

The apparent chaos and disorganised behaviours of the first months of life are not a reflection of some sort of primary narcissism or of an autoerotic stage in which the newborn turns toward the object for the unique purpose of satisfying his needs. These apparently disorganised behaviours are simply a reflection of inexperience. In the absence of pre-programmed behavioural schemata, the newborn needs time to learn how to make contact and organise his relationship with his mother (Greenberg & Mitchell, 1983, p. 156).

In Fairbairn's object relation model of development, the evolving nature of interactions with the mother replaces the rigid Freudian progression of oral, anal, and phallic stages. For Fairbairn, the erogenous zones are nothing more than the channels by which the object relationship is established and maintained. Every child progresses along a continuum, from infantile dependency (in which these channels provide the privileged connections of the relationship) to mature dependency. This last stage of psychic development is characterised by an interpersonal life that reflects intrapsychic life, characterised by reciprocity, the recognition of differences, and the acceptance of healthy dependence.

The Ego, then, develops as infantile dependency (based on primary identification with the object) gives way to mature dependency (based on the differentiation of self and object) (Fairbairn, 1954, p. 163). This evolution is marked by three phases: infantile dependency that corresponds more or less to Abraham's (1954, p. 32) oral phase, a transitional phase, and a phase of mature dependency that corresponds to the genital phase. At first, the infant is in a state of psychological fusion with the parent, relatively undifferentiated and with only an embryonic sense of Self. He must internalise external objects composed of both good and bad, satisfactory and unsatisfactory aspects.

Negative aspects of objects are internalised by introjection. Why does the child internalise something that is bad—why not just spit it out?

Here is Fairbairn's (1954) answer, in a passage that seems to us crucial for any revision of the Gestalt therapy theory of Self:

> At this point it is worth considering whence bad objects derive their power over the individual. If the child's objects are bad, how does he ever come to internalise them? Why does he not simply reject them as he might reject "bad" cornflour pudding or "bad" castor oil? As a matter of fact, the child usually experiences considerable difficulty in rejecting castor oil, as some of us may know from personal experience. He would reject it if he could; but he is allowed no opportunity to do so. The same applies to his bad objects. However much he may want to reject them, he cannot get away from them. They force themselves upon him; and he cannot resist them because they have power over him. He is accordingly compelled to internalise them in an effort to control them. But, in attempting to control them in this way, he is internalising objects which have wielded power over him in the external world; and these objects retain their prestige for power over him in the inner world. In a word, he is "possessed" by them, as if by evil spirits. This is not all, however. The child not only internalises his bad objects because they force themselves upon him and he seeks to control them, but also, and above all, because he needs them. If a child's parents are bad objects, he cannot reject them, even if they do not force themselves upon him; for he cannot do without them. Even if they neglect him, he cannot reject them; for, if they neglect him, his need for them is increased. (1954, p. 67)

Once the negative object is internalised, the negativity is within the child, and his environment is safe. The internalised negative objects are then repressed. Fairbairn speaks of two negative objects: "conditional" (morally negative) and "unconditional" (libidinally negative). Unconditionally negative objects are internalised as persecutors and, to the extent that the child identifies with these objects, he also is "bad". To correct this unconditionally bad situation, he internalises positive objects, which then become the Superego.

At this stage, an internal wrestling-match begins, opposing good and evil. When the good has the upper hand, the child is conditionally good, but when evil dominates, he is conditionally evil—but that is better than being unconditionally evil for, as Fairbairn (p. 71) remarks, it's better to be a sinner in Heaven than an official citizen in Hell! At least the world around us is basically good and there is hope. In the same vein, one might imagine a continuum ranging from unconditionally good (Heaven) to unconditionally evil (Hell), passing through conditionally good (state of grace) and conditionally evil (sin).

If repression fails, the Ego can adopt one of four classic defences: obsession, hysteria, phobia, and paranoia.

The Self, healthy or pathological, can therefore be seen as emerging from a pattern of relations between various parts of the Ego and its objects. For Fairbairn, there are two criteria of emotional maturity. The first concerns the relationship with external reality: for Fairbairn, the question is not whether the reality principle has triumphed over the pleasure principle, but rather if the initial, immature reality principle has evolved into more mature form. The second criterion concerns the cohesion of the Ego, and here the question is not whether the Ego is capable of controlling drives according to the reality principle, but rather if the Ego, source of the drive's tension, is itself structured according to the reality principle, for if not, it is the pleasure principle that will structure the Ego. The Ego continually maintains connections with, and hopes about, internal objects, and thus stalls development in a pathological state. In other words, pathology can be defined as attachment to internal objects (1954, p. 121). Split off internal objects can considerably deform development, and this deformation is not sufficiently developed by Fairbairn (Sutherland, 1994, p. 27).

To sum up: the essence of maturity is the capacity to develop rich intimate, reciprocal relations with others. Psychopathology is a result of interruptions in the natural sequence of the development of relations, compensated by a proliferation of relations with internal objects (Greenberg & Mitchell, 1983, pp. 157–160).

Discussion

For Fairbairn, relations with external reality—Perls et al. would say at the contact boundary—constitute the essence of psychic development. In these relations, the infant must learn how to make contact. Rudimentary capacities for contact must mature in an adequate environment for optimal development. During this process, the erogenous zones described by Abraham are simply the channels—Gestalt therapists would say "contact functions"—by which the relationship to the external object is established and maintained. Optimal development is characterised by an interpersonal life of reciprocity, exchanges, recognition of differences, and acceptance of healthy dependence. Perls et al. would entirely agree with this, speaking of exchanges at the contact boundary that are clarified by awareness of that same boundary, and therefore of the differences on both sides of the contact.

As for healthy dependence, Perls et al. do not really have much to say. Is this because their physical-biological framework does not readily lend itself to this sort of discussion? In any case, in the "Perlsian" version of Gestalt therapy and its corresponding value system (for instance, the "Gestalt Prayer"), healthy dependence never had the same developmental importance as for Fairbairn.

For Fairbairn, the young infant encounters essentially indivisible objects, having good and bad, or satisfying/unsatisfying qualities. These objects must be separated into their constituent parts and then assimilated, by absorbing the nutritious elements and rejecting the toxic ones. But for Fairbairn, it is precisely the toxic elements that are internalised by introjection. Why does the child introject toxic elements instead of rejecting them? In the Gestalt therapy theory of the Self, as well as in Perls' first (1942) text, the answer lies in the conception of introjection as the initial mode of interaction at the contact boundary. The newborn, who does not as yet possess his "organ of oral aggression" (teeth) has no choice but to introject completely nourishment given by the maternal figure. This nourishment is "presumed" to be good, because it maintains the organism in a functional state and permits growth. By a logical development within the biological framework, psychic operations at the contact boundary are seen as having the same form: the natural process is to introject the good and reject the bad, the contrary being pathological. But for Fairbairn, on the contrary, there is no need to introject good elements; it is rather the bad elements that need to be introjected. First, the introjection purifies the environment because the evil is taken within, permitting the child to live in pure surroundings ("It's better to be a sinner in Heaven than to live in Hell", which would be ultimate hopelessness). Second, as the evil is within, the child hopes to master and transform it, before returning it to the world of reality. This could correspond to a clinical reality that therapists can often see (taking the blame as a way of protecting the object), but that could not find a place in the somewhat "hedonistic" picture of Goodman's Self.

The two viewpoints seem to have compatible visions of pathology. For Fairbairn, the efforts of the Ego to maintain relationships and hopes regarding internal objects are responsible for pathology. In other words, pathology is defined as attachment to internal objects, maintaining disastrous loyalties. It is characterized by interruptions in the normal sequence of relations, and by a proliferation of relationships with compensatory internal objects. For Perls et al., psychopathology is defined as the study of interruptions in the process of contact. Reference to Fairbairn could lead to a better understanding of the phenomenology and the psychodynamics of these interruptions, which were more denounced than analyzed in the 1951 text.

Both Fairbairn and Perls et al. reject the concept of repetition compulsion in the Freudian sense. While Fairbairn simply observes that split-off internalised objects can deform development (a question that Sutherland (1994) sees as needing further elaboration), Perls et al. emphasize the processes at the contact boundary that permit the Self's continued existence or transformation. The concepts of emergence and figure/ground should in principle provide adequate tools for the establishment of structural similarities between the theory of Gestalt therapy and Fairbairn's theory of internalised objects.

And health? Although Fairbairn states that the individual seeks good relationships that are essential for healthy development, he does not discuss the lasting impacts of positive experiences, nor the establishment of healthy identifications and authentic values. Finally, in 1984 Rubens published an important text on the meaning of structure in Fairbairn's theory, in which he holds that these impacts must be understood as non-structuring internalisations. (We will return to this notion in our discussion of structure). As Perls et al. more explicitly address the question of optimal health, we can find a more detailed discussion of the fate of these internalisations. They are assimilated to the Self in the post-contact phase and nourish the personality function. Fairbairn does, however, treat the question of healthy development, in which the parents represent the primary actors in the environment, filling certain developmental functions such as satisfying infantile dependence, encouraging separation, establishing limits, introducing the child to the world. Perls et al. give no such recognition to the parents, and for them the environment is seen as either passive or as an obstacle: the parents are simply elements of the environment. Doubtless, here is a question for an integrated theory to answer: how to recognize the predominant role of the parents as first objects, without favouring attachment to "good" internal objects, an attachment that could impede development toward adulthood.

In fact, for both theories, the ideally healthy adult would have no need for attachment to compensatory internal objects: his energy would be completely available for contact and exchanges with real individuals in his environment. But while Goodman remains silent about this utopian aspect, Fairbairn notes that such an ideal state of health is only a theoretical possibility (Greenberg & Mitchell, 1983, p. 161).

Structure: what is the nature of that which gives a person his distinctiveness, regulates his behaviours, life-events, and relations which others, and mediates the impact of the past on current experiences?

Perls, Hefferline, and Goodman

The theory of the Self, as initially presented by Perls in 1942 and then developed by Perls, Hefferline and Goodman in 1951, is based on a fundamental principle of field theory: structure is indissociable from process (Yontef, 1983). Perls et al.'s version of the Self has three functions, of which two have Freudian connotations: the Ego and the Id. However, while Freud saw the psyche as a structure shaped by the action of drives, Perls et al. rapidly distance themselves from this structural perspective, as well as the idea of a psychic "apparatus" (Yontef, 1988), by positing a unitary vision of conscience (Bouchard, 1985). Conscience is itself seen as being the result of the hiatus between the perceived situation and the creative adjustment to the situation. The processes that are produced and that occur during the creative adjustment give rise to characteristic human perceptions of a body, a mind, and an external reality, all three of which are in fact inevitable illusions.

The Self is, for Perls et al., more a spatial-temporal event than a fixed structure that is simultaneously an archive and a generator. The Self is a field phenomenon, and Gestalt therapists go so far as to employ quantitative terms ("more" or "less" Self) consistent with this non-structural conception of the psyche. As a Field phenomenon, the Self is activated only during contact. As shown if Figure 1, the Self's Id function, producing emerging content, appears during the pre-contact; the Ego function, that identifies and sorts the emerging content appears during the contact; and Personality appears during post-contact.

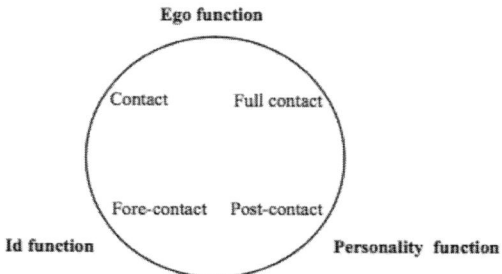

Figure 1. The Self in Perls et al. (1951).

In optimal contacts, one would see only a unified Self, repeatedly regenerated by contact, continuing smoothly along unencumbered by useless existential baggage. In this purified vision of the Self, the cumulative aspect of personality renders the very concept almost suspect, and in fact when Perls et al. discuss personality, the function responsible for contact residues, their position is ambiguous. In a theory of the Self conceived in terms of field dynamics, Personality seems to be oddly out of place, and the authors seemed to have little choice but to minimize its importance:

In ideal circumstances the self does not have much personality. […] Where the self has much personality, we have seen, it is because either it carries with it many unfinished situations, recurring inflexible attitudes, disastrous loyalties; or it has abdicated altogether and feels itself in the attitudes toward itself that it has introjected. (p. 499)

The Personality is the system of attitudes assumed in interpersonal relations; is the assumption of what one is, serving as the ground on which one could explain one's behaviour, if the explanation were asked for. When the interpersonal behaviour is neurotic, the personality consists of a number of mistaken concepts of oneself, introjects, ego-ideals, masks, etc. But when the therapy is concluded (and the same holds for any method of therapy), the Personality is a kind of framework of attitudes, understood by oneself, than can be used for every kind of interpersonal behaviour. In the nature of the case, this is the ultimate achievement of a psychoanalytic interview; and the result is that the 'free' structure thus achieved is taken by the theorists to be the Self. […] But the Personality is essentially a verbal replica of the self; it is that which answers a question or a self-question. (pp. 445–456)

Although the 1951 text contains several references to processes long considered by different schools of psychoanalysis to be crucial for development of the complex psyche, Perls et al. recognise only the distinction between the organism and the environment and not the structural differentiation so dear to most psychoanalytic theorists (Rubens, 1984, p. 433).

Fairbairn's position

Unlike many psychoanalysts, Fairbairn does not hold that normal development implies differentiated internal structures (Bouchard, 1990; Rubens, 1984, 1994). Instead, a unitary Ego is there from the very beginning. The earliest defence (against frustration) is introjection of the bad object; therefore it is clear that the newborn is already capable of defences and object relations. For Fairbairn, the Ego does not evolve from the Id as a result of contact with external reality, but is present from birth as a dynamic entity with its own energy. In fact, the idea of an Ego-structure without its own energy is a contradiction, since the earliest human activities are simultaneously structured and energised (Greenberg & Mitchell, 1983, p. 155). Because it exists from the very beginning, the "whole" has a simple form, a position also held by Lichtenstein (1977). Every organism is "whole", and yet creates other "wholes" for survival. Fairbairn always recognized the existence of these other unified "wholes" (Sutherland, 1994, p. 24).

Fairbairn arrives at a concept comparable to the Freudian trilogy of Id-Ego-Superego, a fundamental psychic structure for which he conserves the term "Ego". The Ego for Fairbairn is a unitary structure oriented toward external reality, with its own energy, and seeking from the beginning a relation to the object (the breast, or the mother). Psychic development proceeds from this primitive Ego which will become differentiated into specialised functions attached to partial objects, through processes of internalisation, splitting, and repression of the maternal object. Thus, in the place of the Freudian trilogy of Id-Ego-Superego, Fairbairn proposes the trilogy Central Ego-Antilibidinal Ego-Libidinal Ego. As a result of inevitable and necessary privations, the child internalises an object that is simultaneously satisfying and unsatisfying, therefore good and bad. Ambivalence and anxiety arise, the sense of security is threatened, and defensive reactions become necessary.

At this point the universal and pathological phenomenon of splitting appears, as a necessary means of surviving the turbulence of early development. Splitting both divides and organises the Self. This division permits the Self to separate the agreeable from the disagreeable, packaging each in circumscribed regions which are then attached to the corresponding parts of the divided Ego. The internal world is born. Partial or complete objects can then be repressed and/or projected upon external objects, modulating the exchange between external reality and the internal world, as a function of the state of the latter.

What is the origin of the Self's partial objects? The mother (or rather, the mother's breast) is what Fairbairn calls an undivided, original object. This object is then divided in two parts as a consequence of the love and hate experienced by the infant, and these parts are introjected into the developing self. The frustrating (exciting) object grows out of interactions with a mother who teases and tempts the child. And when the child (later, the adult) is in relationship with the internalised frustrating object, the dominant experience is frustration and emptiness. As for the Rejecting Object, it is created through interactions with the hostile and/or distant parts of the mother. The dominant experience of the child, and later the adult, in contact with this internalised Rejecting Object, is the sense of not being loved or desired, and the accompanying emotion is anger. There remains a desexualised core called the ideal object, which contains the comforting and gratifying aspects of the breast. The Ego has a libidinal attachment to the object, since it is the libido, or the intrinsic energy of the Ego, that permits it to find the object and connect to it. Because of this attachment, when the object is split, the Ego is split as well. The pre-conscious and unconscious internal world becomes stabilised in a system where components of the split Ego are paired with their split partial objects. The Original Ego is thus transformed, becoming a tripartite structure formed of subsidiary Egos paired with split objects, as shown in Figure 2, reproduced from Bouchard and Derome (1987).

The Central Ego, residue of the Original Ego, is an agent of repression, responsible for relations with objects in reality: Fairbairn calls it the "I". Although Fairbairn speaks primarily of its conscious elements (Moore & Fine, 1990), it also contains preconscious and unconscious components. The Libidinal Ego is a part of the Original Ego that is split-off and repressed, as a consequence of the splitting of the object: it is in a libidinal relationship with the Exciting Object. The presence of the

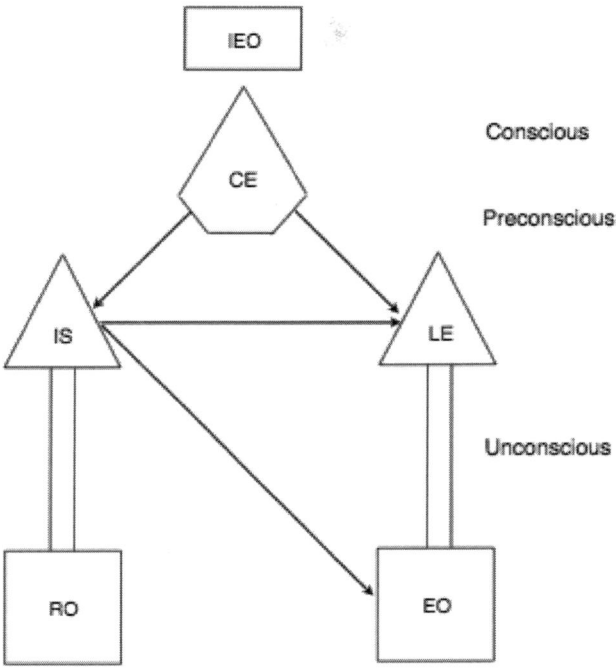

Figure 2. A revised schema of the psyche, adapted from Fairbain (1944 and 1954).
IS = Internal saboteur or Antilibidinal Ego
RO = Rejecting object
LE = Libidinal Ego
CE = Central Ego
EO = Exciting object

Libidinal Ego and the absence of any kind of Freudian "death instinct" allow Fairbairn to do away with the classical concept of the Id as the source of drives. One can thus say that Fairbairn's Libidinal Ego has a function analogous to the Freudian Id. As for the Antilibidinal Ego, it is described as the split-off, repressed part of the Original Ego that is related to the Rejecting Object. It is identified with aggressive parents and represents a primitive persecutory structure that will later fuse with the inhibitory aspects of what Freud describes as the ideal Ego and the Superego. Freud's Superego is thus considered by Fairbairn as a complex structure, including both the Ideal Ego, the Antilibidinal Ego, the Ideal Object, and the Antilibidinal (or Rejecting) Object (Moore & Fine, 1990).

For Fairbairn, normal human relations are fundamentally interpersonal, and he distinguishes between "interpersonal relations" and "object relations". A non-pathological relationship with a real person does not require internalisation because the interpersonal relationship is intrinsically satisfying (Grotstein and Rinsley, 1994, p. 5). Failure at the interpersonal level leads to object relations or an endopsychic structure. For Fairbairn, identifications are always defensive or pathological, and to the extent that splitting is inevitable, the schizoid state is the unavoidable destiny of mankind (Grotstein & Rinsley, 1994, pp. 8–11).

The Self controls and organizes behaviour in an optimally adaptive way thanks to the preservation of its integrity in the face of pressures from the subsidiary selves, pressures that vary as a function of the individual's early experiences and the nature of the external environment that is present. (Sutherland, 1994, p. 26)

Fairbairn concludes that a vision of human nature in terms of drives and zones is so impersonal and inadequate that it could itself be the product of schizoid thought, a travesty of the realities of intimate human life! Fairbairn, as Kohut in a later period, places the accent squarely on external realities.

Discussion

The very concept of "structure" seems foreign to Gestalt thinking in 1951, and it would seem that the only possible answer to the questions asked at the beginning of this section (What is the nature of that which gives a person his distinctiveness, regulates his behaviours, life-events, and relations which others, and mediates the impact of the past on current experiences?) would be: the characteristics of the immediately present Field! With their ideological attachment to Field theory, Perls et al. seem to inordinately stretch their position inordinately by considering only optimally healthy subjects. This level of health, where the Self completely maintains its integrity and never splits, seems to Fairbairn completely utopic; at the very most he seems to consider it as an abstract possibility. Here we encounter the principal weakness of the theory of the Self, with its foundations of "structural naiveties" denounced by Bouchard and Derome (1987, p. 142).

What about the question of internalisation in the theory of Fairbairn? The fate of the satisfactory object was a mystery until Rubens (1984) distinguished two categories of internalisation: structuring and non-structuring. Bouchard and Derome (1987) seized upon this distinction to sketch a possible way of combining our two systems. They point out that Fairbairn never clearly describes how growth occurs, leaving aside questions of healthy contact with real persons, to address instead "endo-psychic structures". On the other hand, the Perls et al. theory of Self directly addresses growth and creative adjustment, leaving aside the question of the development of stable structures (that Fairbairn would call "endo-psychic"). Thus the two theoretical approaches are essentially complementary, in that Fairbairn treats severe personality disturbances that result from introjects and identifications. Growth would result from non-structuring internalisations described by Rubens (1984), which are more or less equivalent to the assimilations of the growing organism discussed by Perls et al. As for "structuring internalisations", they would be the equivalent of Gestalt therapy's introjects, and would be responsible for pathologies, but this point is not developed by Perls et al.

Psychology, then, is the study of relations between the individual and his objects (Fairbairn), or again, the study of creative adjustments (Perls et al.), while psychopathology is the study of relations between the Ego and internalized objects (Fairbairn) or again, the study of interruptions, inhibitions, or other obstacles during the course of creative adjustment (Perls et al.). Concerning the question of health versus pathology, Fairbairn remarks that a completely integrated Ego is virtually impossible, and that all of us are more or less "schizoid" (this remark has lead to some confusion, being interpreted as showing that Fairbairn is only interested in the schizoid pathology. For Fairbairn, "schizoid" does not have the technical sense found in the DSM, but refers to a general loss of unity, common to all forms of pathology (Kohut gives a similar meaning to narcissism, which he sees as underlying many forms of pathology).

The parallels drawn between Fairbairn and Gestalt therapy by Bouchard and Derome (1987) and by Bouchard (1990) need to go further than consideration of "background" pathologies. Bouchard contends that Gestalt therapy can be adequate for understanding "foreground" pathologies, but when a client has a fragmented "background", Gestalt therapy's conceptual tools are not adequate for an understanding of the dynamics involved. A careful reading of Fairbairn, however, shows that all psychopathology is essentially "background" pathology. Translated into Gestalt therapy terminology, this would mean that "foreground pathologies" only seem such because a split "background" has compromised the formation of "foreground" figures.

The process leading to the splitting of the Ego unfolds unconsciously on the foundation of the division between the Libidinal Ego and the Antilibidinal Ego. In other words, the divisions, oppositions, and conflicts within the Ego weigh down and inhibit the formation of "figures". These same divisions of the Ego can go so far as to render this same process chaotic, fragmented, or lethargic. Of course, such a position presupposes that Ego-splitting in Fairbairn's sense proceeds along a continuum from moderate to severe divisions.

As it is the Self that acts at the contact boundary to create and destroy figures, any splitting is also a splitting of the Self. We must not forget that for Perls et al., influenced as they were by the dynamic psychology of Lewin, the Self is not a fixed structure but rather a spatial-temporal event. This may be an interesting concept, but Gestalt therapy pays the price in being deprived of a usable clinical perspective on "background" pathologies. All this leads to the question: is there an inner world for Gestalt therapy? The third chapter of the 1951 text attempts to demonstrate the illusory nature of any such "inner world", but one soon encounters contradictions and inconsistencies: "... then there is the beautiful experience of aesthetic-erotic absorption, when the spontaneous awareness and muscularity drinks in and dances in the environment as if self-oblivious, but in fact feeling the deeper parts of the self responding to heightened meaning of the object" (1951, pp 305–306).

In this passage we find a recognition of two propositions explicitly denied by Perls et al.: the non-structural nature of the Self and the illusory nature of the division " body, mind, and external world". In spite of Perls' declarations affirming a non-structural theory, in watching his filmed interviews one can constantly observe his efforts to bring his client to re-appropriate what has been split off, leaves him fragmented, and prevents him from completing his "figures". Regardless of the technique employed, he constantly returns to the same themes: re-take what was renounced, say "I" instead of "he" or "it", regain a coherent wholeness. It is perhaps in his work on dreams (1969), an important part of early Gestalt therapy, that he is most explicit:

> All the different parts—any part of the dream is yourself, is a projection of yourself, and if there are inconsistent sides, contradictory sides, and you use them to fight each other, you have the eternal conflict game, the self-torture game. [...] Each time you integrate

something it gives you a better platform, where again you can facilitate your development, your integration. (pp. 89, 91)

As Bouchard and Derome, as well as Burgalières (1992) have noted, there is a striking similarity between this passage and Fairbairn's position on dreams: "the view which I myself have now come to adopt is to the effect that all figures appearing in dreams represent either (1) some part of the dreamer's personality, or (2) an object with whom some part of his personality has a relationship, commonly on a basis of identification, in inner reality" (1954, pp. 8–9).

Unfortunately, the mechanism responsible for fragmentation was never clearly explained, except for a brief reference in 1951, which describes it as a result of successful contact.

The theory of the Self in Gestalt therapy has been impoverished by the insistence upon a unitary terminology, and, as a result, its pertinence for clinical phenomenology is limited. This impoverishment and insistence seem to us to be consequences of the choice of a biological framework. If Gestalt clinicians intend to acquire the conceptual tools necessary for a comprehension of the loss of unity of the Self that is at the heart of all pathology (not only "background" pathologies), they must revise their concept of the Self in order to include structuring and non-structuring internalizations, and splitting of the Self as a consequence of specific configurations of the field.

Conclusion

We undertook this comparative analysis of Perls et al. and Fairbairn as a preliminary step in the integration of these two theories of personality, or at least their mutual enrichment. Our analysis has allowed us to confirm and more clearly identify the compatibilities they share and that can guide this integration, notably by applying the analytical grid of Greenberg and Mitchell to the two theories. For both theories, (1) contact or the relationship are the primary realities, (2) both are compatible with general field theory, indispensable foundation of the Gestalt therapy theory of Self (Yontef, 1993), (3) real relations are more important than fantasized relations, (4) optimal development is characterized by reciprocal human relations enriched by the perception of differences, (5) aggression is secondary and is employed as a means by the organism, (6) the bases of pathology are similar. theory contains a more detailed discussion of pathology, while Perls et al. provide more complete descriptions of psychological health that are, nonetheless, essentially similar to Fairbairn's concept: the ideally healthy adult has no need for compensatory attachment to internal objects. His energy is fully available for contacts and exchanges with real individuals in his environment.

The theory of Gestalt therapy, while giving careful attention to the fundamental unit of analysis and to motivation, has little to say about development and flatly rejects the concept of structure, in favour of a unitary vision of consciousness.

Our explorations have uncovered rich zones of material in Fairbairn, unexploited as yet by Gestalt therapy. Although motivation is treated from different perspectives by the two schools, (process for Perls et al., content for Fairbairn) there are fertile possibilities of establishing complementary links. For Fairbairn, motivation is a natural drive of the organism and the primitive Self toward contact which, over time, establishes a relationship.

Henceforth, it will be necessary to limit ourselves to the dynamic (process) aspects of Fairbairn's theory, and leave aside concepts such as libido and anti-libido, even though these terms lose their sexual connotations in his work. In conserving them, we would run the risk of reducing all processes to the single motivational relation and its vicissitudes, as perceived by Fairbairn. As a result, our integrated theory would lose the flexibility that is one of the strong points of Gestalt therapy and that it is important to conserve. On the other hand, some aspects of Fairbairn's thinking on structure can be useful. Fairbairn was highly critical of the reification of instinctive energy in classical psychoanalysis (Sutherland, 1994, p. 18), and yet includes structure in his theory, strongly bolstered by his discussion of development. From his point of view, structural differentiation is both universal and pathological. But it is reversible. And it is the objective of psychotherapy to restore maximal unity in the Self and in the Self's experiences. Table 2 summarizes our conclusions.

A Gestalt theory of the person, more complete and more useful clinically, must therefore recognize that a relationship is a contact that continues in time. As well, the theory must recognize the preponderant importance of the human environment, while accepting and recognizing the impact of internalisations, be they structuring or non-structuring, for the continued development of the psyche. We will attempt to describe such a theory in the following chapters.

Table 2. Summary of comparison Perls et al. vs. Fairbairn.

Fundamental problems	Perls et al.	Fairbairn	Compatibility and complementarities
Fundamental unit of analysis	The individual is an organism living in the Field and contact between the organism and the environment is the primordial reality.	The relation is primordial and zones (oral, anal, etc.) are only channels by which the relationship can exist.	Compatibility and complementarity: the relation is defined as a contact that continues over time.
Motivation	Satisfaction of needs that emerge from the Id function, completion of contact-cycles.	The libido is the energy of the Ego searching for the object. This search is oriented toward external reality from the beginning Compatibility: essential motivation is relational, and is directed toward contact. Complementarity: motivational content for Fairbairn; contact-cycle permitting the satisfaction of needs for Perls et al.	
Development	A theory of growth of the organism but no theory of psychic development.	A developmental theory based on interactions with the mother: infantile dependency, transitional period, mature dependency. Complementarity: Fairbairn completes the lack of a developmental theory in Perls et al.	
Structure	Consciousness is unitary. According to circumstances, the Self appears as Id, Ego, or Personality, but remains unified and is never structurally differentiated.	Consciousness is unitary. Self-object differentiation is not necessarily permanent, but it is universal, pathological, and reversible.	Compatibility: two unitary visions of consciousness Complementarity: the two theories analyse, respectively, the healthy and the pathological case.

PART II

PROPOSITIONS FOR AN OBJECT RELATIONAL GESTALT THERAPY

CHAPTER FIVE

Epistemological and methodological preconditions for a Gestalt therapeutic system

In the preceding chapter, we analysed the theories of Perls, Hefferline and Goodman (1951) and Fairbairn (1954) with respect to four fundamental questions of Greenberg and Mitchell (1983) and concluded that the compatible and complementary natures of these two theories could indeed facilitate fruitful interactions and integrations.

Both theories share a relatively rare unitary vision of consciousness. For both, contact and relation are the primary realities. Contact zones, be they oral, anal, etc., as in psychoanalysis, or visual, tactile, etc., as in Gestalt, are functions that permit the initiation and development of contacts and relations. In both, the Self is seen as possessing its own energy and oriented toward the real Field from the very beginning.

The two theories, as we have seen, present numerous complementarities, in the sense that an area neglected by one will be developed by the other, in mutually respectful ways. For example, as already noted, Perls et al. are silent on the important question of development, while Fairbairn advances a theory of development based on early interactions with the mother, a theory consistent with Gestalt thinking in that there is a passage from infantile dependence (confluence) to mature dependence (contact within the Field). Again, as we have seen, the Gestalt theory of the organism/environmental Field throws a remarkably clear light on the processes by which the Self interacts with the environment, but neglects the structural aspects of a Self that is considered essentially as a unified spatial-temporal event occurring at the contact boundary. In contrast, Fairbairn focuses on the developmental processes that permit an understanding of the intra-psychic dynamics underlying that interaction. However Fairbairn, in turn, does not elaborate, as do the Gestalt therapists, on the object relation modalities that allow the internal object to persist and regenerate.

If a Gestalt theory of human nature is to generate a true therapeutic system in Mahrer's (1989) sense, it must do two things: it must (1) permit comprehension of the internalisation of relations with other—be it by introjection or assimilation—as well as of how these internalised relations are then manifested in the Field, in interactions with reality; (2) go beyond the descriptive phenomenology of the contact moment, to conceptualise the relationship as contact that continues in time.

We propose a revision of the theory of the Self that integrates in a unitary model the compatible and complementary elements of the Perls et al. and Fairbairn theories. The central challenge is to produce a theory that adequately explains the structural differentiation underlying pathology and that allows an understanding of the dynamics of this loss of the unified self.

Before proceeding to the details of the proposed revision, we will briefly return to consideration of certain epistemological and methodological preliminaries as presented by Mahrer (1989), Rychlak (1993), as well as Yontef (1988).

As Mahrer (1989) mentions, certain integrative approaches seem to be doomed to failure from the beginning, while others appear to be more promising, although more difficult. For Mahrer, it is impossible to integrate theories that have radically different conceptions of human nature. By definition, a theory of social learning is fundamentally different from an existential-humanist theory or from a psychoanalytic vision of human nature. A theory of unitary consciousness cannot cohabit with concepts like the dynamic unconscious or libidinal cathexis of the Ego.

At first sight, Mahrer's restrictions seem to contradict the clinical experience of many Gestaltists, who frequently use techniques borrowed from other approaches. Whether it be the "anchoring" of Psychoneuro linguistics, homework assigned in brief therapy, or the immersion techniques of behaviourism, such borrowing is common, although not always explicitly recognised. However, it must be said that no school of psychotherapy has patented concrete techniques of intervention, and use of a technique from another approach is not equivalent to theoretical integration. One is not "doing Gestalt" in asking a client to repeat more slowly what he just said, listening carefully to his voice. One is not "doing Rogerian non-direction" when reformulating what a client has said, just as one is not "doing psychoanalysis" in interpreting resistances. On the other hand, one can certainly add certain elements of a theory of psychotherapy to another approach, but such additions are successful only when the two theories concerned share a similar vision of human nature, or when one develops a new theory that integrates the preceding two theories, as we intend to do with Perls et al. and Fairbairn.

Yontef (1988) on the integration of psychoanalytic concepts in Gestalt therapy

In integrating psychoanalytic concepts with Gestalt therapy, certain rules must be applied. Yontef (1988) advances five recommendations that we intend to respect.

Speak in terms of processes to avoid returning to Newtonian and pre-Newtonian thinking

Yontef advises using a language of processes, in order to minimize the risk of reification: confusing the word with concrete reality. For example, instead of speaking of "splitting" and thus implying the concrete existence of two entities, Gestalt therapy should speak of a person keeping two experiences separate. Again, instead of speaking of "introjects" one could speak of a person attributing to himself aspects of the environment. Without going to the extreme position of a language rigorously and "Gestaltically" correct, we should make the effort to use expressions that respect the dynamic processes of experience. Yontef himself, in a later publication (1993) explains that this recommendation concerns theoretical texts, and should never be so strictly followed that the evocative clarity of an idea is lost.

It is interesting to remark that Polster (1995) rehabilitates the "anthropomorphic reflex" that sometimes leads to reification. Polster maintains that it is perfectly natural to assign human qualities to nature, inanimate objects, and even parts of one's self. If one can say that the wind "moans", that the trees "dance" in the wind, or that the sea is "angry", why is it ridiculous to imagine that our interior world is inhabited by quasi-human entities? This is what we will be doing at a further point when we speak of an introjected field, composed of a "part of one's self" and a "part of the environment", although we know very well that nothing is materially present in the organism, and that we are speaking with anthropomorphic licence in the service of clarity.

Only the complete person acts, never a part of the person

For Yontef, this linguistic quirk has become fixed in our work, and has negative effects on the client as well as the therapist. In a unitary theory like Gestalt, it is clearly contradictory to speak of "parts of the self". Even so, it appears to us that the clinical consequences of an excessively "unitary" discourse are more dangerous than those of a "divisive" discourse. Frequently, the only way that a client can describe the Gestalt of his experience, is in "divisive" language: "Part of me feels humiliated and frustrated by your refusal (negative representation of self and the object). But another part of me is reassured by your sincerity and solidity (positive representation of self and the object)." We feel that our proposed reformulation of the theory of the Self of Perls et al. should help the therapist to more readily accept an internal experience of division, or even fragmentation, and to reflect that experience without losing sight of unification as the global objective of Gestalt psychotherapy.

Action is a result of a choice

Personal responsibility is a cherished value in the existential-humanistic tradition and, for the Gestalt therapist, action must always be seen as the result of a choice, even when complexity and ambivalence can mask the reality of a choice. In particular, prudence is required when importing psychoanalytic concepts, because there is a natural tendency in psychoanalysis to see present behaviour as determined by the past. For Gestalt theory, the past is part of the total Field and does not determine the present. In our revision of Gestalt theory, we intend to clearly place the internalised past in the present Self and to develop a more adequate understanding of the interactions between the internalised past and the present configuration of the Field.

Formulate concepts in a way that respects the dynamics of the Field

The person cannot be isolated from the Field, and thus there is no dichotomy opposing "internal" to "external", even if on occasion it can be convenient to use this distinction in communicating with clients. We intend to clearly illustrate the dynamic interrelation between the internal and the external, but at the same time we recognize the need for Gestalt descriptions to be intelligible, accurate, and understandable. The average everyday experience of our clients is not unitary. The internal world and internal experience exist, and without them contemporary psychology would have no sense. Gestalt should limit itself to holding that the internal world cannot exist outside of the Field, and avoid becoming isolated in a "unitary" doctrine that is too far removed from usual experience.

Better use of psychoanalytic concepts: awareness of fundamental dynamics as well as developmental factors

Obviously, each client is unique and deserves to be treated as such. But even so, it is of paramount importance that the therapist understand the phenomenology of his client correctly, from the very beginning of the therapy (Yontef, 1988, 1993). For this, certain psychoanalytic concepts can be useful, not to reduce the client to a pathological prototype, but rather to clarify the nature of the patient's pathology as well as the underlying, contributory developmental dynamics. To these ends we intend to borrow two concepts from psychoanalysis: internalisation and representation.

CHAPTER SIX

The linear-sequential vision of the Self in Perls, Hefferline, and Goodman: a critique

In Chapter Four, our comparative analysis of Perls et al. and Fairbairn led us to identify certain limits of Gestalt therapy's theory of the Self. In this chapter, we continue this critical analysis, examining some additional shortcomings of the Perls et al. theory of the Self, shortcomings that are a consequence of their strict conception of the Self as a non-structural phenomenon unfolding in time. We will conclude that the Perls et al. conception of the Self, based as it is on a biological foundation, might be adequate for certain simple situations but fails when applied to complex human interactions.

According to Perls et al., three conceptual components are combined in the Self, which (1) is formally defined as a function of contact in the ephemeral present; (2) unfolds according to a strict temporal sequence in the stages of contact, and (3) develops neurotic qualities as a consequence of an inhibition of contact in the present (1951, p. 178).

This conception of psychic life clearly derives from the authors' implicit biological framework: there is a clear intention to ground the realities of psychic life in an irreducible organic foundation in which there is a natural movement of contact and withdrawal. It is not surprising that their text shows numerous references to our primordial, biological nature (Robine, 1994).

Table 1. Conceptual systems relevant to the Perls et al. theory.

Biosphysikos process	Absence of primary excitation	Primary excitation	Orientation toward the environment, conflict and destruction	The Figure is clear and is contacted in a spontaneous unitary action	Interaction between the organism and the environment: the Self loses its clear definition
Contact cycle		Pre-contact	Contact	Final or full contact	Post-contact
Functions of the Self	Absence of the Self	Id	Ego	Ego	Personality
Loss of Ego function	Confluence	Introjection	Projection and retroflexion	Egotism	

The Self's very existence depends upon this natural movement of contact and withdrawal—the Self exists only in the interaction occurring at the contact boundary—and the defensive operations deployed by the Self are strictly connected to the natural contact cycle. In fact, the authors assert (Perls, Hefferline & Goodman, 1951, p. 280) that these various defensive operations are simply variations on one basic neurotic process of interruption, and the precise manifestation of the neurosis depends upon the moment of interruption. Contact follows a natural organic sequence and defensive reactions differ only as a function of the moment at which the sequence is interrupted: no part is played by a conscious choice of the person, by the nature of the ongoing relationship between the person and the environment, nor by the meaning attached to the experience of contact or to the interruption itself.

Their biological model obliges the authors to associate these three conceptual axes in a linear, unidirectional way, producing an organic movement involving an increase and decrease in tension that recalls the Freudian model. Thus, confluence is presented as a defensive operation occurring before the excitation, at a time when, strictly speaking the Self does not yet "exist". But if the Self does not yet exist, how can it produce a defensive operation, and how can that operation protect an entity that does not exist? The only possible answer to these questions presupposes the existence of a physical organism that continues to exist independently of contact episodes.

In spite of these paradoxes, this vision of psychic life has a certain conceptual coherence within a biological framework. But at a more practical level, this epistemological choice does not adequately answer to a number of familiar clinical observations. For example, introjection is considered to be an operation associated with the Id, occurring during pre-contact. But as we know, clinicians frequently observe introjection occurring during contact. As Ginger (1987) remarks, most avoidance mechanisms can be observed at any moment of the contact cycle.

Consistently with the biological framework, the functions of the Self are manifested in a similar temporal pattern: Id, Ego, Personality, in that order. This sequence adequately corresponds to certain simple contexts such as orgasm (Perls, Hefferline & Goodman, 1951), hunger (Zinker, 1977, Robine, 1994), thirst (Katzeff, 1983, cited by Ginger, 1987), or feeling cold (Delisle, 1991). But when it comes to more complex forms of contact, this simple linear model is less satisfactory. It would be extremely difficult to establish adequate correlates between moments of contact, functions of the Self, and defensive operations, in situations such as being undecided between two lovers, or a decision to accept or reject chemotherapy. In fact, almost all clinically relevant examples that one could imagine go well beyond the simple linear structure proposed by Perls et al. As a result of this, some post-Perlsian authors have attempted to remedy the situation by proposing such revisions as micro- and macro-cycles (Zinker, 1977; Polster & Polster, 1973), or meta-needs (Zinker, 1977). But it seems to us that these measures involve resorting to another conceptual framework in order to "save" a theoretical argument: Maslow's (1967) concept of meta-needs refers to meaning, and therefore a biological framework is not, in itself, adequate to the task. These same authors, along with others, have extended the concept of defensive operations so as to include adaptive modes of resistance at the contact-boundary that are conscious, flexible, and adapted to conditions in the Field. In this sense, they are Ego functions. In our view, these adaptive operations go beyond a logic which holds that consciousness is simply a "delay in creative adjustment", essentially the same as that seen in animals.

The concepts of contact cycle and its interruption remain useful, but it is too limiting to confine them to the strait-jacketed Perls et al. model. We apply these concepts in more conceptually satisfying and clinically useful ways, allowing numerous permutations of functions of the Self, contact moments, and defensive operations.

CHAPTER SEVEN

The Self and object relations: a revision of Perls, Hefferline, and Goodman

After making several detours in order to tidy up diverse epistemological and methodological considerations, we now arrive at the revision of the Gestalt theory of the Self that has been our goal all along. As we have mentioned, it is not our intention to rewrite this theory, but rather to revise it in order to permit a more adequate understanding of the loss of the unity of consciousness and how that loss leads to pathologies of the personality. We will begin by setting forth those elements of Gestalt theory that are worth preserving, and as our revision proceeds, we will present omissions, additions, and modifications of the original Gestalt theory.

The development of the Self and the process of internalisation

At birth, the individual is a unified psychophysiological organism, living in a unified Field. The Self is the psychic apparatus that evolves and becomes differentiated as a consequence of contact with the surrounding human environment. A person is born with cognitive, affective, and sensory-motor capacities that can become actualised through contact with a favourable environment. This environment functions to support the child as it lives through the challenges and obstacles to its development. Human life can be seen as a continuing sequence of to-and-fro movements, of contact and retreat. In other words, the Self is progressively constructed through interactions with the human environment, and the component parts of the Self are, in fact, internalised human relations. These considerations have led us to propose an enlarged vision of the Self in which the Self is seen as more than a spatio-temporal process activated during a contact cycle and that evaporates when that cycle is terminated.

For us, then, the Self is above all a system of active structures, stable over time, and produced from interactions between the organism and the Field. What composes this system and how does it evolve? These are the questions to which we now turn.

In spite of its unitary and process-driven vision of consciousness, in which experience can occur only at the contact boundary, the 1951 text contains several references to two processes considered to be essential for the elaboration of a differentiated psychic apparatus and for the construction of the "inner world". These two processes are internalisation and the construction of internal representations.

> When things and other persons have once become outlined and abstracted objects, they can enter into useful deliberate fixed and habitual relations with the self. [...] And the strong emotional bonds of lactation, suckling, and fostering care tighten the sociality. (p. 366)
>
> The persons are formed by the social contacts they have, and they identify themselves with the social unity as a whole for their further activity. [...] There is abstracted from the undifferentiated felt-self a notion, image, behaviour, and feeling of the "self" that reflects the other persons. (p. 368)

It is precisely because there can be this "abstraction" of objects that can then "enter into ... relations with the self" that we confidently assert the existence of an internal world, an internal reality, and internal experiences.

We conclude that experience can be an internal reality, even if all experience originates at the contact boundary, as Brentano held. In the context of Field theory, these internal experiences represent residues of interactions at the contact-boundary, but once these residues are internalised, they become basic elements of internal experience and of psychic life.

From a Logos perspective, it therefore seems justified to define the Self as a processual structure[1] of contacts produced by the organism's activities in the Field, a structure modified by these contacts and that conserves their history. That history is in fact a synthesis of the person's idiomatic meaning of life, as Polster (1987) noted. This synthesis is also the central function of the Self, without which health is not possible.

We therefore break with the classical Gestalt tradition in order to postulate an "archival" function of the Self. As an archive, the Self conserves traces of critically important experiences such as nursing and treatment received during childhood. The structure is largely a function of mother-child interactions, since it is usually the mother that nurses and raises the child. But as the child is also influenced by social contacts, including the father and significant others in the everyday environment, it identifies with the global social unit later in life. For the child, the social unit is primarily the immediate human environment: early experience is coded as a function of this internalised immediate environment.

But it would be a mistake to think that the process of internalisation involves an active Self operating on a passive environment. Field theory holds that all human functioning is a function of the entire Field. Our position differs from that of Perls et al. in that we hold that consciousness is an inherent part of human nature, and the dynamics of the Field do not determine its apparition, although they can help explain its content. A theory of development consistent with Field theory should address internalisation as a phenomenon of the Field. In this sense, dual motivations and processes should be examined. Although the newborn arrives in the world with a genetic baggage and an embryonic consciousness with only intra-uterine experiences as content, the human environment in which it arrives has a history. This history, communicated by the parents, will be one of the active forces in the Field affecting the internalisations of the child. For this reason, Gestalt therapy cannot consider the "mother" as a generalised abstraction, as Fairbairn seems to—particular mothers have particular histories.

As the child develops, and at crucial moments of contact, there is a convergence of multiple forces that emerge from the Field: the genetic baggage and its programmed maturation, the specific genetic makeup of the child, particularities of interactions with the parents as a function of their own history and internalisations, "accidents" in the course of development, the social and cultural environment in which socialisation occurs, etc.

In their 1951 theory of the Self, Perls et al. had no answer to three theoretical questions: (1) by what means does the Self identify with this all-important social unit which comes to guide its activities later in life, (2) at what level is this identification made, and (3) what role does this identification play in figure formation? To answer these questions, we will borrow two concepts foreign to traditional Gestalt theorizing: internalisation and representation.

Internalisation and representation

Laplanche and Pontalis (1967) speak of internalisation in two ways. Firstly, the term is used as a synonym of introjection, notably by the Kleinians, and describes the passage of a good, bad, partial or total object, toward the interior of the person. In a more specific sense, it refers to a process by which intersubjective relations are transformed to intra-subjective relations.

For Moore and Fine (1990), it is a process by which aspects of the external world, including interactions with it, are taken into the organism and represented in its internal structure.

It seems to us that the Field, as conceived of by Gestalt therapists, can itself be the object of internalization. Perls (1942) and Perls et al. (1951) discussed the importance of introjection. In these descriptions, the authors' intention was to denounce introjection as a pathology of contact and a loss of Ego functions, and they gave little attention to the developmental role of the process. In the metapsychological view of the Field, health and pathology are on a continuum: consequently we follow Bouchard and Derome (1987) in describing introjection as the conservative form of internalisation, while assimilation is the creative form.

In the Gestalt conception of internalisation, the element internalised "may have two fates: either it is painful foreign matter in the body and it is vomited forth (a kind of annihilation); or the self partially identifies with the introject, represses the pain, seeks to annihilate part of the self—but since the introjection is ineradicable, there is a permanent clinch, a neurotic splitting" (1951, p. 399).

This is a passage that Fairbairn could accept. What happens to a relation once it is internalised? It lives "inside" as a representation. And what is a representation? Is it a simple memory whose only function is to permit recognition of the Other from one contact to another, or is its role more complex?

The concept of a representation is far from simple: as it relates to the development of intelligence and social capacities, and biological maturation, we could easily question Piaget, Eysenck, and the neuropsychologists as well as psychoanalytical thinkers. For our purposes, we accept the definition of Moore and Fine (1990): a representation is a similarity or an image that gives the impression of the original perception. A psychic representation is, accordingly, a more-or-less faithful reproduction of the perception of an object or of something significant.

In their excellent discussion of internaliations, Moore and Fine stress that all the aspects of the psychophysiological Self will be included in representations of the Self, and all the aspects of to-be-internalized objects that the individual finds important will be psychically represented. We also hold that the content of internalisations includes the organism (the psychophysiological Self) and the environment. Generally speaking, no representations are thought to be present at birth (except for the Kleinians, (Klein, 1959) who consider the Mother to be an endogenous presence). But as soon as experience begins at the contact boundary, there begins to be consciousness of the difference between "internal" and "external" (Skolnik, 1987; Stern, 1985; Zazzo, 1988).

As development continues, the embryonic representations of Self and objects, consequences of early contact boundary excitations, become more elaborate and accessible to consciousness. At the beginning, they are unstable, and the Self-object differentiation disappears with satiety and sleep (Moore & Fine, 1990). This observation reminds us of Perls' claim that the Self exists only when and where there is interaction at the contact boundary. When the baby wakes up and cries, these embryonic representations seem to become more distinct and the Figure is more clearly differentiated from the Ground. This early dynamic resembles the 1951 perception of the contact cycle in general, and this is perhaps why there are frequent references to the newborn in that text. Although this contact cycle can indeed by readily associated to a biological framework, as maturation proceeds these psychic representations become more complex and stable, not necessarily dependent upon physiological needs (Moore & Fine, 1990, p. 166). Perls et al. did not consider the influence of maturation in their formal definitions, and so their theory of the Self cannot adequately explain what object relation psychoanalysis calls object constancy or object permanence.

The Self, then, is a structure that processes contact to create Figures and therefore meaning. As such, it functions to internalise the Field in two ways: assimilation and introjection. Since the concept of introjections is used in Gestalt therapy to describe a neurotic interruption of contact, when we use the term to describe introjection as a primitive mode of internalisation, we will speak of primary introjections. Let us now examine these modes more closely, so as to distinguish those which permit healthy growth from those that lead to loss of unity, structural differentiation, and pathology of the Self.

Non-structuring internalisations: assimilation and growth

Contact can be defined as conscious recognition of something new and useful, as well as an adaptive behavioural response: at the same time it is a rejection of new elements that cannot be of use to the organism (Perls, Hefferline & Goodman, 1951). Assimilation, as a consequence of contact, involves the absorption of those new and useful elements encountered and recognized in the contact moment. In post-contact, the Self elaborates on the assimilated representations to complete them. These representations are then experienced as part of the ever-expanding Self, rather than as foreign elements. They are meaningful and accessible to consciousness via the Personality function of the Self, and are the historical record of completed operations of the Self at the contact boundary. Therefore, contact leads to assimilation, leading in turn to an augmented consciousness of the Self, of the environment, and of the connections between the two. Ideally, this process does not lead to the formation of split structures, and in his analysis of Fairbairn's concept of structure, Rubens (1984, 1994) speaks of non-structuring internalizations. The Self preserves its unity and the individual does not burn up energy to maintain separations among internal structures. Assimilated experiences, good or bad, are perceived as being the Self. Perls et al. repeatedly stressed the reality of this perception, while, however, leaving undiscussed another form developed by Fairbairn: the structuring internalisation.

As accurate as this terminology might be, it has unfortunate connotations for our purposes. Under the influence of Freud and later psychoanalytic thinkers, the terms "structuring" and "non-structuring" have acquired meanings exactly opposite to those developed by Rubens. "Structuring" is seen as desirable—a person who functions well is "structured", while a person in a non-functional state is seen as "unstructured". Despite this inconvenient semantic reversal, we prefer to retain the meaning that Rubens gave to these terms, in order to remain centreed on the idea that structuring, in the sense of intrapsychic structural differentiation, is the opposite of assimilation, and as such is at the origin of pathology.

Structuring internalszations: primary introjection and interruption

Rubens (1984) pointed out the extent to which development was, for Freud, an affair of increasing structural differentiation (Ego from Id, Super-ego from Ego). This Freudian perception found its way into the general culture: differentiation of the Self from the external object implies a structural differentiation within the psyche. In spite of this Freudian heritage, it is possible to imagine a theory of consciousness which would be both psychoanalytic and unitary: differentiation between the Self and the environment does not necessarily imply a structural differentiation. Thus, one could imagine a highly functional person who is well differentiated, without being structurally differentiated. We will return to this distinction at a later point.

For the present, we tentatively accept Fairbairn's point of view to the effect that structural differentiation is not only pathological but universal and inevitable (Bouchard & Derome, 1987; Rubens, 1984, 1994). This pathological structural differentiation is the result of incapacity to complete a contact cycle; the cycle is interrupted by a primary introjection. Now in introjection, the Self represses pain by attempting to annihilate a part of itself (Perls, Hefferline & Goodman, 1951), so it becomes important for the Gestalt therapist to understand the configuration of the Field that conduces the developing Self to this auto-aggression.

In the case of primary introjection, these internalisations, called introjects, are inevitably linked to unfinished situations, more precisely an interruption of the contact cycle at the excitation stage (Perls, Hefferline & Goodman, 1951). What is it that makes this interruption necessary? It is not easy to know if our two theoreticians indeed have a consensual answer to this question, because while Fairbairn examines the question from the perspective of a "naive" newborn, Perls et al. refer to the functional modes of a neurotic adult. Since we are interested in the loss of the unity of the Self over time, let us begin with the phenomenology of contact as it would be experienced by a newborn.

Recent research on mother-infant relationships supports Fairbairn's perspective, as well as that of Gestalt psychology and, by extension, Gestalt therapy. The human infant enters a world of interaction and communication from the very first second, seeking contact and able to organise complex perceptions across sensory modalities simultaneously (Olivier, 1994; Silverman, 1981, 1984, 1986; Skolnik, 1987; Stern, 1985; Walters, 1976; Zazzo, 1988). In this Field of organism-environment, there are already elements that are nourishing and validating, while others are toxic (Skolnik, 1987).

The newborn is immediately capable of a certain form of conscience, even if certain contact capacities are only rudimentary (Skolnik, 1987). As Wertheimer observed in 1925, the infant perceives the whole before the constituent parts. It can feel and perceive, but cannot solve complex problems that demand a superior capacity of consciousness, of creation of meaning, and of action on the environment. As Rubens (1984) points out, major problems occur when an object affectively connected to a fundamental aspect of the self is too intolerable to be absorbed, but too important to be abandoned. Here we have the central dilemma of contact at an early age, defined as becoming conscious of a new, accessible element and production of appropriate behaviour, while at the same time conscious of the need to reject toxic novelty. What, then, can be done with a new object that is simultaneously indispensable and toxic? In such a case, it is impossible for the newborn to find a clear meaning, to construct a clear Figure. Fairbairn holds that this situation leads to the establishment of a psychic structure that is pathological, to be sure, but also "creative", given the rudimentary capacities of the newborn faced with such a situation. The unitary but embryonic Self of the newborn introjects the toxic elements of the environment, because it can neither contact them (they cannot be assimilated) nor reject them (as they are, in this situation, indispensable).

Once introjected, these experiences are retained within the Self, so that they do not re-emerge in subsequent contact cycles, re-creating the intolerable contact boundary event. For Fairbairn, these introjects are maintained in an unconscious form within the Self by a process of repression. This repression involves not only introjected objects, but also parts of the Ego (or of the Self, in Gestalt terminology) that attempt to maintain contact with those objects, judged to be essential for survival. This perception leads to the conclusion that there must be a splitting of the Ego in order for repression to be effective or even possible (Fairbairn, 1954, p. 168).

For Fairbairn, the situation we have just described is inevitable for every human being, regardless of the quality of his or her early environment. Here we encounter a paradoxical situation in Fairbairn's thinking: structural differentiation is simultaneously abnormal (pathological) and universal. It would seem that Fairbairn reached this conclusion solely on the basis of his own clinical observations. Following a widely-used procedure of psychoanalytical epistemology, Fairbairn reaches his conclusions via an induction from a particular pathological observation to a universal-existential generalisation: "... the fundamental position of the psyche is invariably the schizophrenic position" (1954, p. 8).

Given that Fairbairn's clinical experience was essentially with hysterical and schizophrenic adults (Moore & Fine, 1990, p. 71), and that today we are more aware of important differences that exist between the traditional stereotypical child and real children (Stern, 1985), we can consider Fairbairn's position as more the result of a metaphysical choice than of sound empirical underpinnings. Still, the question remains—what should be the Gestalt position with respect to a question for which there is no empirical foundation one way or the other? Only a complete theory of normal development could really answer this question, but in the meantime we will make our own metaphysical choice, one that has clinical utility. This position will be developed in the following chapter, but we can make a preliminary observation here, to the effect that the burden of proof should be placed, not on pathology, but on health. Ideally, the healthy Self is perfectly unified, fluid, and internalises the Field exclusively in a non-structured fashion. As this ideal Self has no introjects, it is meaningless to speak of a dynamic unconscious, and the only unconscious processes are those that Perls et al. identify as physiological. Our position is that although this ideal of health may be within human possibilities, it is certainly not characteristic of most people, and in fact one could hope to encounter such health only in those people who have had an exceptionally favourable development, or have succeeded in neutralising their introjects in order to attain the state of grace of the Perls et al. model. That being the case, it would seem to follow that the clinician who hopes to understand psychic suffering should assume that his or her client has probably not had an exceptionally favourable development, and has not been able to neutralise his introjects. Our default position therefore is that until proof of the contrary, the consulting client has a baggage of unfinished situations, consequences of early contact dilemmas, has lost the original unity of consciousness, and that the recovery of this unity is the overall goal of psychotherapy, even if it may not be entirely attainable. This default position seems to us consistent with the existential position of our two authors, that is to say, the person as a project.

The process described above entails three important consequences for an understanding of the loss of unity of the Self: (1) microcosms of the Field are internalized; (2) these microcosms "live" as representations; and (3) they are maintained outside of consciousness.

Because these microcosms are internalised by a process of primary introjection, and to avoid confusion with other types of internalisations, we will speak of Introjected Micro-fields (IM). Each experience internalised in this way is an IM, and the sum of IMs is the Introjected Field (IF). By way of comparison with Fairbairn's system, we could say that apart from their qualitative properties (libidinal, antilibidinal, etc.), the endopsychic structures of Fairbairn are, from a Gestalt perspective, nothing more than a partial Field introjected and maintained outside of consciousness.

The prototype of an unfinished situation is the early introjection of an element of the Field (an element of the environment, an element of the Self, and the contact boundary between the two) that is simultaneously impossible to assimilate and essential for survival. In order to distinguish between these prototypical events and other unachieved situations that do not result in a contact dilemma and hence remain accessible to consciousness, we will refer to the prototypical case as an Unfinished Situation. As they are incomplete relational experiences, they exist over time, rather than existing only during actual moments of contact. To summarise, each Introjected Micro-field (IM) is the residue of an Unfinished Situation (US) concerning a "contact dilemma", and the sum of these IMs is the Introjected Field (IF).

For Fairbairn, endopsychic structures exert continuous pressure on the central Self so that it will recreate the sorts of experiences that produced them in the first place (Rubens, 1984). For Gestalt, it is the IM that produces pressure on the elaboration of Figure/Ground processes: the first Unfinished Situation (US) seeks to repeat itself, not by emerging into consciousness, but by contaminating the formation of Figures and by penetrating the productions of the Id (Perls, Hefferline & Goodman, 1951, p. 185) in the form of physical sensations, vague perceptions of the environment, and in primitive sentiments linking the person to that environment. Hence, we hold that the Id is not only a function of the Self that appears during pre-contact, but that it also contains an unconscious psychic structure: the IF. Pure pathology would characterise a Self made almost entirely of structuring internalisations, and therefore completely atomised in a multitude of IMs. Pure health would characterise a Self perfectly unified, the only inaccessible processes being of a physiological nature.

As pathology develops, Unfinished Situations contribute to the establishment of internal structures, IMs, embedded and maintained in the background of the psyche. These IMs can be confused with the Field and even take the place of the Field in certain psychotic states. One objective for a Gestalt theory of development would be to clarify the conditions under which USs lead to the formation of split and energetically maintained structures (IMs) that are not accessible to consciousness, and under which conditions the same USs lead to IMs that are less sharply split and more accessible to conscious awareness. For the present, we will mention simply that when early internalisation takes the form of introjection, elements of the environment are carried to the interior and, as they were not disintegrated during contact, they continue to exist in their original form. As such, they form the nucleus of Unfinished Situations that seek to complete themselves by functioning in the background, as it were, keeping themselves hidden from conscious awareness. Productions of the Id are simply derivatives of these introjects or of these Unfinished Situations, in the form of tensions, daydreams, etc. These elements of the Id can contaminate physical sensations and the initial vague perception of the environment, and limit the range of elementary sentiments that normally connect the organism with the environment. These IMs have a very real effect on the Self, motivating it to search out elements in the Field that they need to maintain themselves. In extreme cases, the relations with the Field become so shrunken and deformed that they become practically copies of the IMs.

Human experience, whether normal or pathological, can be understood essentially as the Self continually creating itself by a process of internalisation of the Field. Healthy development involves non-structuring internalisations, which are accessible to consciousness and therefore interpretable. Their action in the creation of Figures can be controlled more easily by the Ego function of the Self, and so the Self can more flexibly manage the organism's needs, and can more efficiently metabolise the psycho-nutritive elements generated by its operations at the contact boundary. In a large sense, we are speaking here of creative adaptation, the elements of the internalised Field serving as flexible guides during contact phases, and furnishing a kind of psycho-immunitary protection against the ingestion of elements that are toxic for the Self. In pathology, structuring internalisations control the contact cycles. These considerations lead to our conclusion: the Self can be seen as the result of processes of the internalisation of the Field, and as the dynamic sum of both structuring and non-structuring internalisations.

Id, Ego, and Personality: process versus structure

Whether we speak of a cycle in four phases, as per Perls et al., six phases, as per Zinker (1977), or eight phases as per Polster and Polster (1973), the cycle of contact has always been at the heart of Gestalt thinking and represents one of the central ideas of Gestalt, organic auto-regulation (Ginger, 1987). It is perhaps this concept that has been most successfully integrated with the clinical practice of Gestalt therapists. We do not see the Self in a limited way as three functions in action only during the contact cycle. Firstly, this limited perception does not account for the archival function of the Self that needs to be considered. In fact we need to proceed to a reformulation of the three functions of the Self in order to more adequately account for the process of internalisation—primary introjection—and of structuring, that we have described above. We can begin this reformulation by remarking that if, generally speaking, the functions of the Self are correlated with the contact cycle sequence (Id during pre-contact, Ego in full contact and the Personality during post-contact), it is always the Ego that mediates contact between the Self and the environment, being the interpreter of the Id and of the Personality.

Reformulation of the Id function

"... the Id is the given background dissolving into its possibilities, including organic excitations and past unfinished situations becoming aware, and the environment vaguely perceived, and the inchoate feelings connecting organism and environment" (Perls, Hefferline & Goodman, 1951, p. 441).

We now turn our attention to that dimension of the Id function that brings forth unfinished situations from the past. Of the four dimensions of the "background dissolving into its possibilities", it is clear that the unfinished situations of the past are in a different category from the other three. Organic excitations, the vaguely perceived environment, and the inchoate feelings connecting organism and environment have a meagre history. Only unfinished situations of the past have a real history, and that history is one of failure.

When an activated background triggers a contact cycle that is dominated by an IM, an inaccessible Unfinished Situation from the past takes control and maintains the emerging element, giving it a highly charged complexity that activates the Self, engaging a complex contact cycle.

An introjected microcosm of the Field that remains in the background destroys the original unity of the Self, and elements emerging from the Id are consequently distorted. At a previous time the Self was unable to contact this experience because of its simultaneously indispensable and intolerable nature, and these newly-emerging elements from the Id must be disguised or else "the intolerable" will once again appear in the Field to emerge as a Figure. We could say that in the Id, there is an IF made up of non-assimilated experiences that rigidly resist the organic fluidity of figure-ground modifications, and therefore remain uninterpreted. These emerging elements are accompanied by distortions that can be detected by an external observer. We will return later to this point. But because these elements are distorted, they create certain difficulties for the Ego function.

As thus defined, this part of the Id would no longer be the Gestalt equivalent of Fairbairn's central Self, as Bouchard (1990, p. 145) supposes. Although the part of the Id which treats the more familiar, classical emerging elements is indeed part of the central Self, the IF is in fact the equivalent of subsidiary "Selves": we have a background layer of the Self, an Id that is no longer simply a function of the Self, but becomes the container of a split, unconscious psychic structure. Bouchard seems to have placed the introjects outside of the Self: in so doing, we believe that he is transmitting the ambiguities of the 1951 text, in its treatment of the destiny of introjections. But, since unfinished situations are part of the emerging elements of the Id for Perls et al., and since there are no functions of the Self other than the Id, the Ego, and the Personality, we must necessarily localise the IF in the Id, and henceforth identify the Id as the container of "structuring" internalisations and Unfinished Situations, as well as supplying the energy that those situations continue to contain, as they remain unfinished. Table 1 summarizes these conceptual equivalencies.

Bouchard's analysis, as reproduced in this table, pinpoints a fundamental problem in the 1951 text that we attempt to resolve here: how to localise, in a unitary self, the processes related to background pathologies. Although the concepts exist, they are poorly defined. The 1951 text focuses on process, and in so doing blurs the distinction between introject and introjection. Consequently, the fate of these introjects remains insufficiently explained, leading to an imprecise, vague theory of the Self, of pathological processes, and, above all, of their effect on the unity of consciousness.

Reformulation of the Ego function

"The Ego is the progressive identification with and alienation of the possibilities, the limiting and heightening of the on-going contact, including motor behaviour, aggressing, orientation and manipulation" (Perls, Hefferline & Goodman, 1951, p. 441).

Perls et al.'s 1951 definition applies equally well to pathological and healthy functioning, and we can accept it as is. In pathology, when the Self is functioning in the Ego mode and is seeking to confirm or disconfirm a contact cycle dominated by an IM, how can its own survival, as well as that of its IMs, be assured in a possibly dangerous environment? Survival is assured by a relationship in the Field, a relationship that implies contact and support functions and is potentially observable externally. In pathology, the Ego seeks above all to reproduce the situations that led historically to the Unfinished Situation; occasionally and secondarily the Ego might seek to modify those situations. Thus the Ego eliminates experiential possibilities in order to maintain the integrity of the Internalised Field. It limits the ongoing contact by a selective orientation in the environment, from which it can aggress and

Table 1.

Fairbairn, according to Bouchard (1990)	Perls et al., according to Bouchard (1990)	Perls et al. revised
Central Self: non-structuring internalisations	Self: organism growing through assimilation	Personality as a matrix of Field representations
Defence mechanisms as seen in clinical phenomenology	Personality Function	Ego as "interpreter" of the Id and the Personality
	Ego Function	Defensive or adaptative modes of contact regulation Creative or conservative adjustment
	Id Function	Id: emerging physiological elements and unfinished situations accessible to consciousness
		Id: Introjected field = sum of introjected micro-fields, products of unfinished situations experienced in contact dilemmas. As such, inaccessible to ordinary consciousness

"Structuring" internalisations: libidinal versus anti-libidinal Self

Internalisation of pathological object relations: repression and splitting of the SelfDistinction between introjects as content and introjection as process

Unfinished Situations. Background pathologies. Conservative, pathological adjustments

---

manipulate that environment. In other words, the Ego acts in such a way that the elements of the Field that could potentially invalidate an IM are kept in the background, while those that reinforce the IM are brought forward as Figure. We will return later to the phenomenology of the Ego's defensive operations.

Reformulation of the Personality function

In our opinion, the Personality function needs not only reformulation, but rehabilitation. In the first place, in a healthy individual this function is not merely a verbal reflection of the Self—when that is the case, we are looking at a narcissistic pathology, springing from the failure to establish relations with the Other. For us, the Personality is an internalised, dynamic matrix of representations that can be seized by consciousness, a matrix in which not only the Self but also the environment is present. After a successful contact, I know more about myself, but also more about the world. This new information enriches the matrix that is always potentially accessible to the Personality. It is incorrect to say that "In ideal circumstances the Self does not have much personality" (1951, p. 499), or that "When the Self has much personality, we have seen, it is because either it carries with it many unfinished situations, recurring inflexible attitudes, disastrous loyalties; or it has abdicated altogether and feels itself in the attitudes toward itself that it has introjected" (1951, p. 499). In our opinion, these assertions confuse personality with introjects, and reduce the personality to its pathological form, Personality Disorder, characterized precisely by inflexibility and poor adaptation (APA, 1980, 1987, 1994). On the contrary, the Self can have "much personality" insofar as that personality is the matrix of complete, assimilated representations of the Self and its environment. We will return later to the nature of this matrix of representations at the heart of the Personality function.

By definition, IMs are hermetic to consciousness, and yet they can trigger a certain number of contact cycles. We have seen how they can penetrate emerging elements of the Id, and how their effect can be detected in the action of the Ego function. We believe that the Personality function contains residual representations of contact cycles, including those contaminated by IMs. In this sense, it is perhaps a mistake to speak, in clinical terms, of a "disturbance of the Personality function". Consider, for example, From's classical patient (who called himself a "poet" although he had never written a poem). Bouchard (1990) and Robine (1994), among others, see in this patient a disturbance of the Personality function. It seems more appropriate to consider this representation of the Self as a consequence of contact cycles triggered by an IM, and thus involving all the functions of the Self. It would be more pertinent to ask just what the patient is reproducing by seeing himself in this way, and just how that is connected to an inaccessible US. We will return to this point in our discussion of psychotherapy in a later chapter.

We see the Personality function as a matrix of Field representations (MFR). This matrix reproduces, at the intra-psychic level, the constitutive elements of the Field: organism-Self and environment-Other. In the context of significant human relationships, the environment's "shape" is analogous to that of an "object" as defined in the classical psychoanalytic theory of object relations. In addition, every representation can take on one or the other of the two basic values of contact theory: nutritive or toxic. In the course of psychomotor development, these basic values will become increasingly complex and loaded with other meanings. That which is nourishing will be seen as good, satisfying, protective, stimulating, true, etc. That which is toxic will be experienced as bad, diminishing, frustrating, false, evil, etc. Figure 1 illustrates this general configuration of the MFR.

As opposed to Polster (1995), for whom the unity of identity is chimerical, we would say that the healthy individual is capable of activating varied representations of himself and the Other, as a function of the current configuration of the Field. Even when there are tensions or conflicts among the diverse representations of Self, the Ego is capable of synthesising these representations in order to give meaning to ongoing experience. On the other hand, when these varied identities or representations have a rigid connection to IMs and are

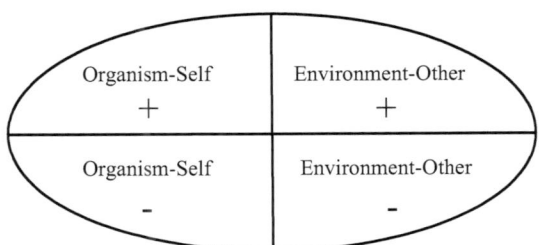

Figure 1. General configuration of the Matrix of Field Representations in the Personality Function.

thus inflexible and poorly-adapted, the individual has a personality disorder, not in the limited sense of Perls et al., but in the more general sense of the DSM.

Modes of regulation and interaction in the Field

A physical organ will rapidly degenerate if it is not nourished and stimulated by the environment via contact and support functions (Polster & Polster, 1973). Now how can a psychic "organ", be it called a subsidiary Self (Fairbairn), an introject (Perls et al.), or an IM, survive without an energy supply to keep it alive? In our perception, as in Fairbairn's, the Field that is introjected following an Unfinished Situation pushes the individual to search his environment for relations and events that will either maintain the Field or transform it. In the same way that a physical organ can deteriorate in the absence of nutritive elements, a psychic "organ", such as an Introjected Micro-Field, will die if it does not find nourishment in the world of objects. "Nourishment" for the IM takes the form of experiences in the External Field to which the person can attach a familiar meaning. In Fairbairn's terms, the Libidinal Ego becomes attached to the Exciting Object, and then must motivate the Central Ego to seek those real objects whose relationships to the Self have the capacity to maintain, modify, or transform the internalised object. The same dynamic applies to the Antilibidinal Ego of Fairbairn.

In its operations at the contact boundary, the Self, pathologically split from its IMs, attempts to give meaning to its experience by projecting the properties of the internally split structures on to the environment at the pre-contact stage. Then, acting during contact, the Ego unknowingly activates a range of tactics motivated by the IMs, tactics whose function it is to manipulate the environment into a shape consistent with the projected image. When this succeeds, the Self is ready to re-introject, in full contact, the object that has now been rendered "edible". Finally, during post-contact, the new introject blends with one or another of the IMs, reinforcing its autonomy, confirming its intolerable nature, and thus maintaining both the force and the necessity of splitting. A concrete example of this process would be the individual who not only fears rejection, but who "succeeds" in getting rejected in an environment that is actually quite tolerant, and who then concludes that the universe is full of callous people and that it's useless to expect anything good from others.

The careful reader of Perls et al. will be surprised to hear of contact, even full contact, in the context of a defensive operation and a conservative adjustment. Those authors limited the concept of "contact" to creative adjustments. But, as Field Theory tells us (Yontef, 1993), one cannot imagine structure without energy, and energy must come from the environment since the organism can be nourished only by comestible novelty. And how can we imaging a nourishing energy flow without contact? We therefore feel that the notion of contact should be broadened to include defensive and conservative operations that do not, after all, refuse vitality, but rather hijack it to profit pathological structures. All the operations of the Self in the Field, be they creative or conservative, are charged with energy and seek meaning. The simple equation "contact = health", apart from its judgemental overtones that Goodman would probably disavow, cruelly limits our understanding of complex pathological or conservative processes.

IMs, as objects that have been internalised pathologically, result in a loss of spontaneity, grace, and creativity in operations at the contact boundary. As the number of split structures increases, so do unconscious pressures on contact cycles, and the Self increasingly seeks, unconsciously, the pathogenic experiences that the IMs demand. One could speak of conservative adaptation, by stretching Goodman's concept.

And so the Self is born and develops in the Field, through a process of interaction at the contact boundary. The interactions affect the development of the Self, but are themselves affected by the extent to which the Self is structured, and by the force of the IMs in the background. When the Self functions optimally, contact is a clear conscious awareness of the distinction between elements that can and cannot be assimilated, and of the appropriate behaviours toward the two. But as we have seen, it is rare to see a person so perfectly unified that he is always in a perfectly conscious contact. So then the question becomes, by what means does a less-than-perfect Self deal with the environment? And above all, how do these processes modulate the relations between the IF and the MFR, on the one hand, and between the IF and the environment, on the other?

In the 1951 text, the authors defined neurosis as a loss of Ego functions, and presented five neurotic mechanisms: confluence, introjection, projection, retroflexion, and egotism. The contemporary clinician sees here one of the limits of Perls et al.'s theoretical system: psychopathology is more or less identified with neurosis. We will return to this point later.

These processes, also called contact regulation modes (Polster, 1988) have developmental and adaptative functions strongly emphasised by Polster and Polster (1973), and Zinker (1977). Each process is treated by the Ego at the contact boundary, and modulates interactions between the Self and the environment. We can roughly say that in confluence, the contact boundary is practically non-existent and the feeling of a separate existence is lost. In fact, it's a state of non-contact. In introjection, a part of the environment is attributed to the Self, while the contrary is the case in projection: a part of the Self is attributed to the environment. In retroflexion, contact energy, that by definition is intended for the environment, is turned back upon the Self. Finally, egotism is "a kind of confluence with the deliberate awareness and an attempted annihilation of the uncontrollable and surprising" (Perls, Hefferline & Goodman, 1951, p. 533). This last mechanism was absent from Perls' first work (1942) and he seems uneasy with it ("For want of a better term, we call this attitude 'egotism'" (p. 533)). Neither Polster and Polster, Zinker (1977) nor Petit (1984) mention egotism. Polster and Polster (1973) present another contact regulation mode: deflection, by which direct contact with another person is partially channelled in a different direction. This concept is found throughout their writings, and was adopted by several authors, including Petit (1984) and Delisle (1991).

As for Fairbairn, the concept of defence or resistance refers to the individual's difficulty in giving up his unconscious, pathological attachments to internal objects (Ogden, 1994, p. 103; Rubens, 1994, p. 163). For Fairbairn, maintaining the internal world as a closed system creates difficulties for interactions with objects in the external world. The individual with a closed inner world can interact with an external object only by means of transfer: the external object is treated as though it were part of inner reality (1958, pp. 380–381). The reader will notice that "transfer" is used in a way that is unusual for a psychoanalyst, but familiar to Gestalt therapists. Fairbairn sees transference not as "from the past to the present" but rather as "from the exterior to the interior". Once again we can see how our two theories treat a fundamental problem from different but complementary perspectives. For Perls et al., resistance is a process at the contact boundary that prevents contact and consequently prevents completion of the contact cycle. In other words, it is an operation in the Field that aims to prevent the assimilation of new elements from the environment and hence, the transformation of the Self. For Fairbairn, resistance is a process that aims to isolate the internal world and maintain it as a closed system, maintaining attachment to internal objects by means of operations like repression, splitting, etc.

At this point, our theoretical question can be formulated as follows: given the redefinition of the Self in the light of the two points of view we have adopted, how should we characterise the five modes of contact regulation? First of all, we will consider them as tactics used by the Ego, in order to modulate interactions between the internal and external worlds. These functions of regulation and modulation can be applied to the IMs in order to modify them or preserve them. We have already seen how these IMs can influence contact. In more severe forms of pathology, the IMs operate further and further from conscious awareness, and incite the Self to reproduce the experiences that produced them in the first place. In this context, we find it useful to speak of a "compulsion" in a larger sense than a simple effort to complete a situation. Indeed, in this configuration, transformational energy is minimal and conservation energy is maximal. Since the individual is attached to his IMs, he seeks primarily to nourish them. As the individual moves toward health, the accent moves to completing the USs and there is more transformational energy.

Reformulation of confluence

Confluence is a process by which the contact boundary is obliterated. The experience of contact is absent or greatly weakened, the person becomes unable to distinguish between himself and the environment. Furthermore, within the Personality function, the MFR is such that representations of the Self become confused with representations of the Other. The Ego function becomes less effective.

Reformulation of projection

In Gestalt theory, projection operates in the same way as the psychoanalytic concept of projective identification, as discussed by post-Kleinian authors such as Langs (1976), Ogden (1979, 1982), and Tansey and Burke (1989). As Freudian and Kleinian theories are not grounded in the concept of a Field, it is possible to think of projection and introjection at a level of pure fantasy: this is impossible in a Gestalt perspective. Indeed, if all human experience is a function of the Field, how can one imagine an experience, even an internal one, without manifestations at the contact boundary? For Gestalt, projection is inevitably accompanied by action in the Field that aims to manipulate the environment into conformity with the projection. Accordingly, the Gestalt concept of projection is similar in structure to the concepts of interpersonal acceptance of projective identification, as proposed by Money-Kyrle in 1956, and as Goldstein (1991) has discussed.

When the concept of projection is placed in the Gestalt framework (1) of the Field, and (2) in the sense of a process both interpersonal and intra-psychic, we can find common ground with a psychoanalytic concept of projective identification and introjective identification. These psychoanalytic concepts are thus compatible with the fundamental principles of Gestalt: the individual situated in the Field, and the adaptative and defensive character of his resistance to contact. Projection produces the perception of the external Field as similar to the Introjected Field, and leads the individual to act at the contact boundary as if the current configuration of the Field were identical to the representations activated in the MRF.

Reformulation of introjection

Introjection is a process by which the Field is internalised without being decomposed and assimilated. Representations of the MFR are therefore dense and heavy, interfering with the creation of Figures. The introjected Field is essentially a clumsy copy of non-assimilated operations of the Self at the contact boundary. Finally, as mentioned earlier, introjection, as well as confluence, is a primitive response of the Self when confronted with a contact dilemma.

Reformulation of retroflection

In retroflection, the person directs contact energy toward himself in an effort to maintain distance between the external and internal Fields. As a part of the Self plays the role of the environment, contact with the latter is impossible. This defensive operation presupposes a more evolved capacity of conscious awareness and action: it appears in development after confluence and introjection.

Reformulation of deflection

A person deflects when he or she acts at the contact boundary in such a way that the events in the external Field are unable to affect the internal Field, in much the same way as a goalkeeper in hockey deflects a shot on goal. One might say that the shot on goal is a part of the environment that aims at an internal target. If the goalkeeper cannot completely stop the shot, he will deflect it away from the goal, returning the puck to the environment. Table 2 summarizes the defensive functions and their role in maintaining the internal Field.

As can be seen in Table 2, each defensive operation is in fact a way of regulating interactions between the internal and the external. From our perspective, it is particularly pertinent to notice the logical connection between these operations and the process by which the Self creates Figures and meanings. The fundamental element of meaning is the internal or external locus of an event, and in this context, the

Table 2. Defensive functions.

Operation	Perls et al.	Function in the creation of Figures and meaning
Confluence	State of non-contact	Erases differences between internal and external
Introjection	Attributes a part of the environment to the Self	Believes what is external to be internal
Projection	Attributes a part of the Self to the environment	Believes what is internal to be external
Retroflexion	Returns contact energy toward the Self	Prevents the internal from contacting the external
Deflection (Polster & Polster, 1973)	Turns away from contact with the Other	Prevents the external from contacting the internal

most severe loss of meaning is that in which the person no longer knows *where* something is happening, *where* his or her experience is occurring.

The Self and contact cycles

In our conception of the Self, contact cycles are initiated in and by the Id. The starting point might be some organic excitation, vague perceptions or sentiments connecting the organism and the environment, thirst, etc. It might also be some unfinished situation from the past that emerges into consciousness.

Whatever the nature of the emerging element, it can be distorted by the action of some element of the Internal Field that is inaccessible to ordinary consciousness. These elements are the Introjected Micro-fields, each of which is born in the interruption of a contact cycle when that contact is a contact dilemma for the Self, a contact dilemma that takes the form of an unsolvable problem for the Self, an element that is simultaneously indispensable and intolerable. The only "solution" for the Self is to accept the indispensable and "forget" the intolerable. To do this, the Ego introjects, or "swallows", neither breaking up nor tasting the intolerable. It then represses the intolerable in the form of an Unfinished Situation (unfinished because it has not been fully contacted), pushing it into a space within the Id that becomes an inaccessible background. This space, called the Introjected Field, is the unconscious zone of the Self. The Ego keeps the introject far from consciousness, because the intolerable must continue to be out of sight. Consequently, the Ego will not recognize the traces of this introject in the elements that emerge from the Id. But since the Introjected Field is formed from contact dilemmas in which an element of the Field is not only intolerable but also indispensable, a part of the Self becomes attached to the introjected element. This Introjected Micro-field, composed of an element of the environment, an element of the Self and the connection between the two, is vital to the Self and must be maintained, unconscious but alive. Therefore the Ego works to manipulate contacts with the environment, by means of the defensive functions, in order to find or create experiences in the environment that can nourish the IF. Acting "in the name of the Self", the Ego modifies the sense of certain experiences at the contact boundary so that the environment will be seen through the distorting prism of the IMs.

Toward the end of the contact cycle, the Personality function appears in the forefront and, with it, the Matrix of Field Representations. The results of the contact episode will be integrated to the Matrix as new representations of the Self and the environment, or else as confirmations of the rigid, inadequate representations of both.

Toward an understanding of development in Gestalt therapy

Classical Gestalt theory does not have much to say concerning the development of the Self, other than that the process of contact with the Field is functional immediately after birth, and that hunger and the aggression that brings satisfaction of hunger are at the basis of the first experiences of the field and the formation of the Ego as a contact process (Perls, 1942). For Fairbairn, there are three phases of development, corresponding to the nature of the relationship between the Self and the environment. First, there is infantile dependence, then a transitional phase, and finally mature dependence. The constant challenge of development is to be able to deal with the frustration inherent in human life, with the resources available at each stage of maturity. During infantile dependency, the infant's only coping strategy is to introject its experience, as we mentioned previously. Then, in the transitional phase, thanks to the development of cognitive and contact capacities, the infant becomes able to cope with interactions between its internal world, made up of introjects, and the world of real people. The infant now has four "tools" for dealing with these interactions: obsessional, paranoid, hysteric, and phobic. Finally, if all goes well, the person reaches the phase of mature dependence, in which interactions involve real people while internal objects, more flexible, serve as reference points in social life. In the revision of the theory of Self in Gestalt therapy that we are proposing, we prefer to see development as a continual process over the lifespan, rather than as a process more or less determined in an early phase of life. For example, we do not think that Unfinished Situations must necessarily occur before a certain age, nor do we use Fairbairn's terminology (libidinal and antilibidinal) to describe developmental experiences.

Along with several authors (Greenberg & Mitchell, 1983; Kuhn, 1977; Pine, 1988; Silverman, 1986; Welt & Herron, 1990), we believe that the apparently contradictory conclusions reached concerning the development of the psyche are the result of inadequate sample size and other methodological flaws. Furthermore, these disagreements are often the expression of differing ideological positions which are the manifestations of conscious or unconscious metaphysical positions. In a more pragmatic vein, the American Psychiatric Association has formally stated that there is no officially established aetiology for any mental disturbance, apart from biologically-based mental illness. Although there have been several etiological systems proposed, none have gained unanimous approval (Millon & Klerman, 1986). Although psychology has seen many theories of development, Gestalt therapy does not have one. At this point, our task is not to propose yet another theory of development, but rather to propose a clearly structured Gestalt theory that will permit us to profit from the clinical and empirical data concerning psychic development that has accumulated since the early days of psychoanalysis. As Gestalt therapy has not pledged allegiance to any particular theory of development, why not try to benefit from the entire range of data, irrespective of the particular theoretical colour they may have? It would be difficult, for example, to understand narcissistic vulnerability without Kohut's insights, or the persistent need to correct an imaginary wrong done to another, without referring to Klein. One could add many authors who have proposed etiological hypotheses pertinent to our purposes, even though they may not have adhered to the our metaphysical position of the unity of consciousness.

The general developmental framework that we are aiming to establish should adequately respond to three questions: (1) At what stage of physiological maturity does a US occur?; (2) What was at stake at the moment of that situation?; (3) What psychic potential was affected in its development because of the US?

To shed light on these questions, we can seek partial answers in competing explanatory models without denying their differences and without grabbing at quick, superficial answers. Even within psychoanalysis, one sees more and more authors favouring openness to different developmental and etiological hypotheses associated with the four principal schools that remain opposed on many points (Pine, 1988; Welt & Herron, 1990). Silverman claims that empirical research as well as clinical observation evolve toward this multimodal openness at the level of comprehension, coupled with a greater rigour and coherence at the technical level.

We therefore intend to profit from the work of the four major schools of psychoanalysis in their attempts to understand the development of the psyche. Have we found the universal integrative principle, which will allow an adequate immediate response to the client without endangering the vital coherence of the treatment, without which failure is inevitable? Hardly, for we are still without a clear criterion for the selection of an explanatory system which could help us understand the representational system that we call the Matrix of Field Representations. We will return to this point in the chapter that presents a theory of psychotherapy, but we can say here that the more an explanatory system is composed of concrete, observable elements, the easier it will be to integrate it with the explanatory framework that we propose here. On the other hand, the more such an explanatory system is built upon a series of inferences upon inferences, the less pertinence it will have for us.

Toward a Gestalt theory of personality disorder

Our primary aim in this book has been to revise Perls et al.'s theory of the Self, making it more clinically relevant, especially with respect to personality disorders. We began by examining the pathological consequences of the loss of unity of the Self. We now continue by clarifying the conceptual connections among several elements, including our revised theory of the Self, Gestalt conceptions of pathology as discussed by Perls et al., a more recent Gestalt perspective—that of Yontef, Fairbairn's "defensive technique", and the DSM classification of personality disorders. Our goal in this discussion is to outline what could become a Gestalt theory of personality disorder, a theory that takes into account the process of internalisation of the Field, and the difficulties associated with that internalisation.

Perls et al. (1951) gave no clear definition of psychopathology, nor did they clearly differentiate different categories of mental illness. Neurosis and character neuroses are lumped together, and psychosis, fleetingly mentioned as a disturbance of the Id function, is never seriously discussed. It is clear that the authors chose, implicitly, to concentrate on "character neuroses", as they were called at the time: "... stereotyped patterns limiting the flexible process of creatively addressing the novel" (p. 271). This vision of neurosis resembles that of Fairbairn, for whom character neuroses are not due to a fixation at some developmental stage, but rather a set of processes deployed to defend the Self against conflicts among its internal objects (Fairbairn, 1954).

These defensive techniques are used by the Self particularly during the transitional phase, when the Self is moving out of infantile dependence but has not yet achieved mature dependence (Fairbairn, 1954).

During this transitional period, the individual matures by gradually giving up internal objects and turning toward real persons in the environment. But this renunciation is not an easy matter, marked as it is by an internal tension that is both desired and feared. Failure during the transitional period is sanctioned by the appearance of pathology in the personality. For Fairbairn, the defences are not employed in a set order according to a particular developmental sequence. Use of one as opposed to another depends rather on the nature of the object internalised during infantile dependence, and the nature of the environment present during the transitional phase. For the adult, these defensive organisations function to protect the Self from either a depressive or a schizoid tendency. If the schizoid tendency is dominant, it is the loss of the Self that must be prevented; if the depressive tendency is dominant, the danger is that of loss of the object.

For Fairbairn, no one can hope to have had a perfectly satisfying object relation during infantile dependency or even during the transitional phase—we are all too helpless and impressionable for that. Consequently, we have all had to resort to defensive techniques in order to survive the inevitable conflicts associated with human development. Intra-psychic splittings tend to emerge when the neurotic defences that protect the Self are weakened, notably during therapy (Fairbairn, 1954).

Perls et al. discuss neuroses in terms of the defensive operations discussed in the previous chapter.

> If we draw our concepts from moments in a present process (namely its interruptions), we can expect that, with awareness, these interruptions will develop into other interruptions; the on-goingness of the process will not be lost. The patient will be found not to have a "type" of mechanism, but indeed a sequence of "types", and indeed all the "types" in explicable series. Now the case is that in applying any typology, rather than finding it in the actuality, one experiences the absurdity that none of the types fits any particular person, or conversely that the person has incompatible traits, or even all the traits. Yet what does one expect? It is the nature of the creative—and so far as the patient has any vitality he is creative—to make its

own concrete uniqueness by reconciling apparent incompatibilities and altering their meaning. Then instead of attacking or reducing the contradictory traits in order to get at the "real" underlying character that the therapist guesses at (character analysis), or of trying to uncover the missing connections to what must be the "real" drive (anamnesis), we heed only help the patient develop his creative identity by his ordered passage from "character" to "character". The diagnosis and the therapy are the same process. (Perls, Hefferline & Goodman, 1951, pp. 524–525)

One can only admire the wisdom in this passage, written (let's not forget!) nearly fifty years ago and yet confirmed empirically by most researchers. The personality disorders of contemporary psychology are nothing more than largely abstract prototypes, and their corresponding diagnostic criteria show considerable overlap (Frances, 1987; Delisle, 1991; McWilliams, 1994; Millon & Klerman, 1986; Tyrer, 1995).

Our task then, is to propose a vision of personality disorders that is consistent with our revision of the theory of the Self which can successfully integrate the various viewpoints that buttress this revision. Here we encounter a troublesome contradiction between the idealistic, anarchistic views of Perls et al. on the one hand, and the necessarily conservative values of an "official" classification like the DSM, which even defines personality disorder as a "an enduring pattern of inner experience and behaviour that deviates markedly from the expectations of the culture of the individual who exhibits it". A definition like that would probably have given conniptions to Paul Goodman! But we will leave to others the job of exploring the social and political ramifications of contemporary psychopathology; meanwhile, and in spite of our hesitations, we suggest that Gestalt therapists adopt the DSM categories, which present the significant advantage of having descriptive and non-inferential criteria, and which facilitate communication between Gestalt therapists and the wider therapeutic community. Gestalt therapy's contribution would be at the level of an understanding of the phenomenology of personality disorders.

We believe that the theory of the Self, formally redefined to adequately take into account the loss of experiential unity, will allow the Gestalt clinician to better understand pathology of the personality, to more readily decode its phenomenology, and to intervene in a nuanced and effective manner.

In contemporary Gestalt therapy, disorders of the Self are presented as the equivalent of personality disorders (Yontef, 1993, p. 104, p. 291) and character disorders (Yontef, 1993, p. 424). Yontef (1993, p. 291) speaks of disorders of the Self as resulting from fragmented, negative, and rigid introjects, resulting in an easily shaken coherence and self-confidence. Consequently, there is no unification of this fragile Self and the ongoing external situation.

In the revised theory of the Self, personality disorder is seen as a habitual mode of stunted, rigid conservative adjustment rather than creative adjustment. All the functions of the Self are involved. Emerging elements of the Id are limited and contaminated by the action of the IF, the Ego function seeks to steer away from contact so as to maintain the IF, and the MFR is habitually at odds with the ongoing configuration of the Field. This summary seems to us to capture the essence of the phenomenology of personality disorder, as described by Yontef. Table 3 illustrates the relationships between the two descriptions and certain elements of the DSM vision of personality disorder.

A hundred years after the birth of psychoanalysis and fifty years after the first formulations of Gestalt therapy, clinical research has given us a richer understanding of pathologies of the personality, their aetiology, their clinical phenomenology, and their dynamics (Abraham, 1993). A clinician could readily adopt our viewpoint to enrich his or her understanding of the aetiology and the phenomenology of specific problems without necessarily accepting the metapsychological framework habitually associated with this enriched understanding: we would speak then of a concrete clinical application of a multi-modal approach, as discussed earlier. It would suffice to consider the Self as the responsible agent of internalisation and the IF as the prototype of a developmental interruption, resulting in a structuring internalisation that fragments conscious unity. At that point we can enrich our clinical reflection by drawing on a universal clinical heritage that can give precious indications concerning the phenomenology of the structuring internalisation and the resulting internal experience. Recent research on the developmental history of specific pathological personalities such as borderline (Wagner & Linehan, 1994), schizoid (Lieberz, 1989), or on personality disorders in general (Crowell, Warters, Kring & Riso, 1993; Dahl, 1993; Dahl & Bordhal, 1993; Paris, Frank, Buonvino & Bond, 1991) could be conceptualized in terms of crucial episodes and contact dilemmas, and

Table 3.

Yontef's description	Explanation of Perls et al. (Revised)	Pertinent DSM elements related to the phenomenological description
Rigid adjustment to the current Field		
A. Experience and behaviour that deviates markedly from the expectations of the individual's culture	New constructs do not harmoniously integrate previous constructs	Constructs (structuring internalisations) are lodged in the IF and are inaccessible to ordinary consciousness: therefore they cannot be integrated to ongoing elaborations
B. The enduring pattern is inflexible and pervasive across a broad range of personal and social situations	Cannot maintain their sentiment of cohesion, of continuity, of security and self-esteem	The IF clogs the creation of Figures and prevents a sentiment of continuity. Internal experience is divided and there is a loss of cohesion and security
C. The enduring pattern leads to clinically significant distress or impairment in social, occupational, or other important areas of functioning	Processes and the experience of the Self are often fragmented	The fragmentation is a consequence of IMs acting in the background to disturb contact-cycles outside of "ego-consciousness" The introjects are IMs inaccessible to ordinary consciousness, that trigger contact cycles that generally have negative outcomes
Presence of rigid introjects		
D. The pattern is stable and of long duration and its onset can be traced back at least to adolescence or early adulthood	Presence of negative, rigid self-images	Negative images of the Self that occupy a preponderant place in the MFR of the Personality function

(*Continued*)

Table 3. (Continued)

Yontef's description	Explanation of Perls et al. (Revised)	Pertinent DSM elements related to the phenomenological description
Elements in the Field can stimulate IMs that, in turn, trigger cycles of contact without the cohesion of a unified Self	Absence of clear and flexible linkages between themselves and the current situation	An incapacity to meaningfully connect internal and external experience

thereby incorporated within a theory of internalisation of the Field such as we are suggesting here.

At this point we are ready to advance a formal definition of personality disorder that integrates the descriptive classification of the DSM and our revised theory of the Self. Personality disorder is a constellation of behaviours and conservative attitudes whose function is to maintain the IFs by seeking and producing in various experiential Fields, contact configurations and relationships that have dynamic links with USs. Sequences of significant contact are triggered by the infiltration of an IM into an emergence of the Id, are maintained by the Ego by unconscious use of five modes of contact regulation, and finally are consolidated by the reinforcement of representations within the MFR.

If our theory is valid, it should be possible to confirm, by systematic observation and clinical research, that patients with personality disorders also show qualitatively different characteristics of Ego function, as well as qualitatively different MFR configurations. As for the nature of the IF, which cannot be directly observed, only longitudinal research will be able to establish relationships between contact dilemmas, IMs, and various personality disorders. Although theoretically possible, such a research program is, at the very least, quite ambitious and for the foreseeable future theoreticians and clinicians who feel an affinity for our model can explore for themselves, in the clinical literature, possible connections between the empirical DSM perspective and the psychodynamic IF model. More immediately, we will see in the chapter on the psychotherapy of the internalized Field, how the therapist can try to work back through the contact cycles by examining the MFR and the functions of the Ego, to finally touch the USs that are at the origin of personality disorder.

Glossary of new concepts and summary of the revision

In conclusion, we present first a glossary of the new concepts introduced in the revised theory of the Self. Then we succinctly resume our revision of the Perls, Hefferline, and Goodman theory of the Self. This summary consists of twenty-six proposals organized along six axes.

Glossary

Contact dilemma: A configuration of the Field in which an element of the environment is experienced as simultaneously indispensable for survival and intolerable for survival. The young Self can resolve such a dilemma only by a process of primary introjection of the element.

US (Unfinished Situation): The prototypical example has capital letters to distinguish it from lower level unfinished situations. The US is the product of an interruption of the contact cycle by a primary introjection when the young Self confronts a contact dilemma.

IM (Introjected Micro-field): Analogous to Perls et al.'s introjects and Fairbairn's subsidiary Selves. A result of the US, it is formed by an element of the environment, a part of the Self, and the contact boundary between the two. By definition, it is practically inaccessible to consciousness.

IF (Introjected Field): The sum of introjected microfields. Analogous to the endopsychic structure of Fairbairn.

Us (Unfinished situation): Written with lower-case to distinguish it from the US. The unfinished situation may or may not be a consequence of the US, and is more accessible to consciousness.

MRF (Matrix of Representations of the Field): A configuration of the personality function, in which one finds representations that are easily accessible to consciousness, which can be verbally described. These representations are of the Self and the Other, and can have a positive or negative value.

S

1. Epistemological foundation

    - Consciousness is a fundamental element of human nature and of Field dynamics. Although it can permit comprehension of the content of the Field, it is not necessarily implicated in the production of that content.
    - Experience, the content of consciousness, can be a part of internal reality, although all experience originates in the dynamics of the Field.

2. Development of the Self

    - The Self is a dynamic structure of contact, of the creation of Figures, and of meaning. It is a product of the internalisation of the Field and the dynamic sum of these internalisations.
    - All the operations of the Self in the Field, whether creative or conservative, are charged with energy and seek meaning.
    - At birth, the individual is essentially a unitary psychophysiological organism, with cognitive, affective, and sensori-motor potentials that can be actualised by contact with a favourable human environment. Through this environment early experience takes on meaning and the Self is the psychic apparatus that is developed and grows by contact with this environment. The Self is composed of internalised human relations.
    - In its development the Self internalises the environment by one of two modes: structuring and non-structuring. Internalisation is the process by which aspects of external reality and relations with that reality are taken into the organism and represented in its internal structure. Primary introjection is the conservative form of internalisation and assimilation is the creative form. Once internalised, a relation lives within, in the form of a representation.
    - In the healthy person, the Self is made up essentially of assimilated internalisations, accessible to ordinary consciousness. Elements of the internalised Field serve as flexible guideposts during contact phases and as psycho-immunometabolic protections against the ingestion of elements that are toxic for the Self.
    - During internalisation, a Contact Dilemma arises when the Field is configured in such a way that the experience is simultaneously indispensable and intolerable. It is then impossible for the young child's Self to find meaning by constructing a precise Figure.

The only solution is to introject the experience so as to have the indispensable while suppressing consciousness of the intolerable. The experience is interrupted and unfinished.
- This process produces a loss of the unity of the Self: microcosms of the Field are swallowed whole by the Self and "live" as representations maintained in an unconscious state.
- As these microcosms were internalised by primary introjections, we call them Introjected Microfields (IM). Each experience introjected during a Contact Dilemma is an IM and is maintained in the background. These IMs contaminate the process of Figure formation and can be confused with the Field. In psychotic states they can even be substituted for the Field. The sum of these IMs is the Introjected Field (IF).
- Introjection of an experience (an element of the environment plus an element of the Self plus the contact boundary between the two) simultaneously indispensable for survival and intolerable is the prototype of unfinished situations. To distinguish these prototypes form other unfinished situations that do not result from contact dilemmas and remain accessible to consciousness, they are capitalised: Unfinished Situations. They are incomplete relational experiences and as such exist over time and not only at the moment of contact.

3. Functions of the Self

- The Id is the "container" not only of the classical emerging elements, but also of Unfinished Situations and of the energy that they continue to contain. In this sense, the Id is not only an active process of the Self appearing during pre-contact, it also contains an unconscious psychic structure: the IF.
- The Ego is the function that connects the Self with the environment and serves as "interpreter" for the Id and for the Personality function.
- In pathology, the Ego seeks above all to reproduce the situation that led to the Unfinished Situation and occasionally, to modify it. It therefore eliminates possible behaviours and perceptions in order to maintain the integrity of the IF, keeping contradictory elements in the background and letting confirmatory elements come forward as Figure.
- The "loss of Ego functions" are regulatory modes of the exchanges between the Self and the environment, between the internal and

the external worlds. Projection is believing that the internal is external; introjection is believing that the external is internal; retroflection is an attempt to prevent the internal from touching the internal, and deflection is an attempt to prevent the external from touching the internal.
- The most serious loss of meaning is the incapacity to localise a phenomenon, to know where to place the experience that is being lived: the incapacity to connect the internal and the external in a meaningful way.
- The Personality function is not simply a "verbal copy of the Self", but contains residues of past contact cycles, including those contaminated by IMs. It is a matrix of Field representations (MFR) theoretically accessible to consciousness and that reproduces intrapsychically the constitutive elements of the Field: representations of the organism-Self and representations of the environment-Other.
- Each representation can take on one of two basic values found in the general theory of contact: nutritive or toxic.

4. The contact cycle

- The IF is maintained by the ongoing relation in the Field.
- The notion of contact should be extended to include defensive or conservative operations, to the extent that these are not a rejection of vitality but rather a re-direction of vitality toward pathological endopsychic structures.
- IMs, object relations internalised in a pathological mode, imply a loss of spontaneity, grace, and creativity in the operations at the contact boundary. The more the Self contains split structures, the more these structures exert unconscious pressure on the contact cycles and the more the Self unknowingly seeks the pathological experiences that the IMs demand.
- In pathological processes, the IMs activate contact cycles and their actions must be masked, or else the intolerable will emerge in a figure. When an emerging element is dominated by an IM, an Unfinished Situation is operating in the background to supply energy. This kind of emergence is more complicated than the others and must be analysed as a distinct process, triggering a much more complex contact cycle.

5. Psychopathology
    - Personality disorder can be defined as a constellation of behaviours and conservative attitudes whose function is to maintain the IFs by seeking and producing in various experiential Fields, contact configurations and relationships that have dynamic links with USs. This functional mode is narrow, inflexible, and a product of conservative rather than creative adjustment. All the functions of the Self are implicated.

6. Development
    - Development is not a matter of an early stage at which the individual is more or less definitively shaped. It is a continuous process that continues throughout life.
    - A developmental path involves the convergence of multiple forces acting in the Field and condensing at certain critical episodes of contact. Among these are: the universal genetic heritage of a human being, with its known stages of physiological maturation, the unique genetic makeup of each person, constitution and temperament, particularities in the contact modes of one's parents which are so many reflections of their own history and their own internalisations, developmental accidents, the social and cultural environment, etc.
    - Aetiological questions must address the crucial contact episodes and the nature of the Contact Dilemmas, in the light of three general questions: at what stage of physiological maturity does the US occur? What was at stake in that situation? What developing potential was blocked by the US?
    - This reflection can be illuminated by any of several competing explanatory systems, insofar as a basic criterion of pertinence and utility is respected: the more a system is constructed of experiential and observable elements, the easier it will be to integrate it in an aetiological framework. On the other hand, the more a system depends upon a series of hierarchical inferences, the less pertinence it will have for an understanding of aetiology.

Note

1. A set of stabilised processes that have acquired a certain regularity and that have, by their nature, a slow transformation. (Yontef, 1993)

CHAPTER EIGHT

Gestalt psychotherapy: from object relations to hermeneutic dialogue

In our revision of the Gestalt theory of human nature, we have attempted to fill in some of the gaps in the original version by incorporating several elements from the endopsychic structural approach of Fairbairn. As we have progressed, it has become clear that both schools see the healthy adult as free from the need for compensatory attachment to internal objects, his or her energy being entirely available for contacts and interactions with other individuals in the environment. This vision of the healthy adult can be considered to constitute the goal of deep psychotherapy, in that the individual with a personality disorder invests an inordinate amount of energy in the introjected microfields, thus limiting his capacity for creative adjustments in the external Field.

In order to arrive at a complete therapeutic system in Mahrer's sense of the term, we need to add a theory of psychotherapy that would be consistent with our theory of human nature. But in the context of our functional-deductive epistemological approach, it would be premature to attempt such a step. As clinical experience progressively validates or eliminates hypotheses, such a theory could develop; in the meantime we will propose a provisional foundation for a Gestalt theory of the psychotherapy of the introjected field—the Gestalt equivalent of object relations—in the context of the treatment of personality disorders. This foundation could serve as a preliminary connection between a revised theory of the Self and a Gestalt clinical practice that remains to be systematically developed. Our aim is not to produce a manual or a guide to clinical psychotherapy, but rather to sketch the boundaries within which, it seems to us, Gestalt psychotherapy should evolve.

We can return to Perls et al. to see that in the original version of Gestalt psychotherapy, the objective was to analyse the internal structure of ongoing experience, according to the nature and intensity of contact within that experience: "By working on the unity and disunity of this structure of the experience here and now, it is possible to remake the dynamic relations of the figure and ground until the contact is heightened, the awareness brightened and the behaviour energized" (1951, p. 273).

No Gestaltist would dispute this general principle. In Gestalt psychotherapy, the goal is indeed to analyse the structure of experience and to energise the relations between Figure and Ground. But when there is a splitting, or an introjected micro-field lodged within the Id, relations with other persons are not so easily established. Gestalt therapy has always been seen as an effort to restore the capacity for contact, contact that is not lost in cases of pathology, but rather deflected from the function of creative adjustment. Consequently, we propose that Gestalt therapy be redefined as an effort to remove the barriers that isolate the introjected micro-field, thus permitting a redistribution of psychic vitality and a spontaneous, graceful flexibility at the contact boundary, characteristics of the graceful flexibility and creativity of the individual himself.

For Resnick (1995), Gestalt therapy functions within a space bounded by Field theory, phenomenology, and dialogue. Consistent with the Logos foundation we have adopted, we prefer to substitute hermeneutics for phenomenology, as the former is closer to the concept of active consciousness that creates meaning. We will return to this question at a later point.

Following Mahrer, we consider a theory of psychotherapy as a conceptual structure half-way between a theory of human nature and a collection of clinical techniques, composed of seven fundamental elements: (1) pertinent data; (2) listening and observation: what and how; (3) a higher-level description of the client and of treatment goals; (4) therapeutic objectives and the direction of change; (5) principles of therapeutic change; (6) general therapeutic strategies; (7) the triad: conditions, operations, consequences. Figure 1, taken from Mahrer (1989) illustrates the various conceptual levels of a therapeutic system.

At present, we feel that it is possible to formulate the first six elements. As for the triad—conditions, operations, consequences—we are speaking here essentially of a "manual of psychotherapy" that we will only briefly explore in the present context. In order to give the reader an idea of the concrete consequences of our theory, we will consider some of the current Gestalt techniques as examples of concrete operative procedures that could be modified by our theory.

This style of presentation has advantages and disadvantages. While it obliges us to proceed in a rigorous and exhaustive fashion, it entails conceptual separations among the elements that, in reality, are interconnected. One cannot reply in a strictly limited way to the first criterion without finding it necessary to refer to the second, or fifth, etc. This interconnected reality will oblige cross-references that we will attempt to minimize.

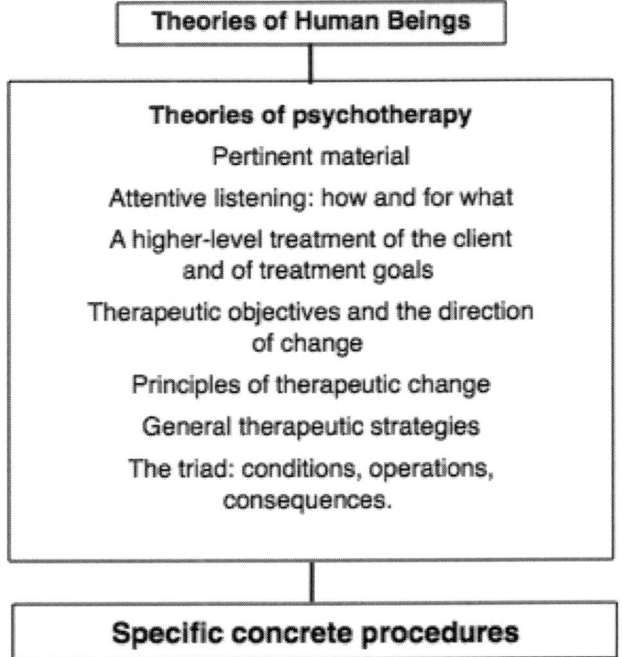

Figure 1. Mahrer's components of a psychotherapeutic system.

Pertinent material

A theory of psychotherapy must indicate the material considered to be pertinent, valuable, or significant at the therapeutic level. For instance, various therapeutic approaches differ as to the importance attributed to dreams that precede or follow a session, or to immediate physical sensations, or to traumatic experiences during infancy.

The Gestalt therapist will be attentive to unresolved situations in the various spatio-temporal fields in order to map the matrix of representations (MFR) related to these unresolved situations. Furthermore, the therapist will be attentive to the manifestation of contact cycles within the therapeutic relationship, in order to observe the Ego in action. Observation of this material will permit the therapist to observe the processes by which the Ego filters the emerging elements of the Id function.

Attentive listening: how and for what

A theory of psychotherapy will indicate to its practitioners how to observe and listen, as well as the goals of these activities. When the client is present, how should we record his verbal and nonverbal expressions? For instance, if the client speaks about her mother or her spouse, should we listen as if we are being addressed personally, or should we attempt to be a "neutral" observer? Should we focus completely on what the client is saying, or should we try to be aware of our own internal reactions to what is being said?

As we have seen, the pathological personality evolves through a series of contact cycles that are repeatedly contaminated by the presence of an internalised micro-field within the Id. This is why the clinician must be trained to recognize contact cycles that are contaminated, when they manifest themselves as distortions and dissonances between expression and experience, either in the therapeutic situation or elsewhere in the client's life. Gestalt therapists have always been trained to detect these distortions and dissonances. By letting their attention "float" somewhere between the content and the contextual information, and by letting their attention oscillate between the client and their own interior reactions, these distortions are recognized, and the therapist can then choose whether or not to bring them to the client's attention. There are of course certain stylistic variations in these processes. Certain therapists will be more inclined to concentrate on the verbally expressed content, others will be more vigilant with respect to non-verbal indications and the moment-to-moment nature of the ongoing process and others will tend to concentrate more on their own internal reactions.

Gestalt therapy has in fact always been notably open to these stylistic variations, because its practitioners believe that a therapist's individual creative style has more importance than uniform obedience to a rule. But even so, the aural receptivity and global presence of the therapist must be disciplined: this discipline, far from blocking the creativity of the therapist, allows him or her to be more focussed, and therefore able to see more deeply into the client. For example, we suggest that the therapist react to detected dissonances not as contradictions, but rather as indications of the inner complexity that the client is attempting to express. A similar reasoning applies to a smile, accompanying a reproach of the therapist. It would not be appropriate to consider this event as indicative of a pleasure—be it sadistic, masochistic, or whatever—that would be more deeply "true" than the content of the reproach. The therapist should instead hear and understand the considerable effort shown by the patient to verbalise an experience rendered highly complex by the infiltration of an IM in the contact cycle. If the dissonance is too rapidly brought to the attention of the client, in a way that suggests a reprimand or a clever unmasking of hidden motivation, the therapist will be contributing, in fact, to that which he should be attempting to combat: the splitting. In this example, the client who became convinced that his smile was "truer" than the reproach made to the therapist, would perhaps miss the occasion to examine the complexity of his relation to "the Other", a complexity in which we could perhaps find a desire to be respected, fear of the therapist's anger, a wish to control the interaction, consciousness of attempting a new, affirmative behaviour that might please the therapist, the desire as well as the fear of being taken seriously, the desire that the therapist, too, feel a little guilty, etc. In addition, as we have mentioned earlier the client often transposes uncompleted situations from one field to another. This is why the therapist must consider the possibility that when a patient places an experience in the field of a romantic relationship, the experience might concern also, or rather, the therapeutic relation. For instance, a client might complain of being neglected by her spouse, and unconsciously use that anecdote as an allusion to a problem in the therapeutic relation. Or inversely, she might reproach the therapist for not understanding her, although the experience of not being understood occurs mostly with her spouse. Transpositions of this nature are frequent because, as we saw earlier, uncompleted situations and internalised micro-fields penetrate contact cycles and contaminate the current Field. Interactions that have been influenced in this way can have the function of bringing another person to behave in ways that create a Field dynamic related to an internalised micro-field, thereby allowing the possibility of either completing the uncompleted situation and thus dissipating it, or of perpetuating the situation, thus nourishing the internalised micro-field and keeping it intact.

Ideally, the Gestalt therapist should assume the position of creative indifference that Perls described in 1942, and that we see as an equilibrium along three axes: content/form, self/other, here-and-now/elsewhere-and-not now. By flexibly maintaining this equilibrium, a Figure will gradually be seen to emerge, and if the therapist skilfully works with the emerging Figure, its contours will become increasingly clear, as well as its linkages with the Ground. Optimal therapy will work with all three axes, and no deep therapy can long neglect one of them.

A higher-level treatment of the client and of treatment goals

A theory of psychotherapy must offer a conceptual framework that allows adequate description of the client and of the treatment goals. Such a theory must, therefore, have a system and a vocabulary that can adequately classify clients, doing justice to their particularities and their ways of being, and also adequately describe the goal of the therapy. In other words, once we have observed and listened in an appropriate way, and have gathered the material in a pertinent way, how then should we organise that information in an intelligible, meaningful, and communicable form?

It is our feeling that such clinical descriptions should be made at two levels: the trans-theoretical DSM classification, and in terms of the revised theory of the Self. The first level will allow the Gestalt clinician to profit from the rich clinical literature that is rapidly developing around the DSM, and thus enrich his or her comprehension of the aetiology, the phenomenology, the epidemiology and treatment of specific personality disturbances, independently of the framework of Gestalt therapy. At this level, the clinical description can usually be rapidly established, and can be useful at the beginning of a therapeutic process, in that it permits the clinician to make a multi-axial diagnosis that will reduce the risks of major errors at the beginning, such as misjudging risk of suicide, violent acting out, effects of pharmacotherapy or organic disorders (Delisle, 1992). This descriptive level is also useful at later times for evaluative purposes: which symptoms have changed and which have resisted therapeutic efforts?

If Gestalt theory hopes to profit from insights made within other approaches, and if Gestalt therapy is to contribute its own significant, often unique insights to others, it seems to us that these exchanges depend upon communication based upon the common language of contemporary psychopathology, the DSM. We do not believe, like Rosenblatt (1995), that preoccupation with diagnostic criteria constitutes a regression that has no place in Gestalt therapy, nor do we share Robine's (1991) belief that the DSM is "incompatible" with Gestalt therapy.

The second descriptive level permits the therapist to maintain contact with the conceptual roots of Gestalt that give a meaningful coherence to his or her interventions. At this second level, the therapist continually updates her observations concerning the functions of the Self and the modes of contact regulation employed by the client. This level of description takes longer, as it does not rely simply upon descriptive criteria. The pertinent elements of this description unfold gradually as the therapist is more and more able to observe the particularities present in the modes of contact, and as the client touches upon his or her experiences in various existential fields.

Therapeutic objectives and the direction of change

This fourth element of a theory of psychotherapy jump-starts the therapeutic process, and guides it toward its destination, forming the foundation of any therapeutic action. It is not simply a matter of repeating what the classical Gestalt theory of human nature has identified as important goals—fluidity of movement, figure/ground, creative adjustment, completion of contact cycles, etc. Between these abstract goals and what might seem to be immediately appropriate at a given instant, there is a middle ground. The therapeutic objectives and the corresponding direction of change should permit a clarification of what seems desirable and attainable for the client within the framework of this therapy.

The overarching objective is clearly the reconstruction of a unified Self. To this end, the general direction of change is a movement away from ingrained, conservative, and inadequate adjustments that characterise personality disturbance, toward functional modes that flexibly combine creative adjustment and conservative adjustment, in the light of consciousness of the meaning of experience. But an objective at this level of abstraction can furnish only a very general orientation to the therapeutic process. Specific objectives vary with the personality of the client and with the nature of the IMs that occupy the deep levels of the Self. Furthermore, the specific objectives can be more or less ambitious as a function of the client's resources, the type and severity of the personality disturbance, and the nature of the therapeutic context. For a narcissistic client, for example, we might have two therapeutic objectives. First, we would probably try to reduce the symptoms as expressed by the specific criteria of the DSM. To achieve this, we would want to bring the MFR toward equilibrium with respect to the interest of the client for representations of himself as opposed to representations of the Other. We would attempt to help him become conscious of his contact regulation modalities, to dissipate many projections concerning others in the MFR. Ideally, we would want to work through the IMs to make them emerge as such in the Id, following which the Ego can identify, then re-metabolise them. But we might well be unable to achieve all that, and would have to be satisfied with a more modest result, such as a reconfiguration of the MFR and a re-education of the Ego, knowing full well that the IMs will continue to contaminate material manifested in the Id. We could at least help the client modify the identification/alienation process used by the Ego to treat these emerging elements, so that the client can find alternative responses to a situation of humiliation, for example. Instead of identifying with this emerging element, the client could learn to concentrate on the phenomenology of the current Field, and to reduce the dissonance between his internal experience and the Field, by according the benefit of the doubt to the Field in a more generous reinterpretation of the sense present in the Field. These different levels of objectives could be arranged as a continuum, as shown in Table 1.

Each objective presupposes work on one or another of the functions of the Self, the lower level objectives being limited to one or two functions, while the superior level objectives necessarily involve all three functions. This point in Mahrer's scheme could doubtlessly be refined as a function of experience with clinical reality.

Table 1. A continuum of objectives in the treatment of personality disorders.

Level 1 Modification of behavioural symptoms	Ego function. Contact regulation modalities
Level 2 Consciousness of emerging elements and their correlates in the external Field	Id and Ego functions
Level 3 Identification of creative adjustment modes that allow perception of relations between subjective experience and Field configuration	Id, Ego, and Personality function
Level 4 Understanding of the source of dissonant subjective experience	Id, Ego, and Personality functions
Level 5 Dissolution of the IM at the root of the dissonant subjective experience	Id, Ego, and Personality functions

Principles of therapeutic change

A theory of psychotherapy must advance a certain number of principles that can engender therapeutic change. Certain therapies are founded on a single sovereign principle while others are based on several principles that are more or less coherently structured together. Gelso and Carter (1985, cited by Mahrer, 1989, p. 46) consider that there are three fundamental principles underlying therapeutic change: insight, experience or awareness, and learning. Each of these fundamental principles is at the origin of a school of thought in psychotherapy. Insight, experience/awareness, and learning are at the heart of psychoanalysis, existential-humanist therapy, and behaviourist therapy respectively.

If we had to choose only one of these principles for Gestalt, it would certainly be experience/awareness. In the logical extension of our theory of human nature, we believe that consciousness, in the larger sense of Gestalt, is the indispensable means for attaining integrated, durable change. In any therapeutic interaction, integrated and durable change can occur only when affective, cognitive, or behavioural processes are rendered accessible to the creative consciousness of the client. This creative consciousness has, in addition, a natural tendency to complete the contact figures initiated in the therapeutic interaction. We might say that this natural tendency to complete figures is like wind energy, the Logos consciousness is like the sail that receives this energy, and the dialogue of the therapeutic relationship constitutes a tiller that gives direction to the incipient change.

General therapeutic strategies

The first five elements prepare the therapist for action, but this sixth element, general therapeutic strategies, directly concerns the therapeutic intervention as such. Unfortunately, the term "strategies" has led to confusion. As Mahrer points out, it is important to distinguish between this strategic level and a lower, more technical level, which Mahrer names "specific, concrete operational procedures". General therapeutic strategies should rather be seen as therapeutic "programs" that include the specific techniques that translate the strategy into successful outcomes. To take an example from the classical Gestalt repertoire, the empty chair technique can be used to achieve the strategic goal of the integration of polarities.

In our conception of Gestalt psychotherapy, durable change is the result of the application of three general, interrelated therapeutic strategies, that seek to capture and transform the energy that is present (1) in treatment of the repetition of dead-ends in the contact cycle, (2) in the various existential Fields of the client, and (3) in the hermeneutic dialogue.

Treatment of the repetition of impasses

As mentioned in the chapter concerning a revision of a theory of the Self, unfinished situations tend to recur by a more-or-less conscious, ambivalent effort to maintain themselves or to finally reach a conclusion. We went on to define personality disorders as constellations of behaviours and conservative attitudes having the function of maintaining the internal Field in seeking and producing within various experiential fields, configurations of contacts and relations that maintain dynamic links with the Unfinished Situations. The goal of the therapeutic relationship is, then, the detection of these object relational dead-ends, the recognition of their experiential dynamic, their dissolution, and restoration of a harmoniously functioning Self.

We call "reproduction" that process by which a person manipulates the environment to perpetuate his or her attachment to internal objects: in other words, externalization of the IF, which is the opposite of internalisation. The meaning of the experience is a product of the Self's actions at the contact boundary, and in fact, this "product" is a re-edition, a reproduction of an internal dynamic, put into place by an Unfinished Situation and perpetuated afterwards by the actions of the Self in the Field. Consequently, the therapist and the client need to concentrate on decoding these reproductions, of their meaning, so as to ultimately dissolve their cause, the IF. In this sense, Gestalt psychotherapy can be understood as having the same final objective as contact cycles. The client's past and present experiences are examined so as to identify those experiences that have been marked by the IF, the meaning is clarified, and the unfinished experience is brought to a satisfying conclusion. This process is achieved by collaborative and interactive attention, and a hermeneutic dialogue between the therapist and the client that engages the cognitive, affective, and sensory-motor dimensions of the client. Although the therapist maintains the central Gestalt orientation of the here-and-now, all the experiential fields of the clients are explored, with special emphasis on the field of the therapeutic relationship itself, to bring the client through the cycle reproduction-recognition-repair.

Experiential fields: from here-and-now to there-and-then

The client transposes, or transfers, patterns of interactions from one experiential Field to another. Why does this client speak here-and-now as if the therapist were a judge in a juvenile court? Why does that client expect his wife to listen to him the way his therapist does? What is it in the present interaction with this client that can help us understand his suddenly remembering a quarrel with his young brother? Or why, in this memory, he sees himself as cruel and unforgiving, while his description of the event seems to indicate the contrary?

Any therapist could add to this list of unconscious transpositions made by a client in a therapeutic session. Because personality disorders are characterized by rigid, inappropriate functioning acquired during adolescence at the latest, it is normal that the client frequently reproduces these blockages in various situations, including the therapeutic relationship. Now even if Gestalt therapy has always been known as the first approach centred on the here-and-now, it is also true that Gestalt therapists have long since ceased to be "prisoners of the present" (Polster, 1985), and recognise the importance of other times and places in human experience, and in the therapeutic process (Yontef, 1988). The therapeutic relation (here-and-now), contemporary relations (there-and-now), as well as past relations (there-and-then) must all be examined. If Gestalt therapy has always stressed the here-and-now, it is simply because in the ongoing present reality, the therapist can directly observe the development of contact cycles and thereby the action of the three functions of the Self. Being present in the immediate Field, the therapist is directly or indirectly involved with contact cycles contaminated by the IF.

In combining two values of space and of time, we arrive at a matrix of four space-time combinations. In our view, each of these combinations can have an internal or an external face, and so we arrive at eight experiential Fields in psychotherapy, as shown in Table 2.

Although theoretically every fragment of a therapeutic interview can be connected to one or another of these Fields, it often happens that a client will not be able to identify an experience clearly with its pertinent Field. For certain clients, the internal Field or the reality of psychic life are denied in a determination to "stick to facts". Others will be so attached to their internal experience that they neglect—deflect— events in the external Field. Others again will not "get the connection" between the different Fields in their experience, and will be unable to see how they themselves have contributed to the creation of their own problems.

If we think of transference as being a movement from the interior to the exterior, rather than from the past to the present, is it not contradictory to then take the past into account? In a Field theory, the past is not denied. "The Field is the largest and least delimited system and, importantly, the Field contains the history of the Field" (Resnick, 1995). In fact, we are not speaking of the historical past at all, but rather the past as it affects the current configuration of the Field. When, for example, we work with a client of forty years to dissolve an IM formed by a contact dilemma when he was five years old, we are not working on something

Table 2. Experiential fields.

	External level *The phenomenology of observable contact in the field* **(E)**	**Internal level** *The Matrix of Representations of Self and Other* **(I)**
Here and now (1)	Here and now therapeutic contact as could be observed by a reasonable third party acting in good faith	Internal representations of self and other in H&N, no matter what is actually happening at the contact boundary
Here and then (2)	A past encounter in the therapeutic relationship about which spontaneous descriptions converge	Internal representations of what went on in the therapeutic relationship at that time and what it meant to the client, regardless of what "actually" happened
There and now (3)	A current significant relationship in the client's life. What could be observed by a reasonable observer acting in good faith	Internal representations of self and other in that relationship in terms of "who is doing what to whom", whatever may be going on in actual fact
There and then (4)	A relationship from the client's past (usually childhood). What really happened and could have been observed by a reasonable observer commenting in good faith	Internal representations of self and other in that relationship in terms of "who was doing what to whom", whatever may have been going on in actual fact

that happened thirty-five years ago, we are working on something that has been repeating itself for thirty-five years.

Optimal psychological functioning would be characterised by the capacity to: (1) clearly distinguish events in the interior Field from those in the ongoing external Field; (2) establish connections between contact episodes in different spatial-temporal Fields; and (3) recognise and reduce experiential dissonance between inner and outer events when necessary. The Gestalt psychotherapist must thus become a master of transitions in a multi-dimensional therapeutic universe, guiding the client in his or her explorations of the different existential Fields, and in particular within the therapeutic relationship itself. To do so, the therapist must develop his capacity to see the connections that the client cannot, and to bring them to their joint attention.

Hermeneutic dialogue

Connections are brought to conscious attention by a process of hermeneutic dialogue between therapist and client. An essentially constructive endeavour, hermeneutics seeks the creation of meaning rather than the uncovering of fixed and fossilised meanings, supposedly long hidden under layers of "defences". The very foundation of hermeneutics, as developed by Dilthey and Husserl, involves a multi-dimensional vision of meaning that is both horizontal (in space) and vertical (in time) (Thines & Lempereur, 1975). Hermeneutic dialogue (Dia-Logos) occupies an intermediate space between simple descriptive phenomenology as formulated by the consciousness of the client, and clinical interpretation as formulated by the therapist. As such, hermeneutic dialogue would seem to be the very essence of a psychotherapy founded on interaction in the Field, and based on a firm Logos foundation.

Since Ricoeur's 1995 work, we can more easily recognize as naive the phenomenologist's claim that reality delivers itself directly and effortlessly to our consciousness. Reality is not given, it must be constructed, even invented. A new epistemology is needed, in which phenomenology can only partially reveal the meanings present in a situation, the rest must be constructed from what was present but hidden. The verbalisations of the client and those of the therapist are accordingly seen as forming an interactive narration that gradually constructs a meaning that is no longer expected to spring forth effortlessly. We are speaking of a massive advance beyond phenomenology, an advance based upon three fundamental principles: reality only responds when it is directly interrogated, meaning can only be constructed on the basis of intended meaning, and truth is more constructed than revealed. (Bouchard & Guérette, 1991, p. 22, trans. James Everett.)

Phenomenology is the initial step in the identification of meaning, in which only meaning that is immediately present to consciousness is grasped. But in our revised theory of Self, the IF is unattainable by ordinary consciousness, and phenomenology is ill-equipped to seek out and construct meanings that have been internalised in this manner. It is therefore necessary to resort to epistemological tools that are equal to the task, hence our choice of hermeneutic dialogue.

Dissolution of an internalised micro-field depends partially on the possibility offered to the client to reproduce an Unfinished Situation in a hermeneutic interaction. In most cases, the hermeneutic effort in itself can bring about closure of the Unfinished Situation. The hermeneutic posture of the therapist is marked particularly by an empathic receptivity to the client's use of contact regulation modes, in Fields 1 and 2. It's a difficult task for the therapist. On the one hand, he must allow the client to reproduce the inadequate contact modes that frequently lead him to dead ends—if not, the therapeutic relationship will not activate the usual functional patterns of the client, or worse, will become submerged in those patterns with neither the client nor the therapist being aware of what is happening. But on the other hand, the client must profit from the therapeutic relationship to become conscious of his functional patterns and of what lies beneath their appearance. Transformation becomes possible because the therapist is not afraid of contact with the client in a form that the client both reproduces and fears, while at the same time refusing to respond to the inadequate contact modes the way others "always have responded". Transformation occurs when the dead end is in fact reproduced, when its meaning has been properly constructed and when the therapist, representing the Other, puts his own contribution in the balance and searches, with the client, the creative adjustment where the client has only been able to find a conservative adjustment.

The model that we propose can be distinguished from other reparative relations by the presence of hermeneutics. While other relationships can have occasional hermeneutic moments, rarely will they show a sustained, intentional hermeneutic. We can speak of a therapeutic contact cycle, similar to the classical contact cycle, that we call reproduction-recognition-reparation. Reproduction emanates from Unfinished Situations, recognition and reparation originate from the therapist, who initiates his therapeutic efforts in a state of "creative indifference", conscious of three levels of relationship, any of which can assume a momentary dominance in the contact: the transference relationship, the hermeneutic relationship, and the real relationship. Each of these is associated with an important aspect of the therapeutic cycle, and it is the therapist's responsibility to direct the process in such a way that each of these aspects can emerge and reach completion. At the same time, the therapist must be attentive to signs of the reproduction of dead ends, and must be able to properly interpret them. In other words, the general therapeutic strategy is pluridimensional, as Mahrer would say. Table 3 illustrates the strategic connections between these dimensions.

The clinician begins by observing the contact episodes present in the client's discourse, as well as the client's internal experience, to work back to the IMs at the origin of the contact distortions. Careful observation of these distortions can lead to etiological hypotheses that can then be examined in the hermeneutic process of meaning creation. If the gap is too great between the phenomenology of the distortions and the explanatory hypothesis that seems to emerge, the client will be

Table 3.

Contact cycle	Pre-contact	Full contact	Post-contact
Therapeutic cycle	Reproduction in a given experiential field	Recognition of links between various experiential fields	Repair or closure of the Unfinished Situation
Therapeutic issue	Activate an internalised micro-field in the external field	Become conscious that the external field is contaminated by an internalized micro-field and become conscious of the connections between the events and the experiences of various experiential fields	Make a creative adjustment that takes into account the Internalized Field, the MRC, and the external field
Relational mode	Transfer	Hermeneutic	Real

unable to participate in the co-creation of meaning, and the hermeneutic process itself becomes meaningless.

Bouchard and Guérette (1991, p. 24) advance five facilitating factors for hermeneutic success in psychotherapy. The therapist can favour hermeneutic dialogue by:

Maintaining a state of creative indifference that allows the client to structure the real field in a meaningful way.

Seeking to construct meaning interactively rather than seeking a meaning that is supposedly waiting to be discovered.

Being less preoccupied by accurately determining historical reality, and more concerned with experiential reality that, by definition, changes over time.

Never losing sight of the overarching goal of therapy: directing the clients energy toward healing, and not being distracted by aiming at an aesthetically pleasing result.

Always remembering to actively seek phenomenological truth, without which an interpretation cannot be genuinely accepted.

The triad: conditions, operations, consequences

As mentioned earlier, it would be premature to attempt to make any substantial contributions under this heading at present. The triad is essentially a practical manual, but even so, we can attempt to make a few suggestions as to what might be included in such a manual. Firstly, we should indicate to clinicians following our approach, the conditions that can justify establishing a connection between one experiential field and another, and the consequences of establishing such connections. Inversely, we should furnish some indications of the conditions conducive to pursuing a dialogue in one field rather than making a transition to another field. Next, we should furnish a reflective tool that can be applied with empathy to the modes of contact regulation that the client employs in the therapeutic relationship. Such an interpretative table would help the clinician discriminate, in the present moment, what emerges from the client and what emerges from within himself. Finally, given that we are restructuring Gestalt therapeutic interventions around the hermeneutic dialogue and the exploitation of the therapeutic relationship itself, we should suggest some guidelines that can help therapists choose among the concrete, specific techniques in such a way that the relation is not short-circuited.

Specific concrete procedures

Without going into an exhaustive enumeration of all of the techniques of Gestalt therapy, we can illustrate the kind of technical restructuring that we envisage with four well known examples: the continuum of consciousness, awareness of immediate somatic experience, dreamwork, and various forms of working with polarities.

The continuum of consciousness

The continuum of consciousness is sometimes considered as the Gestalt version of free association: the client lets his or her attention wander where it wants to go. The therapist applies a kind of focussed attention, in association with a minimalist intervention that, at this stage, consists essentially of four kinds of questions, along with brief descriptive comments. Typical questions include: "What are you doing? What are you thinking? What are you feeling? What do you want?" These questions are typical of Gestalt in the same way that other questions are traditionally associated with classical psychoanalysis: "What is the hidden desire of the client? What is he afraid of, in desiring that? When he is afraid, what does he do to reduce the danger?" (Pray, 1993).

While the client lets her attention wander, the therapist focuses her attention on the micro-processes at the contact-boundary. In our view, the objective at this stage is to permit the client to gradually and uncritically accept elements that emerge from the Id, including those that have been contaminated by the IF. In other words, we attempt to monitor emerging elements of the Id while at the same time neutralising the filtering operations of the Ego that would otherwise have a tendency to reject certain elements. The immediate objective is to allow access to emerging experiences, and then this technique will be gradually replaced by empathic dialogue about background experiences that probably contain elements of Unfinished Situations. As time passes, this technique will produce a corrective empathic effect, in the sense of Kohut and Wolf (1978).

Awareness of immediate somatic experience

The IFs contain energy: therefore we can infer that the splittings that created these IFs consumed energy. Since energy is created by the body, we can conclude that in a sense it is the body that produces splitting.

Now because the splitting is a material reality and not an abstraction, it is observable. Gestalt therapy, influenced by Reich, holds that the contact functions (speaking, moving, looking, listening to, feeling, tasting, touching) contain, in pathological states, chronic neutralisers of experience (Polster & Polster, 1973). Reich believed that the libido had become a mysterious abstraction for psychoanalysis, and he passed on to Gestalt therapists the conviction that it is false to imagine that a person has no energy or is apathetic. The Gestalt therapist believes instead that apparent apathy is in fact a consequence of a re-direction of energy toward contact resistance and, in terms of our thinking, toward maintaining the splitting and IMs. Since IMs are energy and since energy is necessarily connected to matter, it follows that it is in and by the body that they produce their effects. Because of this, the Gestalt therapist will avoid excessively intellectualising the therapeutic process. Of course the verbal channel is important, but it is only one of many ways of accessing the interior reality and its phantasms. Awareness of immediate somatic experience is a precious interpretative tool and, when added to the deliberate amplification of this experience, a fundamental path to transformation.

Dreamwork

Fairbairn and the Gestalt therapists have strikingly similar views about dreams, as Bouchard and Derome (1987) have pointed out. Work on dreams can be a powerful tool for undoing splittings and metabolising IFs. The problem for the Gestalt therapist is to keep dream-discussion within bounds, and to avoid its becoming a convenient way of deflecting important clinical work. It can happen in long-term therapy that a client runs out of gas, for example after an intense session, or a retroflexion of contact (aggression, dependence anxiety, etc.) with the therapist. At such times, if the client or the therapist has trouble tolerating the anxiety of this "empty" period, they may collude to create a diversion. Working on a dream provides the "benefit" of involving material over which the conscious Self (the Ego function) has no control, and therefore for which the client cannot be held "responsible". As Isadore From (1980) noted, the moment and the way in which the dream is brought to attention are often more important than the dream itself.

In any case, Gestalt dream interpretation should permit the client to proceed in a way similar to that of the therapist in general: by trial identifications (Olinick, Poland, Grigg & Granatir, 1973, cited by Tansey & Burke, 1989). As the therapist helps the client enter certain parts of the dream by use of techniques such as reformulating the dream content in the present tense and using the first person, he must be vigilant in detecting dream images that are in fact representations of split parts of the Self. Conscious of the dynamics of these splittings, he will refrain from attempting a premature, even magic, reintegration of these split elements. The dream is rather a vehicle for becoming conscious of the IF and of the splitting, and the client should be initially encouraged to tolerate the splitting rather than try to evacuate it too quickly. We believe that adequate treatment of the IF involves a restoration of the complete object relation, here and now, in the therapeutic relationship. If, however, the therapist shows a preference for one or another of the elements present, he runs the risk of making a Gestalt version of the error cited by Fairbairn, that is, taking the position of a Rejecting Object with respect to that which the client cannot tolerate as a Figure. This can induce the client to force a resolution that is only apparent. The conflict between the elements of the IF, accumulated over years of defensive operations, is indeed banished, but only from the conscience.

Various forms of working with polarities

Any introductory to Gestalt gives significant space to the concept of polarity, and all training institutions insist upon this point. The concept of polarity can be compared with that of the splitting of the Ego. In Perls' demonstrations, one can find several approaches to polarities that merit study. The best known technique, that of the empty chair, has been so badly applied by undertrained individuals, that it is sometimes only a parody of a therapeutic intervention. In addition, as this technique was developed in the context of group therapy, it is difficult to apply to an individual client, who often feels embarrassment. It is no surprise that the bad press of this technique has led to its neglect by an important number of Gestalt therapists. But it is perhaps not the technique in itself that is at fault, but rather its application. There is amateur Gestalt, just as there is amateur analysis. Can this technical innovation be rehabilitated in the context of a revised Gestalt whose goals are the dissolution of the IF and the reunification of the Self?

Here as elsewhere, a Gestalt technique cannot be effectively applied without adequately taking into account the temporal dimension.

Various forms of dialogue can be used in short-term interventions to solve minor problems or treat troublesome symptoms like phobias. In such cases, the technique must be applied in such a way as to respect the limitations inherent in pre-contact situations: in particular, it is imperative to carefully prepare the transition from an internal state appropriate to dialogue with a flesh-and-blood interlocutor (the therapist) to an internal state essential for dialogue with an imaginary person. Failure here on the part of the therapist can quickly lead to an intolerable impression of a ridiculous, futile exercise for the client.

Application of the empty chair technique to the longer-term exercise of personality therapy demands attention to other aspects, notably to the fact that the dialogue produced is in fact between elements of the IF, whatever the identity that might be assigned to the interlocutors. These dialogues must not be allowed to reach hasty conclusions, which would be nothing more than inadequate compromises. The therapist who guides such a dialogue should be conscious of being a witness of an "historic meeting" and act accordingly. Thus, for instance, in the pre-contact period, he should help the client approach the IM by having a comprehensive attitude when the client shows resistances (hesitations, confusions, memory blanks, etc.) that appear as the IMs get closer to consciousness. In the contact phase, the therapist can help the client tolerate the intensity of the conflict rather than deflecting it. As for full contact, it seems to us that this can become possible only over the long term, during which the client gradually becomes tolerant of elements that appear to him to be mysterious and dangerous.

It would be a mistake to reassure the client too much during these periods of anxiety. All too frequently, a therapist can underestimate the dangerous nature of IMs. Paradoxically, the client finds himself in the familiar territory of a lack of empathy known since childhood, when parents who were incapable of tolerating their child's suffering tried to belittle it with reassurances. Yes, the therapist should always begin by being considered a good object, he must also become an exorcist, as Fairbairn concluded: it is not enough to "forgive sins", the therapist must also "expel the demons" (Fairbairn, 1943).

These comments do not do justice to the wide range of Gestalt therapy techniques, and important questions must still be answered. For example, what connections, indications, and reserves can be made between work on the relationship and resorting to techniques that, temporarily, put the relationship "on hold"? How is the fundamental nature of the relationship affected by occasional use of these techniques? Is the traditional format of one weekly meeting sufficient for the introspection needed in the treatment of splittings of the Self?

We conclude this chapter with a reminder of the limits imposed at the beginning of the discussion. It was never our intention to propose a "user's manual" for the practice of the psychotherapy of object relations—that would have been a truly monumental task, and in any case, premature. We did, however, intend to suggest several guidelines for the elaboration of a more complete theory of IF psychotherapy, a task for the future. In so doing, we have hopefully put into place some essential elements of a therapeutic system, in Mahrer's sense of the term.

CHAPTER NINE

Neuroscientific perspective of ORGT: neurodynamics of the Self in therapeutic dialogue

Can contemporary neuroscience make substantial contributions to the theory and practice of psychotherapy? New possibilities of observing the brain *in vivo* have spurred growth of two major axes of research, each of which holds great potential pertinence for psychotherapy. The first addresses the pathogenesis and malleability of certain pathodynamic elements, and asks questions such as: what is the neurodevelopmental history of impulsiveness, shame, the incapacity to remain calm, separation anxiety, and so forth. In fact these questions are not limited to the history of development, but touch as well upon the conditions that can permit these mental states or tendencies to be reversed. The second axis of research addresses the functional mechanisms of psychotherapy such as, for example, the generality and the permanence of the effects of psychotherapy on synaptic function.

Historical background

To begin with, let's not forget that Freud was a neurologist. In his day, neurology was a young science closely linked with psychiatry. As Shterenshis wrote:

> It is frequently said and believed that the history of clinical neurology of the nineteenth century has much in common with the history of psychiatry. Though neurology and psychiatry are neighbouring clinical disciplines, the development of clinical neurology differs from that of psychiatry in nineteenth century Europe. The history of bedside neurology is that of a gradual separation of nervous diseases from other internal diseases. Despite the efforts of the German psychiatrists, any influence of psychiatry on that process was very limited. (1999)

Realizing that the scientific method of his day could do little to advance his research, Freud initiated a movement that so rapidly distanced psychiatry from clinical neurology that during the twentieth century, these two disciplines might never have crossed paths again. In fact, serious contact had to wait till the end of the 70s, when Eric Kandel, psychiatrist and future Nobel prizewinner in medicine, reunited these two mental disciplines:

> I want to consider the simplistic but perhaps useful idea that the ultimate level of resolution for understanding how psychotherapeutic intervention works is identical with the level at which we are currently seeking to understand how psychopharmacologic intervention works—the level of individual nerve cells and their synaptic connections. (1979)

Without examining this text in detail, we can note that it clearly announces the conceptual convergence under discussion in this paper, a convergence that has continued with increasing speed over the ensuing years. The Journal of Neuropsychiatry and Clinical Neurosciences appeared in 1989, followed by the Decade of the Brain, the 1990s, during which there was an explosion of brain research, perhaps somewhat disorganised but nevertheless rich in potential.

At the beginning of the third millennium, this conceptual convergence is no longer hypothetical but an established fact, consecrated by the foundation of the International Neuropsychoanalysis Society in July 2000. It should be noted also that according to Kupfer, First, and Regier (2002), the APA, in its preparatory text for the DSM-V, devoted a fifty-page chapter to the contribution of the neurosciences to the pathogenesis of mental disturbances. We are witnessing the birth of a new paradigm with the potential to unify a fragmented field of study, of theorisation, and of clinical practice. I will term this axis of convergence neuropsychotherapy. In using this term, we are not attempting to "validate" psychotherapy by neurosciences, but rather, as Solms (Solms & Turnbull, 2002) has proposed, a dialogue between an objective and a subjective approach to the brain, between a worker who observes neuro-images and a worker who proceeds by taking his own subjectivity as an object and his own objectivity as a subject. As such, our implicit epistemological framework is one of reciprocal orientation and support. For those whose aim is to understand central nervous system function in psychotherapeutic situations, this epistemological dialogue is between Eros and Psyche on the one hand, and between Neuros and Psyche on the other.

The brain in the third milennium

So what does the brain look like in the third millennium? In fact, the brain itself has not changed much over the past several thousand years. It's still "the size of a coconut, the shape of a walnut, the colour of veal liver, and the consistency of an overripe peach" (Sykes-Picot & Simon, 2004). This rather odd fruit is formed of billions of cells, each of which is electrochemically linked to roughly 10,000 others making it, in fact, the most complex biological entity on the planet. Previously, the brain was considered to be the organic, material reality that determined our emotions. Perspectives were invariably dichotomist, the body being opposed to the head, the physical to the psychological, nature to culture. Today we understand that the brain is a highly plastic organ that grows via renewed internal integrations all through life. Although the brain itself has not changed, our perception of it has. In the not-so-distant past, it was thought that the brain was a finished product, comprised of a fixed number of cells that determined the limits of our affective experiences. It was matter, the literal incarnation of "nature" in the classic "nature/nurture" dichotomy. Innate, it pre-determined the limits of future learning. More recently, we have come to understand that the genetic heritage is not in itself a good predictor of the appearance of mental illness. Current models are invariably multifactorial, combining the genetic heritage with environmental factors that sculpt their expression (Gabbard, 2000). Turning, as it were, the ancient idea on its "head", we can say that this highly interpersonal organ is "created" by emotions that structure and organise it!

As Freud anticipated, it is from here only a small step to imagine neurodynamic correlates to psychic structures or functions, but this small step has proved difficult to take. It is relatively easy to consider that the limbic system is related to the Id and the prefrontal lobes to the Ego, but that does not get us very far. Damasio (2000, 2003) and Panksepp (1998) have adopted the more promising perspective of affective phylogeny. Panksepp distinguishes four phylogenetically transmitted systems of emotional activation: pleasure-seeking, anger-rage, fear-anxiety, and panic-distress. At the dawn of humanity, these systems were necessary for individual and species survival. They are "economical" in the sense that they permit rapid, automatic, and adequate responses to biologically significant events. The precise temperament of a given individual would depend upon the relative strengths of these systems in his or her affective profile.

These hypotheses are still rather speculative and, indeed, it would take a foolhardy neuro-psychoanalyst to advance any of these ideas with firm certainty. We are on even shakier ground when it comes to dynamic concepts such as repression and splitting. At the neurodynamic level, concepts such as these seem plausibly related to the various forms of memory, because in fact that is exactly what is at stake in these phenomena: How can it be that we do not know, or no longer know, what it is that happened to us? How is it that in spite of the absence of a clear memory, we behave as if the memory is still influencing the present? The study of long-term memory and its complex links with affective life dominates neuro-psychoanalysis. We now know that memories are not "stocked" intact in an archive somewhere in the brain. Instead, the constitutive elements of a memory are distributed to various regions, and several cortical and subcortical functions are implicated in their storage and retrieval. In these complex processes, the amygdala and the hippocampus play very different and essential roles, as we shall describe later.

Psychotherapy: an intervention that has permanent effects on the brain

Psychotherapy can change gene expression and create long-lasting modifications in the force of synaptic connections (Kandel, 1998). During verbal exchanges between a client and a therapist, there is more going on than observable visual and verbal contact: the therapist's nervous system exerts an indirect but quite real and, hopefully, long-term effect on the client's nervous system. This influence is probably reciprocal.

As recent data have shown, psychotherapy and certain psychoactive medications have similar neurophysiological effects.

Both psychotherapy and fluoxetine (Prozac) produce a reduction of cerebral metabolism in the right point of the caudate nucleus (Gabbard, 1994).

Certain psychological interventions can modify the brain's response to biochemical influences (Shear, Fyer & Ball, 1991).

Psychodynamic therapy significantly impacts serotonin metabolism (Vijnamäki, Kuikka & Tiihonen, 1999).

As for Gestalt therapy in particular, Cozolino (2002) remarks that

> … Gestalt therapy … is a unique expression of psychodynamic therapy that is particularly relevant to the notion of neural integration. […] The Gestalt therapist believes that maximizing awareness of all aspects of the self—including cognition, emotion, behaviour, and sensation—will result in increased maturation and psychological health. This process depends upon the integration of the neural networks responsible for each of these functions.

In typical Gestalt concepts such as the continuum of awareness or Figure/Ground movements, one can easily see that Gestalt psychology and Gestalt therapy have been marked by a constant effort to integrate behaviour, affect, and cognition; the perennial preoccupation with this triad is a trait that the Gestalt tradition shares with contemporary neuroscience.

Another important idea for Gestalt therapy is that of integration. Full awareness of emotion, and the co-construction of the meaning of emotionally charged experience is at the heart of the Gestalt process, and these depend upon integration.

Fries (2005) sees integration as a communication between brain regions that depends upon "neuronal coherence": a synchronisation of activity that would permit receptivity to activation arriving over channels of communication. The network is composed of dense local circuits interconnected by large communication pathways. Coherence also permits recruiting of larger neuronal populations for a given activity, thus enhancing the potential for adequate and fast treatment of information. "Oscillations of a neuronal group rhythmically open and close the group's windows for communication." But this communication must be precisely controlled.

> It is the very nature of a communication structure that communication is facilitated in a structured or selective way and not globally. Global phase locking is found during states of epilepsy and is obviously incompatible with normal cognitive functioning. The fact that the brain normally manages to avoid epileptic states, but rather generates an intricate communication structure, suggests that it is equipped with robust regulation mechanisms.

In Fries' vision, selective attention would be the manifestation of a selective rhythm in a subsystem, as for example the circuit corresponding to an attended part of the visual field. A top-down message from executive regions establishes the preferred rhythm which then spreads through the system, blocking off competing rhythms and therefore competing information.

> I hypothesize that neuronal communication is mechanistically subserved by neuronal coherence. Activated neuronal groups oscillate and thereby undergo rhythmic excitability fluctuations that produce temporal windows for communication. Only coherently oscillating neuronal groups can interact effectively because their communication windows for input and for output are open at the same times.

It is not difficult to see how these ideas could be applied to situations where affect and cognition are not integrated. Consider an individual whose neuronal processes are frequently destabilised by stress-induced perturbations. Oscillations within a group of neurons would easily fall out of phase, because many neurons would respond not only to the oscillation frequency, but also to stress input. As a result of these perturbations, coherence within the oscillating circuit is reduced, information is lost and information that remains is treated in a less adequate fashion. As the perturbation increases, coherence could be reduced to a point at which integration fails, and contact between "emotions" and "cognition" would be lost.

Memory in psychopathology and psychotherapy

Anyone who hopes to successfully navigate in the complex universe of inter-psychic communications and influences must necessarily examine and understand the properties of memory. Surprisingly, little attention is paid to memory as such in the psychotherapeutic literature. Psychoanalysis has long rejected the notion of a passive, static, and totally accessible memory, and the theoretical universe of psychoanalysis is rich in concepts such as splitting, repression, and retroflexion, that label some of the surprising properties of memory. Now clearly this psychodynamic memory is not some immaterial entity, but rather depends upon activity in various subsystems of the central nervous system. It would require hundreds of pages to give a detailed explanation of the neuronal bases of memory: we shall be content to concisely outline this complexity, underlining whenever possible the pertinence for today's clinician.

In the universe of cognitive neuroscience, memory is not one and indivisible: it has multiple forms and functions. Memory can be short-term or long-term, but it can also be explicit, implicit, declarative, episodic, or semantic. Clearly, the general psychotherapist will be particularly interested in long-term memory and its properties. Recent research gives us a complex, intricate image of memory functions and of their localisation. We know today that the hippocampus and the temporal lobes, as well as the limbic structures connected to them, interact in complex ways during the consolidation of long-term memory. The hippocampus seems to act as a dispatching agent, guiding associations among the various modules of cortical and limbic regions (Moscovitch, 1992). But the hippocampus matures only during the second year of life: earlier on, the amygdala participates in memory formation. Amini (1966) finds that implicit memory of early attachment, communicated by affective language, forms a durable neural structure that influences later affective autoregulation and interpersonal interactions. During psychotherapy, clinicians often observe behaviours that are poorly adapted to present circumstances, but were pertinent in an earlier stage of development. Each therapeutic system applies its particular set of conceptual structures to explain this phenomenon. In Object Relational Gestalt therapy (ORGT), we speak of an infiltration of some Unfinished Developmental Business from the past, a sort of introjected microfield in the current figure formation. In terms of the neurodynamics of memory, we will speak of an intrusion of early implicit or procedural memory into adult consciousness. Now this implicit memory is essential raw material for the therapeutic process. Early attachment relations that have been internalised and consolidated as procedural memory are a mainspring of transference (Amini et al., 1996). As we will discuss later, certain dialectical techniques can favour awareness of implicit/ procedural memories. It could well be that the cardinal process of the psychotherapy of personality disorders is in fact this continual interaction of implicit and explicit memories. This is why psychotherapy can be seen in a neurocognitive context as a relationship that aims to revisit the implicit memory of attachment.

Plasticity and memory

The developmental plasticity of the brain, and therefore of the memory modules, is well illustrated in recent research such as that of Driessen et al. (2000). This German research team found that subjects with personality disorders had smaller (16 per cent) hippocampuses and smaller (7 per cent) amygdalas than did normal subjects. Gurvits et al. (1996) had already shown that subjects who had experienced post-traumatic stress had smaller than normal hippocampi. And in 2002 Gilbertson et al., in a twin study, showed that hippocampal size predicted the appearance of personality disturbance. It is still early days for major conclusions from this current of research, especially since longitudinal studies are lacking and dissimilar populations have been studied. But even so, the results are consistent with the theoretical positions of several forms of relational psychotherapy. ORGT among others holds that early traumatic relationships, experienced in a context where the indispensable coexists with the intolerable, leave memory traces normally inaccessible to consciousness but nonetheless active in the form of introjected micro-fields. Furthermore, these micro-fields tend to shape experience in ways that recall the themes of developmental trauma. In the research cited here, early trauma appears to hinder development of essential memory structures, thus affecting later recall of the trauma. Another study showed that this neurodevelopmental blockage is correlated with the appearance of post-traumatic states: it is plausible to imagine that subjectively these stress states would have thematic affinities with the original traumatic events.

Neuronal plasticity is implicitly demonstrated by Bruner's (1990) study showing that memories are modified at each recall. Other studies (Ceci & Bruch, 1993; Loftus, Milo & Paddock, 1995) also demonstrated this malleability and especially the importance of the co-construction of meaning during the process of recall. Taken together, these neuroscientific results underpin the hermeneutic axiom of the vertical multiplicity of meaning: The meaning that I now give to this or that event is necessarily at least minimally different from that which I accorded to the same event during the last therapeutic session ...

Neurotherapeutic functions of hermeneutic dialogue

When childhood experiences are revisited by an adult during therapy, attention is focussed on diverse forms of long-term memory, with the primary aim of rendering these memories accessible to emotional consciousness. One of the fundamental goals of ORGT is to create or augment the capacity to consciously experience emotions associated with unfinished business. But activation of limbic and other subcortical structures does not automatically result in a conscious experience of an emotion. Cortical participation is necessary for emotional experience (Lane & Garfield, 2005). Since memories are slightly modified at each occasion of recall, it follows that the hermeneutic dialogue of Field 4[1] can permit a positive, creative re-writing of the client's history. The neurosciences can furnish tools that allow an understanding of: (1) how hermeneutic dialogue can modify the cognitive-affective-behavioural schemas that make up contact blockages; (2) the nature of memories related to contact dilemmas; and (3) the introjected micro-fields.

Substantial data show that psychotherapy has long-lasting effects on the activity of the brain, and that specific changes are related to a positive therapeutic result. These changes occur primarily in the frontal lobes (Gabbard, 1994). By definition therapeutic dialogue is fully suited to exploit the most powerful auto-regulation tool of all: language. During early development, language is the means by which prohibition becomes inhibition, abstract ideals begin to structure a personal ethic, and affective hetero-regulation becomes affective auto-regulation.

By its very nature, psychotherapeutic dialogue favours the establishment of neurodynamic conditions similar to those found in early development. When hermeneutics are properly calibrated, the regressed state is modulated by frontal lobe activity, thereby augmenting the Ego's control. Verbal descriptions of an emotion modify both our perception of that emotion and the way the emotion is subjectively experienced (Lane & Garfield, 2005). The hermeneutics of Field 4 allow a "revisiting" of the developmental past, and with each repetition, memory of the experience is gradually modified. This process involves both the semantic functions of the left hemisphere and the affective networks of the right hemisphere. In addition, as Gestalt therapy has taught, the body is mobilised in body language and during enactments. Thus reactivation of our history modifies the nature of our memories and reorganises neuronal circuits, thereby favouring long-term neurophysiological integration.

The contact boundary and the therapeutic relationship[2]

The capacity to infer what another person is thinking and feeling is at the core of human interactions, and this basic quality reaches its highest levels in relational psychotherapy. Whether it be called mentalisation, intentional stance, or mind theory, this capacity rests upon highly complex neurological functions, including perception, emotional activation, and the attribution of meaning. Current neuroscientific methods such as neuroimagery permit us to observe neural activation produced when a person strives to interpret the mental state of another person (Calarge, Andreason & O'Learly, 2003). These recent data hold the promise that in the future we will be in a position to understand the neurological underpinnings of the interactions among the three axes of therapeutic competence: reflexive, affective, and interactive. In the perspective of ORGT, therapeutic interactions are optimal when the therapist maintains fluidity in all three axes, as the relation evolves through the tranferential, reality-based, and hermeneutic modes.

Every psychotherapeutic approach, at some point in its history, has had to define what is and what is not a therapeutic relationship, beginning with Freud. Freud's "free-floating attention" permits the psyche of the therapist to act as an antenna that captures unconscious communication from the client. A functioning antenna obviously presupposes a broadcasting agent: the Kleinian concept of projective identification permits conceptualisation of this unconscious emission. Here is the question: How does an unconscious system emit messages that influence the receptive elements of another unconscious system? The same question can be framed in Gestalt therapy language: By what pathway(s) is the awareness continuum modulated within the therapeutic relationship? The key to answering these questions lies in the context of early development, from which consciousness and awareness emerge in the first place. Contemporary neurocognitive science has acquired the tools that make it profitable to revisit development and the therapeutic process.

And although Melanie Klein's (1946) work with infants has augmented our understanding of that sometimes less-than-idyllic period of life, modern neuroscience obliges us to reject the elaborately constructed fantasies that she attributed to young infants: such psychic phenomena demand a mature cerebral cortex.

Affect regulation: a critical developmental process

For the affective neurosciences, the most important developmental process is affect regulation. Lane and Garfield (2005) go so far as to affirm that one of the most basic goals of psychoanalysis is the development of the capacity to consciously experience emotions associated with unfinished business. These authors go on to state that emotional consciousness is a process that is distinct from other cognitive domains, whose development can be interrupted whilst other functions continue to mature.

The first "mental" states in early life are in fact psychobiological states. As Winnicott (1942) said, they emerge in mother/infant interactions and develop through rapid, essentially non-verbal communication at a highly efficient contact boundary. By means of this communication of essential psychobiological states, the intra-psychic becomes inter-personal, what is internal is communicated to the external environment.

Current data point to a link between affective states and neurobiological processes in the right hemisphere, which matures more quickly than the left and dominates psychic life during the first three years. As all object relation authors have held, it is this critical period that sees the establishment of secure attachment, and consequently of adequate affect regulation. Affect regulation is of paramount importance in the treatment of pathological personalities, more so than interpretation, insight, or awareness. Contrary to general opinion, this is probably particularly true for patients who lack introspective skills.

During neuro-affective development, the young infant uses a precocious, unconscious "strategy" in order to "survive" intense affective states. As evolution has shaped us to be relational creatures, we naturally seek help from others in stressful situations. In this context, emotions obviously have an adaptive function (Damasio, 2000; Frijda, 1994; Panksepp, 1998). Panksepp states that the basic systems of emotional activation are the fundamental tools of survival. Thanks to the normal, predictable activation of essential emotional systems, the self becomes rooted in the body. Because the human species would perish without a caretaking Other early in life, we are programmed to communicate our primitive somatoaffective states. Schore (2003b) considers this to be the process that Klein identified as projective identification.

Affect regulation and the therapeutic relationship

In Gestalt psychotherapy, memories have never been studied with the aim of understanding the past as such. Psychoanalysis and neuropsychoanalysis increasingly hold that memories are studied for what they can reveal about the client's strategies for affect regulation. In this context, an understanding of the neurodynamics of the Self in interaction can be a useful guide. Psychotherapy necessarily implies an interaction, which must be bidirectional and interactive. In an optimal therapeutic relation the psychotherapist internalises, contains, and tolerates the "intolerable" part of the client's experience, even his or her emotional identity, in much the same way that the client's mother performed these functions earlier in life. This "holding" continues as long as necessary to prepare the co-construction of new meaning for this intolerable yet indispensable experience. In cases of severe personality disorder, these intolerable experiences are so massive that the co-construction of meaning, and therefore the metabolism of introjects, can progress only by fits and starts. We can say that the client's strategy for affect regulation amounts to an implicit and unconscious communication of his intolerable affective states to others. The therapist must not refuse to internalise this intolerable burden, but rather must do so with full awareness of what is at stake. Underdeveloped personalities have internalised an early experience of being "used" as a projection screen for repudiated elements of their parents' identities. These individuals were unable to establish and maintain a relationship with a parent who could mirror diverse aspects of their developing Self, thus permitting differentiation and integration of these aspects (Robbins, 1996). These early interactions at the contact boundary hold an intense affective charge that rapidly "deregulates" the child. This is the essential feature of a traumatic relationship that engenders a twofold psychobiological response described by Schore (2003a): hyperactivation and despair. Hyperactivation is a form of protest, composed of screaming, crying, and head-turning to avoid visual contact. The sympathetic nervous system (activation) is fully active during this phase. After hyperactivation comes dissociation, analogous to the despair mentioned by Bowlby. Dissociation involves detachment from external reality and an attention directed exclusively toward internal stimuli. Cortisol (which inhibits behaviour) and opiates (which diminish pain) are released, and the parasympathetic nervous system (energy conservation) has taken control. From a neurodynamic perspective, this sequence of hyperactivation/dissociation could be seen as a real-time representation of projective identification, but we should be cautious here. This sequence could well be the phenomenological manifestation of one of the frequently seen forms of projective identification, that is, that emerging from developmental issues involving attachment. But it would be simplistic to think that this sequence applies to all the forms of projective identification discussed by post-Kleinian authors such as Langs (1976), Ogden (1979, 1982), or Tansey and Burke (1989). To the extent that "projective identification" can involve repudiated parts of the self in narcissistic or Oedipal dynamics, it would appear unlikely that all these forms of projective identification could be explained uniquely in terms of hyperactivation/dissociation (Delisle, 1993, 2004). These other, more subtle and less primitive forms of "contagious affect" still await explanation in neurobiological terms.

These cautionary considerations aside, it seems clear that individuals who have lived their early years in a traumatic relational field learn to make excessive use of projective identification, in order to survive repeated episodes of stressful interactions that can disorganise the budding Self. It is this very process of affective "survival" that simultaneously energises and paralyses the therapeutic relationship, occasionally rendering it paradoxically hyperactive and hopeless Just as an infant's screams can provoke highly inappropriate responses from caretakers, the manoeuvres of borderline patients can provoke partial disorganisation of the therapist's Self. And precisely because this process of hyperactivation/despair provokes increasingly maladapted responses from the environment, the young Self "learns" to inhibit it. In adults, only subtle signs of these primitive states remain.

The contact dilemma produced during a developmental trauma in the context of attachment generates successive reactions of hyperactivation and despair, accompanied by the underlying sympathetic and parasympathetic processes that are themselves linked to the maturing limbic system. These reaction cycles eventually become permanent strategies of affect regulation. Early negligence and abuse result in severe disruptions of attachment as well as serious malfunction in maturing psychobiological systems, particularly in the early-developing right hemisphere. These experiences of Field 4 (early development) are stored as implicit procedural memories and can produce dissociation later in life.

A primitive contact boundary regulatory strategy can become manifest when, in the therapeutic relationship, thematic elements appear that are related to early disturbances in attachment; this can happen, for example, when the therapist displays a poorly adapted response to the client's disorganisation. The reflexive capacity of the therapist is disabled, while his affective capacity is severely distorted, and the transference/counter-transference dimension dominates the therapeutic situation. Contact is severely deformed by successive projections, introjections, deflections, and retroflections, with no awareness of what is transpiring (Delisle, 1998).

The therapeutic relationship, at least with respect to transference and hermeneutics, is basically a two-way communication between right hemispheres, and even limbic systems (Buck, 1994). While the left hemisphere communicates with other left hemispheres via conscious linguistic elements, the right hemisphere communicates non-verbally with other, receptive right hemispheres. Therapy largely involves implicit communication, in which emotional, non-verbal species-specific signals are captured by a receptor, resulting in an instant, implicit understanding. But unless the therapist can induce the neurodynamic conditions that favour a hermeneutic dialogue, there will be no true two-way communication and instead of reparation there will be another repetition of inappropriate reactions and behaviours. Perhaps therapeutic receptivity should be interpreted as a voluntary interruption of left-hemisphere activity and a concomitant synchronised reverie of right hemispheres! In any case, this is what Gestalt therapists seem to be doing when they bask for a time in the mood created by the client, or when they allow themselves to be taken into the client's universe and to experience its textures and colours. Alpert et al. (1980) have found that when therapists drift into these reveries, their right frontal lobes show increased electrophysiological activity. It seems to be important that the therapist precede the client into this "reverie" state: the client's unconscious perception of the therapist's receptive right hemisphere allows this "unusual conversation" (Park & Park, 1997).

These neuro-affective states form the Ground before becoming the Figure of the dialogue, and are communicated by prosody (rhythm, volume, tone) rather than by verbal elements of language. This is why the effective therapist must be sensitive to prosody from the very first moment of contact with the client. The therapist must modulate his state in order to synchronise it to this prosodic rhythm, thereby allowing his inner world to contact that of his client. Beneath conscious awareness, this receptiveness and empathetic resonance with the client's constantly changing internal states unconsciously determine and maintain the therapeutic alliance.

But this resonating presence, this controlled confluence, comes at a price: the therapist is stripped of certain psychic defences. When the client's moods enter freely and the therapist floats in a stream of reverie, the usually-vigilant border guard is off-duty, and dangerous material can permeate: the intolerable experiences of the client. This penetration—sometimes invasion—destabilises the therapist's right hemispheric function, and his self-confidence and competence are menaced by unnamed and chaotic material that behaves like a bull in a china shop. The therapist's reflexive competence seems disabled, his or her affective competence evaporates, allowing affective emergences to attain a full primitive, un-nuanced intensity. Finally, interactive competence is engulfed by involuntary prosodic communication of un-modulated affect.

The reparatory function of affective regulation

In the psychotherapy of personality disorders, the therapist is continually interacting with a client struggling with his or her intolerable load, and the therapist's response is an essential element of treatment. This response is the channel through which the co-creation of meaning can lead to reparation. As Ellman (1991) remarks, the most difficult aspect of psychotherapy is to recognise and adequately deal with the negative affects that arise through this intimate contact with the client. In neurodynamic terms, the difficulty arises from the fact that the painful experience of developmental trauma is stored in the implicit-procedural memory of the right hemisphere and communicated to the therapist at a non-verbal, psychophysiological level (Schore, 2003a). The therapist must offer, in the here and now, that which the client's environment could not offer previously. This task is all the more difficult because these early experiences, reactivated in the here and now, trigger strong defensive reactions in the therapist's own internal Field. The analyst who is continually conscious of not only his own experience but also of his contribution to the ongoing process, experiences as much stress as his patient, if not more. In these intense moments, the critical question is: will the therapist be able to conduct an interactive co-regulation with the client, while conserving sufficient psychic energy to maintain an essential auto-regulation? In certain cases, the therapist's internal field becomes so turbulent that somatic signals are blocked, and consequently there is an instant loss of empathic communication with his own suffering as well as that of the client. When the right-hemisphere communication channel is lost in this way, the therapist can only switch to the left-hemisphere channel, to offer an "interpretation", a "hunch" or a "hermeneutic hypothesis" of the client's resistance, which could have the effect of increasing that "resistance". Studies of subliminal perception and of emotional contagion teach us that a therapist's refusal to take up the patient's intolerable burden is undoubtedly perceived by that client. The therapist's facial expression can, unknowingly to him or her, express disgust or irritation, the tone of voice becoming sarcastic or aggressive. These fleeting perceptions are unconsciously registered in the right hemisphere of the client. Research on the psychophysiological communication of emotions shows that verbal expression of anger produces electromyographic changes in the facial expression of the recipient (Hietanen, Surukka & Linnankowski, 1998). We can infer that the therapist's facial expressions briefly reflect negative emotion expressed by the client. These findings support my assertion in the 1990s, concerning the dimension of integrity in the therapeutic relationship: the client is capable of unconsciously detecting the emotions that are consciously experienced by the therapist (Delisle, 2000). Consequently, the therapist should always assume that the client "knows" what the therapist is feeling. The challenge is to find a way to move this "awareness" from an unconscious background to a conscious foreground, while ensuring that the awareness can be assimilated and metabolised by the client.

Recent neurobiological research has also shown that early aberrant experiences can compromise the capacity to adequately process facially-expressed emotions, which further complicates therapeutic interactions (Pollak & Kistler, 2002). These unconscious processes are doubtless part of the foundations of reproductive synergy, as conceived by ORGT. It is now clear that in the context of reproduction, the most significant enactments transpire in the non-verbal and unconscious interactions within the therapeutic dyad (McLaughlin, 1991; Schore, 1997). When reproduction cannot connect with the recognition or the co-construction of meaning, the affective competence of the therapist is unavailable, and regulation of inner reality is compromised. His or her interventions become projections of a non-metabolized, co-created affective state: the therapeutic alliance is diminished and possibilities for reparation become more remote. Reproduction is total and complete. Here and now, just as previously in life, the client is psychophysiologically destabilised by contact with an improperly regulated object. Consequently, the client regresses to cycles of hyper-activation and dissociation that were present in earlier life. During a therapeutic session, when the client passes rapidly from a hyperactive state (intense emotions, emotionally charged language, motor hyperactivity) to a more-or-less dissociated state (mutism, interrupted affect, avoidance of eye contact, etc.) we can infer that the affect has not been "discharged", but is still present, anesthetised and dissociated. This dissociation is not an interruption of reproduction, but rather its continuation in another form.

And projective identification?

It is often claimed that these processes of affective contagion, called projective identification by Kleinien psychoanalysts, are in fact attempts to control the therapist. Current neuroscientific data cast doubt on this interpretation. This form of affective regulation appears too early in life to be the product of neural structures associated with intentionality, that are far from mature at that age. In any case, it is implausible to interpret intentionality behind these affective explosions, which are more the result of despair, helplessness, and the absence of coping mechanisms.

In cases where primitive affective communication is seen in a person who is not seriously dysregulated, the emotions are accessible to consciousness and empathetic therapy can favour a positive evolution. In other words, the affective state is accessible to the personality function, which can identify with this state and render it partially explicit, thus facilitating the processes of recognition and reparation. On the other hand, when the process is undertaken by a person with serious personality disorder, the affects are not accurately verbalised by the personality function—the verbal version of the Self—and thus are not subject to therapeutic dialogue. Only a non-dissociated therapist, with reflexive competence, will be able to contain them.

The experience is not, however, exempt from pain, and it can become difficult to distinguish content that belongs to the therapist from that which belongs to the client. In these cases, we can say that affective competence remains high, but that reflexive competence is more slowly activated. Since the client is unable to access material for therapeutic dialogue, the therapist has difficulty verbalising his own experience, and is forced to maintain retroflexion, a prefrontal activity that inhibits the therapist's right hemisphere, rendering it less able to produce the state of reverie so important for effective therapy. If the situation is unduly prolonged, the therapist will eventually feel the emergence of negative affect. Although this negative affect indeed belongs to the therapist, it is produced by the sustained containment of the client's negative affect. This fundamental clinical experience of solitude and uselessness is one of many that every therapist must come to terms with: one might say that it's "part of the package".

Neurodynamic aspects of reparation

The therapist's autoregulation of negative states is an important and frequent process occurring during interactive reparation. The most significant reparatory work, touching the very heart of the developmental dilemma, is done by the therapist in situations of affective stress. At these critical moments, all three axes of therapeutic competence (affective, reflexive, and interactive) converge in a focussed interdependence. The therapist's capacity for containment initiates a movement toward reparation, in that it represents a form of contact that the client has not sufficiently experienced. This "contained" contact is critical, because the therapist is a target for two intense, but probably unconscious, desires of the client: on the one hand, the client attempts to reproduce the same type of response (or non-response) that he has always known, but on the other hand he is simultaneously trying to finally elicit, from the Other as well as in himself, a regulatory response (Fosshage, 1994; Migone, 1995).

Winnicott identified "holding" as a dominant process in early development. This supportive function, assumed principally by the mother, provides the basis for the species-specific neurophysiological development that will transform an infant into a person. With the early presence of a good-enough mother, maturation will go beyond the pure neurological level, to allow expression of the unique genetic make-up and interpersonal influences of the developing person. At this early age, neuronal plasticity is at its highest point. If, during this period, the infant is "held" and "contained", its primitive emotional activations will establish neuronal connexions that will later permit affective regulation, an essential function of the right prefrontal lobe. Ideally, connexions between the right and left hemispheres will be both numerous and highly integrated, as will be connexions between the limbic system and the cortex.

In clients suffering from personality pathology, one or both of these neuronal integrations will be deficient, and the therapist who accompanies the client in revisiting the developmental path will have to become this supportive environment and exercise the important "holding" function to a greater or lesser degree. In psychotherapy, "holding" often means "listen and wait", but a neurodynamic perspective gives us a more detailed understanding. In "holding", the therapist allows unstable right-hemisphere states to persist, resisting the impulse to activate the conceptual machinery of the left hemisphere to take a certain distance from the discomfort. The key to maintaining a right-hemisphere mode is to resist the tendency to seek "closure" via a conceptual explanation that assigns meaning (Schore, 2003a). As Rotenberg (1995) notes, the right hemisphere is activated in complex, intrinsically contradictory experiences that are irreducible to an unambiguous interpretation. In hermeneutic terms, to contain is to avoid assigning meaning! Containing implies an elevation of tolerance of uncertainty, ambiguity, and unclear figures. In psychotherapy, affective competence permits the therapist to detect and tolerate dissonant affect emergences within herself. Although containment is essential, even indispensable, it is not sufficient. Eventually, the dialogue between therapist and client must produce an understanding of these dissonant experiences and, for that, the therapist must regulate herself and then co-regulate the client. These regulatory capacities involve two-way communication between the inferior (limbic) and superior (cortical) layers of the right hemisphere: What am I feeling? How should I react? A regulatory interaction with the client is intimately dependent upon these alternations between affective competence and reflexive competence.

In these intense and potentially destabilising interactions, the therapist who is continually challenged by strong and unexpected affective emergences might well wonder if it would be therapeutic for him to communicate his subjective experience to the client. Opinion has always been divided on this question, with as many arguments for as against. Historically, humanists favoured this communication, while analysts were opposed. But as we all know, these divisions are not as strict as they once were, and today several contemporary psychoanalytic authors share with humanists a support for cautious, limited revelation of the therapist's experience in the therapeutic session. From a neurodynamic perspective, a selective and reflective communication of the therapist's ongoing experience has a hermeneutic and reparatory function. In optimal therapeutic interventions, a therapist who is dealing with a difficult projective identification is willing to partially share the neuroaffective impact of the patient on her own experience: the therapist's willingness to share will encourage exploration and sharing on the part of the client. These moments of affect-reflexive interaction favour hemispheric integration and maximize the pertinence of the therapist/client dialogue (Stark, 1999).

Revelation of the therapist's inner experience is not cognitive, but rather a counter-transferential/corporal process (Freedman & Lavender, 1997). In fact, Schore (2003a) claims that the capacity or incapacity to understand the somatic experiences generated by a projective identification can determine therapeutic outcome. It is perfectly natural that this intense, complex, implicit, and essentially prosodic communication produce somatic sensations during a therapy session. These sensations can produce two types of response: an interpretative response that frequently evolves into a series of reciprocal reprojections, or an empathic-developmental response in which the therapist contains and regulates her own and the client's inner experience. When the therapist is in a state that favours a "limbic conversation", a dialogue between right hemispheres, her viscero-somatic experience includes a slower, softer, deeper speech, and a calm expression. The client's pre-conscious observation of this process permits the creation of an "unconsciously secure" context (Schore, 2003). Essentially, passage from a dysregulated negative affect to a positive regulated affect is communicated by prosody.

Neurobiological data show that even very slight variations in facial expression can be detected in less than 100 milliseconds (Lehky, 2000), and processed by the right hemisphere in less than 400 milliseconds, well beneath the threshold of conscious awareness (Stenberg, Wiking & Dahl, 1998). These processes of reciprocal regulation help the client internalise the therapist's empathic resonance to his suffering, thereby reducing dissociation and eventually permitting verbalisation of his internal experience. New neuronal connections are established between implicit and explicit memory.

When a child experiences a strong affect that threatens to submerge him, he externalises his distress. The parent internalises this projection, contains it, modulates it, gives it meaning and returns the transformed affective experience to the child as part of the process called "holding". The child can then accept the metabolised affective experience, and the new resulting inner experience as his own. He will eventually learn to internalise the metabolic process as well, thus acquiring the capacity to contain his own affective experiences in an autonomous way. In therapeutic interactions involving intense affective experiences within the client, the therapist reproduces this parental holding process.

Six principles for optimal neuronal growth and integration in psychotherapy (Cozolino, 2002)

We will conclude this neuropsychotherapeutic overview with an interesting summary by Cozolino.

> "We appear to experience optimal development and integration in a context of a balance of nurturance and optimal stress. The disruption of this balance during development can result in symptoms, maladaptive defences, and psychopathology. The creation of this balance in the therapeutic relationship optimises the neurobiological environment for neural growth and integration. Although stress appears important as part of the activation of circuits involved with emotion, states of moderate arousal seem optimal for consolidation and integration. In states of high arousal, sympathetic activation inhibits optimal cortical processing and disrupts integration functions. States of moderate arousal maximise the ability of networks to process and integrate information. The ebb and flow of emotion over the course of therapy reflects the underlying neural rhythms of growth and change." (2002, pp. 62–64)

Empathic attunement with the therapist provides the context of nurturance in which growth and development occur. By activating processes involved in attachment and bonding, as well as moderating stress in therapy, empathic attunement may create an optimal biochemical environment for enhancing neural plasticity.

The involvement of affect and cognition appears necessary in the therapeutic process in order to create the context for integration of dissociated neural circuits. It has been said that, in psychotherapy, "understanding is the booby prize": it is a hollow victory to end up with a psychological explanation for problems that remain unchanged. On the other hand, catharsis without cognition does not result in integration either. The mutual participation of affect and cognition are required for optimal neural functioning.[3]

Repeated simultaneous activation of networks requiring integration with one another most likely aid in their integration.[4] The repetitive play in children and the phrase "working through" in therapy best reflect this process. This concept parallels the principle from neuroscience that "neurons that fire together, wire together" (Hebb, 1949). The simultaneous activation of neural circuits allows them to stimulate the development of connections within association areas to coordinate and integrate their functioning.

The ability to tolerate and regulate affect creates the necessary condition for the brain's continued growth throughout life. Increased integration parallels an increased ability to experience and tolerate thoughts and emotions previously inhibited, dissociated, or defended against. Affect regulation may be the most important result of the psychotherapeutic process across orientations, because it allows for a reconnection with the naturally occurring growthful experiences in life.[5]

Language is an important tool in both neurological and psychological development. The co-construction of narratives between parent and child or therapist and client provides a broad matrix supporting the integration of multiple neural networks. Autobiographical memory creates stories of the self capable of supporting affect regulation in the present and the maintenance of homeostatic functions into the future. Memory, in this form, may maximise neural network integration as it organises vast amounts of information across multiple processing tracks.[6] Stories serve to bridge and integrate neural networks both in the present moment and through time (Siegel, 1999).

Conclusion

As we have seen, recent theorising and research are bringing neurosciences and psychotherapy into a stimulating and promising contact from which both can hope to benefit. A deeper understanding of the neural processes underlying human experience will guide therapists who seek to modify that experience by means of interventions that must, necessarily, affect those very neural processes. The therapist equipped with a deep understanding of the neural processes underlying the suffering of her client will more clearly discriminate the targets of her interventions. Mindful of the complex, interactive neural systems involved in the processes of containment, holding, and hermeneutic dialogue, she will more adequately take into account the dynamic nature of the dysregulation that leads to reproduction of the symptom. And in return, psychotherapists, with their vast experience with the complexities of memory, affect, dissociation, and impulsivity, can provide neuroscientists with virtually endless research questions. Intercommunication between the two disciplines appears irreversible and can be ignored only by a voluntary denial of the biological basis of psychic experience.

Although this convergence cannot be ignored, it could backfire if tomorrow's therapists choose to concentrate entirely on neurobiology while ignoring the reality of the human encounter and the accompanying subjective experience, if they passionately study theories of harmony but dislike music and no longer know how to sing.

To conclude—a more personal reflection. My recent explorations of this new neuroscientific territory have helped me reach a better understanding of what I do and what I teach. Having lived the greater part of my professional life navigating between the "how" of Gestalt and the "why" of psychoanalysts, I now explore another universe of meaning and I can perceive, on the planet Neuros that the "how" contains the past and the "why" shapes future experience.

Notes

1. In ORGT, Field 1 is the here-and-now of the therapeutic relation, Field 2 refers to other moments of that relation, Field 3 represents the other significant ongoing relationships, and Field 4 is the developmental past.
2. This section borrows from the chapter that Allan N. Schore (2003b) devotes to the neurobiology of projective identification, in his book *Affect Regulation and the Repair of the Self*. The complete reference is in the bibliography.
3. This principle is at the very heart of hermeneutic dialogue, in which the therapist constantly strives to keep affect close at hand during the co-creation of meaning (Delisle, 2001).

4. Neural networks that are dissociated or inadequately integrated have to be activated simultaneously or alternately. In ORGT we speak of optimal inter-Field transitions, repeated movements from inner to outer Fields and vice-versa. This principle underlies a fundamental working hypothesis of GROR concerning hermeneutic dialogue: construction of meaning is facilitated when a moderate affect is maintained alongside somatic consciousness.
5. In ORGT, this regulative capacity depends on the therapist's tolerance for the reproduction of ambivalence in the client, which in turn depends on the therapist's affective competence.
6. In ORGT, the therapist adjusts his language to the regressed mental state of the client and can thus address the developmental blockage present. This intervention involves two-way communication between the two hemispheres as well as the limbic system and the cortex, activating the right prefrontal lobe to achieve regulation and adjustment of the affective elements accompanying the emergences.

CHAPTER TEN

ORGT and evidence-based practice

Marc-Simon Drouin, Ph.D.[1]

Introduction

Object relation Gestalt therapy (ORGT), as developed in the writings of Gilles Delisle (1998, 2004) has become an influential model of therapeutic intervention, particularly in Quebec and in Europe. In recent years, a large number of therapists have been trained in ORGT, or have at least been introduced to its principal concepts through a series of seminars and didactic activities offered to mental health professionals. ORGT can be defined as a treatment of contact failures within various domains of experience by means of a hermeneutic dialogue: the approach was developed for the treatment of pathological personalities. This rigorous therapeutic model has substantial theoretical support and satisfies Mahrer's (1989) criteria for coherent psychotherapeutic models: a theory of human nature, a theory of psychotherapy, and a set of concrete operational procedures.

Delisle (2008) has shown that recent research in the neurosciences has given some support to the application of the ORGT model in the clinic. But in spite of this non-negligible validation, ORGT, along with several other psychodynamic and humanist models, has remained largely outside the mainstream of evidence-based psychotherapy.

In spite of a general opinion that psychotherapy is an effective form of intervention for many mental problems (Lambert & Ogles, 2004), recent years have seen something of a credibility crisis with respect to the objective validation of psychotherapeutic interventions. In 1998 for example, the Clinical Psychology division of the APA undertook an empirical validation of certain treatments. This project, considered as fundamentally important for the survival of psychotherapy in North America (Barlow, 2008; Chambless & Hollon, 1998; Nathan & Gorman, 2002), sought to standardise the characteristics of psychotherapists and clients by applying a pharmacologically-inspired medical model with its rigorous criteria of effective treatment. Thus, a psychotherapeutic treatment is considered empirically based when it produces results superior to those of a placebo or of an alternative treatment, and when this superiority is confirmed by at least two independent studies. Following this verification, the treatment is recorded in a manual that lists the precise treatments possible for a given psychological problem, and this manual becomes the official guide for the choice of an intervention (Lecomte, Savard, Drouin & Guillon, 2004). This entire procedure is copied directly from the criteria of the Federal Drug Administration (FDA) and appears to constitute the logical foundation of current attempts to validate psychological treatments. As we shall see, the validation procedure described here cannot be uniformly applied to all current forms of psychological intervention.

In the light of these stringent criteria of effectiveness, what can we say today concerning the validity of humanist or psychodynamic interventions? Is ORGT less credible because there are relatively few empirical studies of this model's effectiveness? These are the questions we will be examining in this article.

To begin with, we will consider the various ways in which therapeutic effectiveness has been measured since the 1950s. In doing so, we will give special attention to data pertaining to humanist models. Following that, we will review the relevant data obtained by studies of the empirical validity of psychotherapeutic models.

Following this critical analysis, we will present the contribution of a group of researchers headed by Louis-Georges Castonguay and Larry Beutler (2006), who propose a new perspective on the validation of psychotherapeutic interventions. The perspective of Castonguay and Beutler seems to respect the spirit in which ORGT was developed, as we will see by comparing the fundamental principles of ORGT with the conclusions of their study. Our intention is not to provide an exhaustive validation of ORGT, but rather to compare its fundamental precepts with principles recognised as empirically valid.

Evaluation of therapeutic effectiveness and the evidence

Since Eysenck's (1952) conclusion that psychotherapy was no more beneficial than spontaneous improvement over time, many workers have tried to demonstrate the effectiveness of psychotherapy. Several rigorous meta-analyses conducted between 1952 and 1993 have concluded that psychotherapy gives positive results. In particular, it has often been shown that humanist psychotherapy is effective. Elliot's recent (2002) meta-analysis of the effectiveness of humanist psychotherapy arrived at the following conclusions.

Clients of humanist therapy show significant change:

1. Post-therapy gains are stable over 12 months or longer.
2. Clients of humanist therapy show significantly greater improvement than clients not receiving therapy.
3. In comparative randomised group studies, humanist clients show changes comparable to those of clients of other approaches, including cognitive-behavioural approaches.
4. Humanist therapies are particularly effective for clients in distress induced by a variety of issues, ranging from depression and anxiety to adjustment problems and interpersonal difficulties.
5. The effectiveness of humanist therapies has been clearly demonstrated in the treatment of major depression and personality disorders.
6. Therapies based on a directive process are particularly effective.

Although this meta-analysis did not include studies that explicitly used the ORGT approach, it remains clear that ORGT, as a humanist psychotherapy, shares many therapeutic characteristics with the approaches used in the studies of the meta-analysis. In this sense, Elliot's meta-analysis gives implicit support to ORGT. In any case, no evidence has as yet demonstrated the superiority of any one particular school of psychotherapy (Lambert & Obles, 2004; Wampold, 2001, 2006). How else can one explain the fact that forty meta-analyses have shown an absence of significant differences among "bona fide" therapeutic approaches when the analysis controls for therapeutic allegiance?

Hypothetical interpretations of these consistently obtained results

1. Various therapies obtain similar results through different means.
2. The therapies obtain different results but our current analytical tools are not sufficiently sensitive to detect them.
3. The majority of these therapies share a certain number of common factors that have beneficial effects but that are not clearly identified by the therapists applying their appro ach.

The third hypothesis would seem to have the clearest implications for clinical practice, and, over the last decades, has attracted the most attention from researchers. This hypothesis of shared common factors also seems to emerge from studies that seek to identify the active "ingredients" of psychotherapy. Current thinking identifies two types of factors that contribute to positive results in psychotherapy: treatments that are specific to one approach, and treatments that are common to many approaches. Both categories of factors have received empirical validation, and the results of these meta-analyses lead us to conclude that all the major schools of psychotherapy are effective.

In 1993, however, the evaluation of clinical effectiveness changed. As mentioned earlier, the Clinical Psychology division of the APA undertook to evaluate the empirical validity of certain treatments by creating a task force with this mandate. Since then, we have seen a proliferation of "evidence" and "empirically validated" treatments (Nathan & Gorman, 2002).

But just what is "evidence" to begin with? We can accept the following definition, proposed by the Canadian Foundation of Health Service Research (March, 2006):

> Evidence is information that comes closest to the facts of a matter. The form it takes depends on context. The findings of high quality, methodologically appropriate research are the most accurate evidence. Because research is often incomplete and sometimes contradictory or unavailable, other kinds of information are necessary supplements to or stand-ins for research. The evidence base for a decision is the multiple forms of evidence combined to balance rigor with expedience—while privileging the former over the latter.[2]

The spirit of "evidence" is thus an integral part of the new procedures for the validation of therapeutic interventions. For these validations, evidence takes the form of empirically validated treatments (EVT) using randomized clinical trials (RCT). Clients suffering from a particular disturbance are considered to be equivalent with respect to all other variables and are assigned randomly to an experimental group. The experimental design attributes a specific treatment for a specific problem.

A treatment can be considered effective if:

1. At least two studies with group comparisons demonstrate a statistically significant superiority of the treatment when compared with a placebo, or
2. If the treatment is equivalent to an already validated treatment, or
3. At least nine case studies with an appropriate experimental design and a comparison with another intervention demonstrate the effectiveness of the treatment.

In addition, the studies testing the treatment must have used a treatment manual, the characteristics of the clients must have been clearly specified, and the effectiveness of the treatment must be demonstrated by at least two independent research teams. These studies generally recommend treatments involving six to sixteen therapeutic sessions. Given the clear links between the methodology imposed and the clinical context of cognitive-behavioural approaches, it is perhaps not surprising that cognitive-behavioural treatments are more frequently "validated" than those of other approaches. For example, in 2007, more than 150 treatments were empirically validated. Of this number, more than ninety-five per cent were cognitive-behavioural treatments.

These results might seem at first to confirm the overwhelming superiority of cognitive-behavioural approaches, but it would be wise to be prudent before jumping to this conclusion. The validation procedure employed presupposes several improbable conditions: (1) that the therapists are equivalent, and (2) propose a similar and standardised procedure to (3) clients that are equivalent. These presuppositions raise important questions.

If the clients are to be considered similar, these studies must exclude any client presenting a psychological disturbance other than that targeted by the treatment. Any form of co-morbidity automatically excludes a client from the research protocol. The problem is that co-morbidity is the rule rather than the exception in clinical practice. Westeon (2006) affirms that up to seventy per cent of the clinical population suffers from more than one clinical syndrome, and thus would necessarily have to be excluded from research protocols.

Leaving aside the question of co-morbidity, the very notion of "similar" clients is implausible: what clinician has ever encountered two "similar" clients? "Similar" in what way exactly? Wampold (2006) raises the question of the uniformity of therapists. Studies have shown that the population of therapists can be divided into three roughly equal groups that consistently obtain superior, average, and inferior results with their clients, independently of the approach employed. In spite of efforts to minimise this variability by the use of standardised manuals, the quality of the therapist seems to seriously affect the results of the therapy (Lecomte, Savard, Drouin & Guillon, 2004). As for the treatment itself, how standard can the treatment be? Even this would appear to be illusory: markedly different therapists treat markedly different clients, and so how can one imagine that the "same" treatment is being applied in each case? In the course of a therapy, there are inevitably technical adjustments of an apparently minor nature—can these have significant effects on treatment outcome?

The clinical experience of active professionals casts further doubts on the adequacy of the official validation methodology: the number of clinical encounters imposed would seem to be insufficient. Westeon (2006) has shown a high rate of relapse for a variety of mental disturbances that are treated by a programme of six to sixteen encounters. Treatments that continue for more than a year are more effective, and the effect is greater when the clients have a personality disturbance (Howard, Moras, Brill, Martinovich & Lutz, 1996).

Should we conclude that this kind of "evidence" is useless? Probably not. It would not be helpful to throw out the baby with the bath water, but as Lecomte (2007) remarked, it might be more appropriate to speak of "suggestive results" rather than "evidence". As for ORGT, should we abandon all hope of eventually obtaining empirical validation just because the validation methodology used presently is tailor-made for cognitive-behavioural therapy and its objectives? Elliott (2002), addressing this question, encourages humanistic clinical researchers to develop research methodologies adapted to the specific variables of the models that they use and seek to validate. ORGT has, at its heart, a hermeneutic dialogue that presumes the uniqueness of each client and of his experience: an approach with this fundamental assumption cannot be validated using an "official" methodology that presumes uniformity. However, recent developments in the study of therapeutic effectiveness give hope that ORGT can and will receive a significant and rigorous validation.

Empirically validated relational variables

As a response to criticisms levelled at the attempt to validate treatments with randomised clinical trials, a task force was formed to explore the contribution of relational factors to the success of psychotherapeutic treatment. This committee, led by John Norcross (2002) of Division 29 of the APA (Psychotherapy), was mandated to empirically verify the importance of relational factors that might contribute to therapeutic success. Particular attention was given to variables such as alliance, empathy, overcoming resistances, etc., and their contribution to treatment seems to have been empirically confirmed.

At this point, we are faced with two independent bodies of research results. The results gathered by Division Twelve (Clinical) identify specific elements of treatments that contribute to successful therapeutic outcome, but ignore relational variables as well as client or therapist characteristics. On the other hand, the results gathered by Division Twenty-nine (Psychotherapy) identify relational variables but ignore techniques specific to the various approaches. The conclusions of these two bodies of research are generally considered to be contradictory, even antagonistic, and this perception encourages, to some extent, a radical division between partisans of the relationship and partisans of techniques and models. However, our clinical experience has taught us that a relationship without a technique is useless, and a technique without a relationship is insufficient.

Empirically validated therapeutic principles

In an attempt to reconcile the opposition between partisans of these two bodies of research, while adequately taking into account the substantial literature concerning therapeutic effectiveness, Wampold (2001) proposes a contextual model of psychotherapy based on the dominant contribution of common factors. For Wampold, a model that focuses on the specific elements of a particular form of therapy cannot adequately identify the true source of change in psychotherapy. Wampold's unique position seems to be in contradiction with the results of the two "task forces" reporting to Division Twelve (Clinical) and Division Twenty-nine (Psychotherapy) of the APA.

In 2006, Castonguay and Beutler attempted to reconcile the split that had been growing between the perceptions of Division Twelve and Division Twenty-nine, proposing a new vision of the role of common factors in therapeutic interventions, a vision that seems to approach that of Wampold. By taking into account characteristics of the clients and therapists, aspects of the therapeutic interaction, as well as the specific techniques used in several approaches, they succeeded in identifying a set of therapeutic principles that can guide therapists of various orientations in their interventions. This set of principles in fact constitutes an ensemble of common factors that were (1) identified by the previous task forces, or (2) confirmed by numerous rigorous studies.

Castonguay and Beutler (2006) concentrated on affective disorders, anxiety, substance abuse, and personality disorders. As ORGT was primarily developed as an intervention for clients with personality disorders, it would be particularly interesting to verify the extent to which the fundamental principles of ORGT are in harmony with their conclusions. It would perhaps be premature to attempt an exhaustive comparison of ORGT with the principles of Castonguay and Beutler, but a preliminary survey would be a worthwhile undertaking.

Personality disturbance, empirically validated therapeutic principles, and ORGT

In the universe of mental illness, personality disturbances are in a distinct class. Since they are egosyntonic, most clients with these disturbances consult initially for some other Axis One pathology, such as mood disorder or anxiety. Consequently, these clients have more than one pathology: as mentioned previously, for them co-morbidity is the rule rather than the exception. In this context, the identification of empirically validated therapeutic principles emerges as the methodology of choice. It is difficult to validate a particular treatment by means of random clinical trials, since these protocols exclude clients showing co-morbidity. Although some workers claim to have demonstrated the effectiveness of specific treatments by means of random clinical trials (Giesen-Bloo et al., 2006), these studies have a particularly rigid experimental design that is ill suited to the realities of private practice.

While the majority of therapeutic principles have been clearly identified for mood disturbances, anxiety, and substance abuse, things are not as clear for personality disorders, because in this case we are dealing with multiple dimensions of the client. It is sometimes difficult to isolate therapeutic action targeting the personality within the broader scope of the therapy. As a result, few of these therapeutic principles have been empirically validated in an unambiguous, satisfying way. This state of affairs seems to us to be a direct consequence of a clinical reality rather than a negative reflection on the goal of validating recognised therapeutic principles.

Castonguay and Beutler (2006) identified three groups of common principles that contribute to successful therapeutic outcomes. These principles were associated with the participants (client and therapist), the relationship between the client and the therapist, and the therapeutic techniques used in the therapy. Critchfield and Benjamin (2006) studied these three groups in the specific context of personality disorders; we will review their results, paying special attention to how ORGT can be seen in the light of these principles.

Principles associated with the participants

The client

As each personality disorder client is unique, it is difficult to identify client-related therapeutic principles. We can say that outcome becomes less favourable as severity increases. On the other hand, chances of success are greater when the client agrees to invest in intensive therapy.

These principles may appear self-evident, but it is important, at the very beginning of the therapy, to determine realistic therapeutic objectives and to clarify the client's capacity for commitment to the therapy. Delisle (2001) underlines these considerations in the application of his model.

The therapist

Principles associated with the therapist seem to be more fully identified. Therapists should:

- Be comfortable with long-term, emotionally intense relationships.
- Show patience and the capacity to tolerate modest therapeutic gains over time.

- Have the capacity to tolerate and regulate their own emotions, particularly those related to the client and to the therapeutic process.
- Demonstrate openness and flexibility.
- Be highly creative while constantly striving for coherence.
- Have specialised training for this type of pathology.

This list neatly summarises the affective, interactive, and reflexive abilities identified by Delisle (2004) as essential for the application of his therapeutic model. For example, in speaking of "affective abilities", Delisle mentions the therapist's capacity to experience a large register of emotions at a moderate level, the importance of being constantly aware of his client's uniqueness, and the ability to be highly creative while at the same time being certain that the therapeutic interventions remain consistent with the overall objectives of the therapy. In order to sustain the abilities required by this approach, therapists must continually refresh and consolidate their training.

Principles associated with the therapeutic relationship

These principles can be divided into two subgroups, the first concerning the characteristics of the therapeutic alliance and the second concerning more directly the role and the attitudes of the therapist.

The therapeutic alliance

Concerning this alliance, studies have shown that:

- It is imperative to develop a solid alliance and to attentively repair alliance ruptures that can occur at any moment during the therapeutic process.
- It is important to establish a clear agreement concerning the objectives of the therapy and to establish a continuing collaboration with the client with respect to attaining these objectives.

The ORGT model exemplifies both of these principles. Delisle (2004) describes the therapeutic process as being composed of cycles of varying length, organised in a trilogy of reproduction-recognition-reparation. In order to progress through these cycles, the client must be able to perceive the therapist as open to his complexity and his unique experience. The therapist's openness must be maintained in spite of the reproduction of blockages in therapy, the client's distorted perception of the therapist, and the resulting psychological pressures that the therapist inevitably receives from a frustrated or impatient client.

The role and attitudes of the therapist

Studies have identified the following five principles: in each case, we will attempt to evaluate the extent to which ORGT exemplifies the principle under discussion.

An active but not necessarily directive role for the therapist
The hermeneutic dialogue at the heart of ORGT seems to perfectly exemplify this principle. During this dialogue, the vigilant therapist contributes to the collaborative creation of meaning while carefully avoiding imposing a predetermined conclusion. Recent developments in neurosciences have given empirical guidance to research on the optimal level of activity in the therapist.

A structured intervention that clearly separates the acceptable from the unacceptable in the therapeutic context
Although Delisle and his collaborators have never specifically addressed these questions, it is clear that therapists who apply the ORGT approach base their interventions on the models developed by major authors who have treated personality pathologies (Allen & Fonagy 2006; Clarkin, Yoemans & Kernber, 1999).

The therapist must develop and maintain a high level of empathy toward the client
Empathy is a multi-dimensional construct that includes: (1) a cognitive dimension that permits comprehension and validation, (2) an affective dimension that permits communication and interaction, and (3) a particular form of interaction (Bohart & Greenberg 1998; Drouin, 2003). Here again, the three cardinal clinical abilities identified by Delisle (affective, reflexive, and interactive) correspond to the three dimensions of empathy, and emphasize their importance for the satisfactory progress and positive outcome of therapy.

The therapist must maintain a positive perception of the client
Although "positive perception" is not explicitly mentioned in the relational vocabulary of ORGT, therapists are invited to permit the

reproduction of unresolved developmental issues, and such a reproduction clearly presupposes a positive perception of the client.

Coherent emotional expression on the part of the therapist, including a certain measure of self-exposure as well as transmission of conceptual understanding
Here it is again a question of interactive abilities, clearly established as essential to the optimal utilisation of the ORGT model. Among other things, the therapist is expected to develop a mastery of his contact and support capacities.

Principles associated with therapeutic techniques

These principles can be classed in four categories, all of which are correlated with positive therapeutic outcome.

Salient elements of therapy

- A flexible approach that permits the therapist to tailor interventions to the client's ongoing subjective experience.
- The therapist must focus on problems presented by the client. A respect for the client's frame of reference.
- An initial formulation that identifies the affective, cognitive, and behavioural repetitions that tend to perpetuate the problem.

By its very essence, ORGT recognises and respects the unique experience of the client. The therapist adjusts to this reality in order to encourage the re-emergence of the contact failure. Moreover, active search for inter-field similarities in the presenting problem favours the formulation and identification of affective, cognitive, and behavioural patterns that maintain that problem.

Principles related to therapist transparency

- Honesty, particularly the capacity to honestly explain the limits of the therapeutic framework and of therapeutic interventions.
- Openness to frank discussion of the nature of difficulties encountered in therapy, as well as the rationale and the objectives of the treatment.

- Interventions that favour comprehension of the relationships between difficulties, emotions, the environment, cognition, and behaviour.

The honesty and transparency mentioned here correspond to the notions of integrity discussed by Delisle (2002) in his article on the tri-dimensional relationship.

An objective-based treatment plan

- In collaboration with the client, the establishment of a treatment plan with explicit, clearly identified objectives.
- A clearly oriented treatment plan with a coherent theoretical foundation and a defined sequence.

The theoretical coherence of ORGT needs no further demonstration: it is an epistemologically valid model. Directionality is clearly established in the framework of ORGT by the sequence reproduction-recognition-reparation.

Principles targeting change

- The constant effort to harmonise objectives and motivation for change on the one hand, and empathetic support on the other.
- An emphasis on the development of better-adapted cognitions and behaviours.
- Principles that accentuate the reduction of ill-adapted behaviours and irrational thinking.

These technical preoccupations find a clear echo in the fundamental postulates of Gestalt therapeutic intervention. Gestalt therapy's approach has always been both phenomenological and behavioural. The search for meaning is never conducted in a manner that neglects maladapted behaviours.

Many authors have strongly recommended personal psychotherapy and clinical supervision for therapists working with clients who have personality disorders. ORGT, in its training programmes, strongly encourages personal psychotherapy as well as didactic supervision.

Conclusion

This review leads us to the conclusion that ORGT respects a great majority of principles that have been empirically validated for the treatment of personality disorders. Even though Castonguay and Beutler (2006) state that these principles are less clearly-defined for personality disturbance than for other disorders, we can safely conclude that ORGT is in clear harmony with data currently available for the treatment of personality pathologies.

It remains true that ORGT cannot be considered to be empirically validated in the strictest sense. As we have seen, current methods employed for this strict form of validation are not, by their nature, applicable to ORGT. Consequently and in conclusion, instead of being "empirically validated", ORGT can be considered to be "empirically supported".

Notes

1. Professor at the Department of Psychology of Université du Québec à Montréal. Director of the Centre for University Consulting of UQAM. Didactic supervisor at CIG in Montréal.
2. Jonathan Lomas and Chris McCutcheon (on behalf of the "What Is Evidence?" team)
   CHSRF Annual Workshop 21–22 March 2006, Vancouver.

PART III

CASE STUDIES

INTRODUCTION TO THE CASE STUDIES

The following case studies were written by clinical psychologists with varying degrees of experience and mastery of the ORGT approach. Michel Dandenault, Ph.D. has been in private practice in Ottawa for twenty years, and recently completed the third level, the highest of the ORGT training program offered by the CIG. Guilhème Pérodeau, Ph.D., is a professor of psychology at the Université du Québec in Outaouais. She also recently completed the third level of the ORGT program and began private practice a few years ago. Finally, Dorothy Scicluna, D.Psy., has been in private practice in Malta for several years. Unlike the other two, she did not complete the clinical training program offered by the CIG, but was introduced to ORGT during an introductory workshop that I gave in Malta in March of 2009. None of the three are native anglophones.

The authors were asked to begin with a general framework featuring a multiaxial diagnosis and a structural diagnosis, as well as a global summary of the psychotherapy conducted in terms of the theory presented here. Apart from these minimal requirements concerning the structure of the presentation, each author was encouraged to express their personal vision, using their own style. The resulting texts were sometimes concretely detailed, sometimes global and abstract. Sometimes the diagnosis was described in detail, while sometimes the author chose to more deeply explore symptom reproduction in psychotherapy.

It goes without saying that the authors took all the necessary precautions to insure confidentiality and protect the identity of their clients.

In spite of the significant contribution that such case studies can make to clinical practice, there are, surprisingly, precious few clear guidelines for their presentation. These three clinicians accepted the challenge to put into writing their concrete application of the theoretical model presented in these pages, and doing so, they exposed their own clinical work to the critical evaluation of their peers.

The clinical diversity of these case studies and the unique personal vision of each author are immensely satisfying for me personally: these texts illustrate the wide clinical applicability of the theory proposed here. In the nebulous and often speculative universe of Gestalt theory, it is to be hoped that their example will be followed, and that therapeutic concepts—these or others—will be put to concrete test in similar case studies.

I heartily thank them for their contributions.

CHAPTER ELEVEN

Bob

"I dream of shining as captain of the team, but I end up not being picked"

A case study presented by Michel Dandeneau, PhD, C.Psych.[1]

He slowly walked into my office with the trace of a smile thinly veiling a shy and gloomy demeanour. He discretely scanned the environment as he waited to be asked to take a seat. He was well-groomed, polite and very cooperative during the interview, expressing little feeling until he talked about his marriage and his work: then distress choked him up and seeped through teary eyes. I was touched by this man who came across as a young boy struggling with his grief.

Bob was referred to me by a psychologist working in his organisation. He was particularly distressed about his marital relationship and complained of feeling frustrated with his lack of promotion at work. Although he had no plans to end his life, he felt depressed with recurrent thoughts of death.

When I met Bob for his first consultation, he was in his mid thirties, held a university degree, and worked in a large government organisation in a low management position. He was married with two young children. At the time of writing, I have seen Bob in my private practice for close to five years. With a few exceptions, he has come in for weekly sessions.

Developmental history—Field 4

Bob is the last of five boys in a family of "macho men". He would not be invited to parties with his brothers, even when cousins his own age were invited: he always felt left out. His father was a successful businessman, very well off until Bob was in his teens when his father lost everything and their standard of living dropped dramatically. Bob was afraid of becoming a clone of his father who was depressed and fell from success. On the eve of his sixteenth birthday he provoked his father by sitting in his chair and demanding that his father say "please" to get it back. His father stabbed a knife into the table and pulled him up by the hair demanding respect. One of his older brothers had to pull them apart. Later that summer, his father went to a track and field event in which Bob was competing, embarrassing Bob by being the only parent there, and the event turned out to be a fiasco for Bob. His father criticized him for "walking on his toes like a girl". Bob saw his father as "an idiot who crowded me by trying to tell me how to live". Even after his fall from success, he continued to boast and make himself the centre of attention. At Bob's graduation ceremony his father mocked him and told him "you're still walking on your toes". "My father could not leave me be on the podium, it still had to be his show."

His mother was a homemaker. Keeping a low profile and avoiding conflict, she didn't intervene much in Bob's life other than to try to cheer him up by asking him to put a smile on his face.

At school Bob was the butt of jokes, bullied and ridiculed. He dreamt of being the leader of the pack, the "star" athlete, impressing girls. In reality, he rarely made the team, and when he did he was almost always picked last: he felt rejected and isolated. One time he was kicked off the team. "As they drove away with my hockey sweater, I fantasised that one day they would regret their mistake after realising how great I was and would beg to have me back."

Current situation—Field 3

During the first years in therapy, he felt he was above average and should be moving up more quickly at work. He dreamt of being the expert whom everyone respects and seeks out for advice and direction. "I want to shine, be seen as an expert, a leader, someone who pleases people and impresses them with his charm; but I feel held back." Despite repeatedly asking for promotion, he was repeatedly passed over. In spite of his fantasy of being superior he also complained of being a failure, of not being organised, always late, procrastinating, forgetting things, losing focus, and not properly completing his work.

In the initial phase of treatment, he felt particularly anxious and worried about his marriage to "the woman of my dreams". He felt his wife was moving away emotionally and he was feeling depressed. Early in the first year of treatment, his wife left him for another man.

He summed up his life story with: "I dream of shining and being respected as captain of the team, but instead I end up not making the team or getting kicked off".

Multi-axial DSM diagnosis

Axis I   Major Depressive Episode

When Bob started therapy, he met the criteria for Major Depressive Episode. The Depression lifted within the first year of psychotherapy; however, Bob reported feeling "down" and gloomy for most of his life, which raised the possibility of Dysthymic Disorder or an Axis II diagnosis. It became clear over time that his dysthymic mood was due to depressive features in a Depleted Narcissistic Personality profile (cf. Psychodynamic Diagnostic Manual (PDM)[2]). Hence, the dysthymic symptoms were seen more as a function of his personality rather than a mood disorder.

Axis II   Personality Disorder, NOS

Bob complains of a chronic pattern throughout most of his life which caused significant subjective distress. Although he fantasises of being successful, he perceives himself as a failure which makes him feel depressed and frustrated. Occasionally, he expresses a mixture of admiration and envy towards others whom he sees as "having it together, succeeding and earning respect". He experiences these feelings at work and in his relationships. Bob meets the general diagnostic criteria for a Personality Disorder, that is, an enduring pattern of inner experience and behaviour that is inflexible and pervasive across a broad range of personal and social situations and which leads to clinically significant distress.

The specific category of Narcissistic Personality Disorder in the DSM was considered but not retained due to the insufficient number of criteria being met.

Given that his functioning meets the general criteria for Personality Disorder but not for any specific Personality Disorder, the DSM Axis II diagnosis is Personality Disorder Not Otherwise Specified.

The Personality Axis (P Axis) of the Psychodynamic Diagnostic Manual (PDM) was applied in an effort to supplement the DSM. Bob meets most of the criteria for Narcissistic Personality Disorder, Depressed/Depleted subtype. He also presents many traits of the following: Depressive Personality Disorder; Masochistic (Self-Defeating) Personality Disorder; and Dependent Personality Disorder, Passive-Aggressive Version. The use of the PDM considerably enriches the understanding of Bob's personality and the issues he struggles with.

Axis III   No diagnosis
Axis IV   Marital distress; lack of promotion at work
Axis V   GAF: 45–50 (at intake) Serious symptoms and difficulties in a conjugal relationship, thinking, and mood. At times unable to work.

GAF: 75–80 (current) Symptoms tend to be transient and appropriate reactions to psychosocial stressors; has appropriate and meaningful relationships with his children; is doing better at work.

Structural analysis of the self[3]

(Based on the revised theory of the Self–Delisle, 1995–1998)

Function/structure of the Self

Id: *Fluidity and relative strength of emergences. What seems to emerge most easily and least easily?*
What emerges most:

- Depressed thoughts and feelings; feels like a failure. Some sadness.
- Feelings of rejection and of being ridiculed by peers (at school and at work). Feelings of humiliation.

- Wants to shine, be admired as an expert, a leader, someone who pleases people and impresses them with his charm. *"But I feel held back"*. And that is when he loses focus, procrastinates, gets absorbed in TV, leaving little time to sleep.
- Complains of lacking the discipline and concentration to achieve his goals.
- Anger and contempt, mostly directed towards his father.
- Alternates between despising self and despising others. Rarely feels equal to others.
- Frustrated with his lack of promotion; feels he should move up faster than the average.

What emerges least:

- Feeling of self-confidence and self-acceptance.
- Determination, perseverance, and self-discipline.
- Happiness, joy, pleasure.

Ego-function: *Ability to correctly give voice to the Id and the MFR in relations with the current environment. What are the specific elements most often affected by each of the regulation modes? What does the client project? Introject? Deflect? Retroflect? In which field configurations does the client seek confluence?*

Projection: tends to project contempt. When his boss compliments him, he believes he is *"just saying that to make me feel good; deep down he sees me as weak and inferior"*.

Introjection: introjects his boss's perception of him as a "Badluck Schleprock"[4], that is, someone who falls prey to bad fate, having accidents, forgetting or losing things.

Deflection: deflects any positive comment from the therapist. For example, when I comment on his ability to make intelligent connections, he smiles and quickly downplays anything good he might have inside, for fear of becoming arrogant, boastful, and grandiose like his father.

Retroflection: retroflects the energy necessary to achieve his goals, and thus resorts to fantasising of being the best as a defence against feeling inadequate.

Confluence: there may be some confluence in his "accepting" my suggested strategies to overcome his procrastination. He agrees on the surface in the session, perhaps as a wish not to upset me; however he rarely puts it into action outside my office. This could also be seen as a form of passive aggressive or self-defeating behaviour.

In addition to the classical modes of regulation listed above, Bob employs the following defences or coping styles listed in the DSM-IV:

- Fantasy of omnipotence: he tends to embellish his past accomplishments and to dream of impressing and pleasing others with his expertise.
- Devaluation: at times he devalues his colleagues who, in his opinion, have less potential than he.
- Idealisation: sees certain people as having it all together, that is, some of his brothers and his therapist.
- Passive aggression: missing appointments, coming in late, and procrastination at work.

These defences or coping styles are used predominantly as a minor image-distorting mechanism to regulate his self-esteem.

Personality function: Configuration of the MFR and nature of representations

Configuration of MFR

Oscillates between "I am better than others" and "Others are better than I"

Self +	Other +	Self +	Other +
Self–			
Other–			

What seem to be the nature of Self-and Other-representations?

Self	*Other/Object*
+ I am very careful not to come across as arrogant or self-centred (like my father). As long as I'm not like my father, I'm OK. However, secretly dreams/fantasises about being admired as the best. Fantasy of being superior and capable of "beating them all".	+ My brothers are successful Others have it together

(Continued)

Table1. (*Continued*).

I want to shine as the captain of the team, but I end up being picked last or rejected. I am a failure.I lack self discipline, am lazy and depressed. *I don't deserve recognition (or, if ever I accept recognition I risk turning into my father, that is, someone who believes he knows better than everyone else).*	*My father was self centred, arrogant, obnoxious, always needing to be the centre of attention. Father succeeded socially and lost everything. Co-workers have been promoted without deserving it anymore than I. People are insincere with compliments.*

In the initial stages of therapy, Bob's MFR was predominantly made up of a negative self or underdog (a failure, a reject, a loser) and the other was seen as top dog (in control, having it all, admired)[5]. As the therapy unfolded the MFR configuration occasionally reversed itself and he became the top dog attempting to control the other (represented mostly by his father) now seen as the underdog. In the past his father would put him down by criticizing him and telling him things like "you're walking on your toes like a girl". Recently Bob is fighting back more, confronting his father and trying to dominate and control him. In so doing, he is reversing the MFR configuration, becoming the top dog who "demands respect". However, the two configurations remain incomplete: if one is good, then the other is bad. His challenge is to integrate the good and the bad in the same MFR configuration.

Inferences concerning the IF

Inferential hypotheses concerning the presence of Introjected Microfields in the background of the Id, taking into account observations of the Ego function and the MFR

1. What dynamic does the client seem to be trying to set up (process of repetition of impasses) in the relationships he or she mentions and/or in the therapeutic relationship? Can you describe this process of "repetition" in terms of some unfinished developmental issue?

    Bob fantasises about being recognized and admired. He wants to "please and impress others". But when he induces his co-workers, superiors, or myself to give him some positive feedback, he deflects it, at first because he believes the feedback is not sincere and is "just a way to make me feel good". In fact, he may not be wrong in his assessment. He talks about certain accomplishments or good deeds in a hesitant or self-deprecating manner inducing the listener to highlight the positive in an attempt to "repair" him (projective identification). Upon further analysis we discover an underlying fear of becoming like his father. When given positive feedback, he translates it into something like "you are the best in the world", which he argues he isn't. This "translation" evokes the image of his father's arrogance. This is his unfinished business or developmental issue, his Contact Dilemma: he needs genuine recognition, validation, and respect (indispensable), but if he takes it in, it becomes intolerable as it evokes the image of his father's inflated ego. This may be seen as a defence against grandiosity and could explain why he does not meet the criteria for NPD in the DSM.

2. How are defensive operations used to maintain/reproduce this unfinished developmental issue?

Through a process of projective identification, Bob induces others to give him positive feedback. This prevents him from believing and taking in positive nourishment because he "knows" that "they are saying these things only to make me feel good or perhaps as a way of making themselves look good". He deflects similar positive comments, out of fear of inflating his ego and becoming like his grandiose, boastful father whom he despises. The projective and deflective operations conserve his introjected father's view of him as not worthy of respect and admiration.

In addition, he tends to retroflect his energy into daydreaming and fantasising about admirable success as an attempt to compensate for a negative self view instead of channelling it into constructive action in the outside world. He complains of a lack of self discipline that leads him to zap on the television or surf on the Internet, to go to bed too late for proper sleep, thereby lacking energy to get things done during his day, and feeling bad for it. As he fantasises about ways to impress his superiors at work, he procrastinates and hands in substandard work. He harvests negative work evaluations instead of admiration, which further confirms his painful introjected negative self-view. As he struggles against a painful self-perception with these defensive operations, he feeds into a vicious cycle, a conservative adjustment as opposed to a creative one.

3. What were the known risk factors and resiliency factors around this specific issue in the client's developmental past?

A major risk factor in Bob's developmental past is his relationship with his father who treated him in a tyrannous and despising manner, ridiculing and criticising him. Being the last of five boys, Bob needed to fit in and belong as a male. He needed to feel valued by his father and sought his love and approval by identifying with him. Yet when he internalised his father, he also introjected the cruel contempt his father expressed towards him. Bob couldn't be himself with his father without being criticised or ridiculed.

There is some limited resiliency perhaps with one of his brothers who defended him at school. However this was short-lived because it meant that Bob lived in his shadow and had difficulty making his own mark and being seen for who he was.

Unfolding of therapeutic process

Reflexions on therapeutic process (adapted from Delisle, 1995–1998, CIG, Montréal)

1. Essentially, what is my experience with this client?

    I am touched by a boy struggling with grief, someone who is looking for help, and who trusts me to provide it. I want to help him. As time passes, he displays some passive-aggressive behaviour, basically rejecting my help. He knows this is not helping him and complains about it. My experience becomes one of frustration with his lack of progress, with his tendency to self sabotage. I feel myself to be going around in circles, powerless and helpless. Although he is a nice guy, I sometimes feel like "shaking" him to get him to move out of his rut. I could turn into his domineering father.
2. Can I find some thematic affinities between my experience with the client and some of what he reports as occurring in Field 3?

    In Field 3, he feels frustrated by a lack of promotion at work, and by his lack of organisation. He complains about a lack of self discipline, procrastinating, falling behind at work, and feeling overwhelmed. His boss sees him as a "Badluck Schleprock", a Flintstone character who is ill-fated.

    In therapy (Field 1), he sets himself up for failure with behaviours that prevent him from achieving what he desires. There is a chance that people in his environment experience feelings similar to mine, that is, a nice guy who procrastinates, makes mistakes, and who ends up frustrating to be with or to work with. Is this the result of anger toward his father turned against himself? Is he indirectly expressing this anger via mistakes and failures?

3. Can I find some thematic affinities between my experience with the client and some of what he reports as having occurred in Field 4?

He reports feeling frustrated with his failure to make the hockey team. He felt he didn't fit in with his peers at school nor within his family. His father demanded respect; pulled him up by the hair; ridiculed him for walking on his toes. At school he tried to impress his classmates by pretending to eat cat food and to drink mouthwash. The whole incident backfired and he became the butt of jokes instead. This hapless, ill-fated image is carried over into his work environment and filters through his therapy as he "forgets" what we are working on. As his MFR and his Contact Dilemma seep through his modes of regulation, I feel a certain pressure to react in forceful ways that may resemble his father and that would maintain his negative self and other representations. The primary introjection (Contact Dilemma/Unfinished Business) lives on in the Id and in the MFR and continues to shape his behaviour in such a way as to maintain an introjected negative image of himself.

4. How could I express this construction of meaning in hermeneutic terms?
a partial hypothesis …
that does not exhaust the entire meaning of the phenomenon …
that stimulates the clients' own constructive creativity …
and that keeps affect alive …

He appears to externalise an internal conflict, a form of Projective Identification whereby I feel pressured to behave according to his internal representation of his father. I could say something like: "If I were to go with the flow of what happens or doesn't happen here in therapy, I could feel an urge to shake you up, to get you unstuck and to move forward, to work so hard to help you that I could end up feel frustrated and powerless; but my sense is that we would be repeating an experience that you probably know all too well: a sense of failure, of not achieving what you want, not having the respect you want, or feeling like a loser, not making the team. I wonder how what I'm saying just now resonates emotionally inside you, how does it fit?"

There is a good chance that as the Reproduction is played out, he will disqualify me as a father figure and reject any "teaching" that I might offer.

5. Can I think of a restorative response that ...
would be different than those that the client tends to evoke ...
that I feel I could maintain with integrity over time ...

Not a one-time response, but a way of being with him, that is, a blend of warm positive regard, empathic attunement with his genuine developmental needs (*à la* Kohut) and empathic confrontation in Field 1 (*à la* Kernberg). Not lose touch with the narcissistic rage in the background, a rage tied to not being recognised and validated. Confront the projective identification whereby he projects his rage without expressing it openly and without owning up to it. For example, I could point out that his forgetting our appointments or what we discussed in therapy is a message he is communicating to me-what might it be?

The course of the therapy

Overall, the therapy moved like a spiral, repeatedly circling back over themes, at times discouraging, but overall with slow, gradual progress in acknowledgement and reparation.

The initial phase of therapy consisted of monitoring his mood and energy. He met the diagnostic criteria for depression but refused to take medication until the third month of therapy. He was distressed with his marital relationship. His wife was away much of the time, travelling as part of her new work. "She laid a bomb on me", as he put it, by confessing that she no longer felt attracted to him and that she was no longer sure of her feelings for him. He noticed that she was taking greater care of her looks, rarely called him, and avoided talking about their future. They had very little sexual and emotional intimacy. Bob suspected that she was having an affair. However, he didn't really want to hear from her that she was cheating on him—"it would be too hard on my self-esteem". They saw a marital therapist, but after a few sessions it became apparent to him that there was little hope in saving his marriage. This was painful, devastating, and humiliating to Bob.

Intimate relationships

As he and his wife were discussing selling the house as part of the separation process, he got involved with Cynthia, a married woman he met at a conference and who saw him as "an expert" in his field of work. This encounter was a balm on the self-esteem injury caused by the separation. A few weeks into their eight month liaison, she told him about a time in her life when she had sex with multiple partners and reminded him that she was married and was thinking of working things out with her husband. This revelation was upsetting to Bob as it triggered familiar painful feelings related to suspicions of his wife having an affair. As he floated back in time with these familiar feelings, he remembered a girl he was dating in high school (Field 4) who had asked to keep their relationship secret because her previous boyfriend felt jealous and could cause trouble. He felt that he had to submit to her wishes and saw this as a way of "respecting" her. She finally accepted to go with him to the graduation dance, but later cheated on him. As he was telling me about this, he had flashes of his current relationship with Cynthia (Field 3): it too was secretive and she also cheated with other men; she too was in control and dictated when they could see each other, placing him in a position of subjugation. He made a connection between Fields 4 (his high school girlfriend) and 3 (his current liaison with Cynthia), and began to acknowledge a possible recurring theme in his love life. His wife also played into this theme by leaving him for another man with whom she was having an affair.

Soon after Cynthia's disclosure about multiple sexual partners and her reminder that she was married, Bob experienced difficulties performing sexually with her. However he had no difficulty engaging in sex with two other women, sharing this with Cynthia who was hurt by the news. This suggests the possibility of a sadomasochistic feature in his love relationships. For example, he later met a woman who he felt "talked down" at him and who "held an important job". He seduced her into his bed and as he was on top of her he suddenly left her to check his pager, feeling the satisfaction of "getting back at her". He nevertheless felt some shame in telling me the story. He didn't want me to see him as one of "the guys who disrespect women". Nevertheless, he was able to acknowledge that his behaviour toward Cynthia and the other woman was an expression of his anger toward his wife for cheating on him and leaving him.

In the history of his relationships there is a recurring alternation between seeking admiration and fearing embarrassment and rejection. Shortly before he ended his relationship with Cynthia, she had seen an insecure side of him. He felt embarrassed and wanted to distance himself from her and hide. "When she first met me, I was well dressed for a conference, I was the expert, her rock; now she saw me dressed in grubs with torn jeans, and she saw how nervous I was with her parents". This event triggered a memory of him at age eleven, walking down the street, noticing a girl that he finds attractive, wanting to impress her just as he trips over his boot laces and feels embarrassed. "Here I am thinking of impressing this girl, and I end up embarrassing myself". "I felt like a social reject".

He continued to reproduce this dilemma in his contacts with women. Before going out on a date, he would be particularly concerned about his image, wanting to impress and afraid of embarrassing himself and scaring his date away. This wish to impress and fear of embarrassment together formed an impasse which he reproduced in his relationships.

After Cynthia, he dated a colleague widely admired for her looks and her intelligence. He placed her on a pedestal and was flattered by her interest in him. However, he was also uncomfortable with her. She seemed to have some insight into how he truly felt, for example about not getting the promotions. Resenting that, he kept her at bay.

His need to impress and be admired affected his marriage. When he was with his wife, they would scuba dive and the fact that this impressed people made him feel good, proud, and admired. But did he feel loved? Perhaps he was mostly motivated at the time by his need to "shine and stand out as special". He got caught up in dreaming about shining at work, in courses, in social clubs, and in having his wife admire him for all these accomplishments. Spending an inordinate amount of time surfing on the Internet for ways to improve himself, he neglected his marriage and his wife "fell for another guy". Across most of his life, his fantasies of self-fulfilment became ultimately self-defeating.

Through hermeneutic dialogue and mentalisation he made some progress in the acknowledgement of his dilemma and started to differentiate between admiration and true intimacy, that is, sharing vulnerable feelings. He began to recognise that perhaps his desire to be admired, respected, and to shine reflected a deeper need for true love and intimacy. I asked him "Wouldn't it be nice if you could show a vulnerable side of you, a part that you feel ashamed of, and hear her say

'I see your quirk but I will stand by you and still love you'?" He seemed touched by my remark, saying that he felt he could show me his quirks and not be judged or rejected for them. This was a "weird feeling" for him. He began to recognise how he confused love and admiration, believing that in order to be loved he first needed to accomplish something impressive that others could admire and look up to. With me, he acknowledged his fear of being seen as weak and vulnerable. To his surprise, he didn't feel like I would reject him, despite his apprehension. This was a new feeling for him, and he had some difficulty trusting it. He nevertheless gave me and his "weird feeling" the "benefit of the doubt", perhaps an attempt to erode an IM (Introjected Microfield) and to move toward a new experience, a creative adjustment. I invited him to risk sharing some of his vulnerable feelings in his relationships.

Gradually he developed meaningful intimate relationships and was able to introduce a significant partner to his children. Although the reproductions recurred, they became less powerful as he mentalised and recognised them through constant hermeneutic dialogue within the context of his relational dilemmas. He is now progressively more able to make sense of his relationship experience and to experiment with new ways of being.

Work life

His priority at work was "to shine, to be seen as an expert, a leader, someone who pleases people and impresses them with his charm". "But I feel held back". Here too we see the dilemma between the wish for admiration and the fear of humiliation. He became unfocussed, procrastinated, got distracted by TV and the Internet, lacked sleep, felt depressed and tired. He was consistently late for work and had difficulty concentrating on the task at hand. He felt overwhelmed: "All these things to do, yet when I think of it, it isn't all that much". He wanted to apply for a promotion, yet he confessed that he would not select himself for the job because of his difficulty concentrating and producing. He alternated between personal and work tasks on the computer, was easily distracted by personal emails and moved from one thing to the next without getting much accomplished. We worked on various strategies to help him keep a better focus on productivity, but with little success. He became convinced that he was suffering from Attention Deficit Disorder and obtained an evaluation. The results of the assessment showed he had no ADD and that his problem was his tendency to base his self-worth on outward achievements, setting very high expectations for himself and being very self-critical for not achieving them.

Through hermeneutic dialogue and mentalisation, he gradually became aware of an internal struggle. He saw himself caught between a critical, demanding, and punitive part of himself (top dog), a rebellious childlike part that refused any form of control (underdog). This rebellious part was seen as responsible for his lack of self-discipline, recurrent procrastination, and self-defeating behaviour. His boss once asked him to do some important work that needed to be completed within a couple of days. Bob thought he would impress him by getting it done that very evening. However he let himself be distracted and at nine o'clock he only had half of it done. He was fed up and angry. During the next two days he worked on other things until his boss asked him about the work, and he felt disappointed and bad for not having it done. The disappointment he saw in his boss's eyes made him feel even worse. Scenes such as this had become reproductions of an impasse in his relationship with his father.

I invited him to continue to observe and to stay in touch with feelings tied to this internal struggle between the critical parent and the rebellious child, and he developed greater awareness of his destructive habits of procrastination, not following up on actions, and being neglectful in general. He seemed to take pride in resisting the demanding part of himself, at times turning it into a question of "being a free spirit". Yet he chastised himself for not meeting the demands of his superiors, thereby sabotaging his chances of promotion. "I ended up getting my boss to hate me". Although he acknowledged a possible reproduction of his relationship with his father, he was not yet able to work it through on a more emotional level.

On Bob's performance evaluation his superior made negative comments about his being late with his work. Although Bob agreed that he was late, he felt it was unfair to put it in writing, because it compromised his chances for promotion. Yet at other times Bob felt he didn't deserve to be promoted, saying "I wouldn't select myself for promotion if I were in their shoes". This suggests a form of role reversal (in his MFR) between the critical parent and the rebellious child. I pointed this out to him but he remained focused on seeing himself as a victim of circumstances: "I was dealt a bad hand", referring to events such as his wife leaving him (Field E3) and his father "crushing my self-esteem"

(Field I4). "I know it's foolish, but I wish someone would give me a pill or something so that my life could change".

In my countertransference I often felt that he was bringing me a mess, expecting me to fix it all. When I gave him suggestions, he found them important and didn't want to forget (Field E1). Then as he walked out, it all fizzled away and he forgot. Nothing stuck, nothing changed, and he returned with the same mess, hoping again that I would clean it up (Field I1), the way his mother cleaned up his room (Field E4).

He reminisced about a time a few years previously when he felt respected and recognised, at a high point in his career. He dreamt then of "having power, being respected, and looked up to, like a politician". Currently however, he was stuck feeling worthless at work, experiencing a large gap between where he dreamt of being and where he actually was. This is not unlike the tension that exists between the ideal ego (reminiscing about a past where he was powerful, a form of infantile omnipotence) and the ego ideal (what he would like to achieve). As he talked about what he referred to as "the high point" in his career, he gave the impression of idealising the past with a tinge of omnipotence, as though it were now forever lost, resembling the notion of ideal ego as described by Freud (1914)[6]. He gave another example from his undergraduate days: "I was shining in the top ten out of 250, dreamt of completing a doctorate, and then I stopped caring and finally turned out to be an average student, even though I profoundly dislike being just average". It could be argued that Bob tried to regain some of the lost omnipotence in his fantasy of "shining as captain of the team" as well as through the embellishment of his past work. The ego ideal, on the other hand, is not born out of illusory omnipotence, but fashioned after parental ideals, after the Freudian superego. The fantasy of the ideal ego escapes the work required by the ego ideal, functioning as if its goals were already attained. A manifestation of this would be his distraction from the work that needs to get done, in order to dream of exceeding expectations and thus impressing those above him. His fantasy could be seen as a form of retroflection of energy, which becomes a conservative adjustment confirming his MFR, a negative representation of self as a failure.

He remembered being demoted to a lower hockey league as a young teenager, but as they drove away with his uniform, he fantasised that someday they would regret their decision, realising that he was a great hockey player after all. As he shared these stories from Field E4 I asked him what it felt like inside as he talked with me. He switched to his contemporary world (Field I3) confessing that inside he often felt superior to others, secretly confident that he could beat practically anybody. He felt somewhat embarrassed and ashamed to tell me this, but with some empathic encouragement he gave me greater access to his ideal ego and was able to express his inner/secret feelings quite openly. I felt closer to him and shared that with him. He said "it feels weird to hear you say that, but, I don't know, I guess it also feels good". This was a touching moment, the beginning of reparation where he felt himself to be seen in authentic feelings without being rejected or "crushed". As he let me into his secret fantasy world, I felt as if I was in the presence of a young child playing superman and the last thing I wanted to do at that moment was to crush him as his father had done.

He continued to put his name in for promotion, becoming restless and unfocused, applying for all kinds of positions without taking the time to reflect on what he truly wanted to achieve. The job title seemed more important to him than true enjoyment of the work. As a result he was ill prepared and never made it through the selection process, triggering a self-defeating cycle of feelings of inadequacy which he tried to overcome by desperately trying for other promotions without sufficient focus and preparation which only resulted in more failures and feelings of inadequacy. He acknowledged that he was caught in fantasy (a remnant of his ideal ego), wishing that somehow through the magic of a promotion he would be respected and admired as a great person without having to "earn it or work for it", without any effort (required by the ego ideal). "Give me a pill, and all my problems will vanish and people will be proud of me" or "If I slip on the captain's sweater, I will be seen and admired as captain, which will make my 'badness' go away".

His focus on external validation/admiration prevented him from concentrating on the task at hand, and set him up for failure. For example when he was invited once to give a presentation on a work-related matter, he read the requirements superficially and accepted with the belief that this would be good for his image as an expert. But he realised afterward that he had not adequately responded to what was demanded. When he went back to the invitational message, he realized that the demands were clearly stated and that if he had paid more attention, he could have delivered what was required. Hence, his focus on external validation/admiration prevented him from concentrating on the task and set him up for failure.

I encouraged him to be more realistic in his self-assessment, grounding him in the here and now as opposed to getting distracted with dreams and fantasies. He made some progress in focusing on the concrete task at hand and putting in more effort to bring his current work to completion, focusing on the work and not on the praise he wanted to get for it (see Table 8: level 1, in terms of therapeutic objectives, i.e., a change in symptomatic behaviour).

Later he declined applying for a promotion to a position with an "attractive" title because the work involved was not suited to him and would have interfered with his ability to be there for his children. For the first time since the beginning of his therapy, he based a decision on his personal values and genuine needs, letting go of the pursuit of external validation (level 3 in terms of therapeutic objectives, i.e., identifying creative modes of adjustment that allow congruence between subjective experience and field configuration). His self-representation softened and became more fluid. He sought feedback from some members of the selection board in order to better prepare for promotion.

In spite of the possibility of finally moving forward in his career, he ignored the feedback he was given, explaining that he didn't have the energy to follow up on it and he failed in his next two attempts to obtain a promotion, becoming frustrated and angry. Although he felt he had the knowledge and the tools to change (via the feedback), he wasn't doing anything about it. It was as if in resisting the "ghost" of his arrogant father, an internal struggle was created (a form of IM). Bob felt he knew better than his father, who continuously criticised him and told him what to do. However, he came short of realising that by rejecting the feedback for promotion, he was reproducing a pattern created by the IM with his critical father. In this instance he was close to a level 4 in terms of therapeutic objectives, that is, achieving a relative understanding of the basis of his dissonant subjective experience.

Floating back in time on his frustration and anger, he visualised scenes from his childhood when he was bullied and ridiculed by peers or by his father. He realised the importance of anger in his life and said he wanted to hold on to it as a lifebuoy. "It's all I have left. Being put down is how others want to define me. I don't want to let go of the anger. If I do, I will give up." This important insight facilitated a change in the way he used anger. Instead of using his anger to reverse the top dog/underdog positions, as he had attempted to do in the past, he used it in a more constructive fashion (level 3, creative adjustment). When he was not given recognition for replacing his immediate superior but was still expected to do the extra work, he used his anger to speak up and refuse to do the extra workload, since he was not recognised for it anyway. As a result he was given recognition and, having asserted himself appropriately, he was able to refocus on his work. This is an example of levels 2, 3, and 4 in terms of therapeutic objectives. Although level 5 was not achieved entirely, there was nevertheless an erosion of the IM at the origin of his dissonant subjective experience. He acknowledged feeling less anger toward his father, recognising however that it was not resolved.

    He was able to concentrate better on his work and received positive feedback. He joined a new team which he found stimulating. He was excited, on a "high", but he was apprehensive about the "next low", recognising his past pattern of getting himself overwhelmed and behind in his work, and feeling rejected by the team. Together we worked on consolidating his progress by helping him to be a legitimate team member without having to be the best. We discussed potential traps he could fall into with his new job. For example, in his desire to shine and impress superiors he could spend too much time on side projects, run behind in his core work, feel the stress of that, get a signal from his superior that he is behind, feel overwhelmed and envious of his boss. I suggested that he focus on his role in the team—"stop looking at the captain with admiration/envy wondering why you're not in his position, and concentrate on playing a good defence, lest the puck passes you and you get into trouble." He agreed to keep his superiors informed of his work and to discuss setting limits: this helped him keep a better focus on the work at hand.

    He was excited by his work and was offered praise and appreciation which triggered his dilemma (indispensable *vs.* intolerable) and he defended with a negative projection of intention, that is, "they don't really mean it", deflecting the praise. The mechanics of that became clearer: he converts praise into a scale comparing him to others and placing him above them. This in turn triggers two reactions: fear of becoming swollen like his arrogant pompous father, and a pressure to keep up the positive impression that others have of him. This prevents him from taking in and savouring the appreciation. Since he doesn't assimilate it and spits it out immediately, he remains hungry for more, and this fuels his compensatory dreams and wishes of being seen as the expert, shining as the captain, better and above others, an image/impression that is hard to maintain and which remains fragile and vulnerable, leading by a decompensation into depression.

I felt touched seeing him work and struggle so hard to free himself from a toxic emotional trap where he ends up hungry. I felt closer to him, and shared that with him. I felt respect and some admiration for his work. It felt "weird" for him to hear me share this with him. He nevertheless seemed to take it in as tears welled up in his eyes.

Throughout our sessions, he was increasingly able to identify and accept the various struggles within himself. He enacted a dialogue between two conflicting parts within himself: 1) Dante—the achiever, the "should" side, who wants to be a better person, who has drive and passion; but who can also fall in the trap of external validation to the point of becoming vulnerable to feeling like an impostor; and 2) Dopey—who refuses to get flustered, who takes it easy and just lies down; but who can also become lazy and depressed. Bob, the observing ego, wants to be proud of himself and needs to be healthy and whole, to care and be compassionate with himself. He recognized that each part had a core quality to be developed, and a possible trap to avoid. The parts would need to collaborate instead of fighting to win and dominate. This reflects an integration of the positive and negative representations in the MFR (akin to a level 5 in the therapeutic objectives).

Finally, he got a significant promotion. He felt proud. As he expressed his pride, his attention turned to his internal conflict between feeling "pompous" on one hand, and like a failure on the other. He talked about triggers (accomplishments he is proud of) which can inflate him to the point of imagining that he could be the best prime minister. Then he "caught" himself and felt ashamed of being a "pompous ass", like his father. He was able to initiate greater mentalisation. Instead of going into his familiar anger against his father, this time he stayed with the feeling of being "pompous". He felt ashamed admitting to having a pompous side to him, yet he was surprised that he wasn't as ashamed as he had anticipated. He thanked me for my "demeanour" and reiterated the deep respect that he felt for me. It was a touching moment of acknowledgement and reparation.

Notes

1. Dr. Michel Dandeneau is a registered psychologist who has been in private practice for the past eighteen years. He has taught clinical

psychology courses at the University of Ottawa for nineteen years and is a graduate student of the CIG in Montreal. Dr. Dandeneau wishes to express his warmest thanks to Line Girard for her invaluable help in preparing this case study.
2. PDM Task Force. (2006). *Psychodynamic Diagnostic Manual* Silver Spring, MD: Alliance of Psychoanalytic Organizations.
   Note: The Psychodynamic Diagnostic Manual is a psychodynamic nosology of mental disorders meant to supplement the DSM. Its purpose is to assist in psychodynamic case formulation and treatment planning. Whereas the DSM is a categorical taxonomy of symptoms and disorders of function, the PDM is more dimensional in nature as it describes a continuum of human mental functioning.
3. See Appendix.
4. Badluck Schleprock is a character from the 1970s *The Flintstone Comedy Hour*. The character has since been assimilated into popular culture and become an icon and stereotype for unlucky or hapless individuals.
5. Perls, F. (1969), *Gestalt Therapy Verbatim*. Moab, UT: Real People Press.
   NB. "Topdog vs. underdog", labelled by Perls, refers to intrapsychic polarities. The topdog, much like the Freudian Superego, is an introjection of societal, familial, or authoritarian demands. Opposed to the topdog is the underdog, similar to the Freudian Id, the manifestation of resistance or internal sabotage assuring that the demands will never be met.
6. Freud in "On Narcissism" (1914).

CHAPTER TWELVE

Brian

Case study presented by Guilhème Pérodeau, Ph.D.[1]

Identification

Brian (pseudonym) is a man forty-one years old at the onset of therapy. He was born, raised, and still resides in a small rural area in the province of Quebec (Canada), and has cohabited for the last fifteen years with Sheila who manages a small gift shop in town. They have a twelve-year-old son, Maxime, who was diagnosed with cancer at age six, but who has been in remission for the last five years. Brian worked as a plumber at his family-owned business until the time of his motorcycle accident. Following the accident he had his right leg amputated at the knee (he now has an artificial leg), suffered a traumatic brain injury, and had to quit his job.

Clinical context

Therapy took place in a private practice setting over a two-year period. Brian was seen weekly (during the first nine months), then bi-monthly (for the next twelve months) and finally on a monthly basis (for the last three months). He came regularly and cancelled only seven times due to illness, medical examination, or transportation difficulties (during the winter). Costs for the sessions were covered by the Société de l'Assurance Automobile du Québec or SAAQ (Quebec Automobile Insurance Corporation), which provides insurance for personal injuries following road accidents. The SAAQ is responsible for evaluation, treatment, and financial compensation in such cases. Brian was assigned a caseworker to whom we sent progress reports on demand.

Chief initial complaint and associated symptoms

Initial contact was made over the phone. Brian indicated that he was badly in need of psychological help because he continually felt unhappy, experienced a great sense of emptiness, was very depressed, and did not care if he lived or died. Through therapy, he hoped to "muster a bit of happiness and the will to live." Since the accident, his life had turned upside down. "I used to be happy. I liked to tease my friends and have a good time: now I feel unhappy and pitiful."

At the initial face-to-face encounter with the therapist, Brian was casually but neatly dressed. A good-looking man with bright blue eyes and an engaging smile, he exuded a strong vitality in spite of using a cane. He seemed open to engage in therapy and I could sense a certain hopefulness in his demeanour.

Although counter-transference was mostly positive because of Brian's obvious vitality and zest for life, it was tempered by the perception of a certain underlying slyness, as if he were somewhat fearful of being swindled.

History

Brian's father is a self-made man with little education but enough know-how to launch a successful plumbing company where his three sons were employed. Brian is the middle child. His older brother is a hard-worker, still in the father's employ and the favourite son, according to Brian. The younger is an alcoholic and a drug-addict. Mother is a tearful homemaker who stayed home to look after her husband and growing boys. Father does not talk much and spends the little free time he has in the basement working on his stamp collection.

Brian reports that he was well taken care of as a child and had a religious upbringing. He believes in God and prays every day in spite of his lack of concentration. He did not go beyond Grade Three because he did not like school. Nonetheless, he feels smart and resourceful. Before his accident, he was a hard worker, proud of his skills as a plumber.

Between the ages of fifteen and twenty-six Brian roamed the bars with various gangs, got into fights, and became a drug-addict, doing cocaine and acid. At one point, he was hospitalised due to a bad "acid trip." To sustain his drug habit, he stole from his parents. He also engaged in criminal acts such as breaking and entering (with violence) various properties. He was caught, did time in prison, and went through a drug rehabilitation program. He changed his outlook on life, controlling his drinking thereafter. His "bad boy" days were over and, as he says, he resumed being a "good person", which he feels is his true nature. He met his present life partner, Sheila, who is also a "good person", whereas his previous partner was a drug-addict like himself. In his early thirties, he launched a business venture which went awry, and had to file for bankruptcy. It was hard on him: his dream of getting rich was shattered.

Some years later, Brian got depressed at the news of his son's illness, taking antidepressant medication (Zoloft) to pull through. Just before the accident, Maxime was in remission and Brian decreased the medication. He was still working at his father's company and had a good life with Sheila.

Two and a half years before entering therapy, Brian's life turned upside down very abruptly. While riding his Harley-Davidson, he collided with a large recreational vehicle. He was thrown twenty feet, lost consciousness, woke up in hospital, and was amnesic for two weeks. His right leg was amputated; he had multiple fractures throughout his body and severe brain injury among other things. Neurological and other medical tests indicated that the after-effects of the accident were severe, numerous, and permanent, that is, severe brain injury affecting his concentration and memory, restricted mobility, and tinnitus with its ensuing hearing difficulties. He now tires very easily, has headaches, and has grown more impatient and more aggressive. After a two-month hospitalization, Brian was discharged and spent the next four months at a rehabilitation centre. He then received treatment on an outpatient basis. He refused any kind of psychological help throughout his ordeal, because at the time he felt strong enough to pull through on his own.

Multi-axial diagnosis

Brian presents with the following diagnoses (based on the DSM-IV[2])

Axis I: clinical disorders

Major depressive episode F32.x (296.2x) based on the following symptoms: 1) period of at least two weeks during which there is a depressive mood on a daily basis; 2) the loss of interest or pleasure in nearly all activities; 3) weight gain; 4) insomnia; 5) decreased energy; 6) feelings of worthlessness; 7) difficulty in thinking, concentrating (probable interaction with the medication); 8) recurrent thoughts of death or suicidal ideation.

Acute stress disorder F43.1 (308.3). He A) has been confronted with an event which was a threat to the physical integrity of self and; B) after experiencing the distressing event, he had a subjective sense of numbing, a reduction of awareness of his surroundings, and dissociative amnesia; C) afterwards the traumatic event was persistently re-experienced via recurrent images, thoughts, or dreams; D) there is an avoidance of certain situations the client would have engaged in prior to the accident and a marked increase of anxiety (e.g., sleeping difficulties, irritability, poor concentration, hypervigilence); f) social-emotional dysfunction in various areas of life.

As he sustained a major injury and his physical integrity was affected, it is possible that some of his symptoms reflect the physical injury and subsequent pharmaceutical treatment.

Axis II: personality disorders

Narcissistic personality disorder (F301.81) based on the following symptoms: 1) has a grandiose sense of self-importance (e.g., exaggerates achievements and talents, expects to be recognized as superior without commensurate achievements); 2) is preoccupied with fantasies of unlimited success; 3) requires excessive admiration; 4) is interpersonally exploitative, that is, takes advantage of others to achieve his or her own ends; (7) lacks empathy: is unwilling to recognize or identify with the feelings and needs of others; (8) is often envious of others or believes that others are envious of him.

Brian presents himself as a man of importance who wants to become a millionaire. He enjoys being admired for his feats. He uses his wife as an intermediary to become a successful business man through the gift shop she owns; he has a very harsh interacting style with the employees. He is envious of others who appear to be more successful than he is, such as neighbours with "bigger boats or newer cars."

His narcissistic personality is permeated with paranoid traits: he projects malevolent intentions on to others and exhibits a pattern of pervasive distrust and suspiciousness, quickly assuming that other people will exploit, harm, or deceive him.

Axis III: acute medical conditions and physical disorders

Severe and chronic physical pain, phantom leg, severe traumatic brain injury, tinnitus, diminished cognitive functioning.

Axis IV: psychosocial and environmental factors contributing to the disorder

Various highly stressful events over time: motorbike accident, son's cancer, bankruptcy.

Axis V: global assessment of functioning

In this axis we rate overall social and occupational functioning, taking into account limitations due to physical or mental impairment. At the onset of therapy Brian was functioning at level 50 that is, with " serious impairment in social, and occupational functioning" (e.g., he was suicidal, was staying home with no social contact except for his immediate family) At the end of therapy he reached level 70 that is, with "some difficulty in social, occupational, but generally functioning well." He still experienced some difficulties but had resumed or initiated some meaningful interpersonal relationships and social activities with friends. He was actually thinking of getting married. He was slowly integrating his loss and feeling hope for the future.

Psychodynamic diagnosis

This diagnosis is based on the Psychodynamic Diagnostic Manual (PDM)[3].

Personality patterns and disorders—P axis

Level of personality disorder: borderline high level of functioning

Brian has been living under highly demanding conditions since his accident. He displays a certain rigidity, especially under stressful circumstances, and is able to use only a limited range of coping mechanisms. He still experiences relational difficulties under difficult conditions, that is, a SAAQ evaluation process or business dealings. He uses projective identification, for example, attributing malevolent intents to others while being unaware of his own ill feelings directed towards them. He also entertains a split view of the world: on one hand there are the good people he loves such as his life partner, son, and parents, as well as a few hand-picked family members and friends. On the other hand, there is the rest of the world that he deeply distrusts; he must constantly "protect my own interests." Nonetheless, before his accident he was successfully holding a job and had a satisfactory family and social life. One can speculate that during his adolescence and early adulthood Brian functioned at a low borderline level of personality organisation (multiple drug addiction, criminal activities, fights, etc.), but benefited from rehabilitation following his prison sentence. He attained a higher level of function within the borderline range, settled down, and ceased hard drugs and criminal behaviours. He was able to establish a relationship with a woman who was not doing drugs or engaging in erratic behaviours, as was the case in his previous relationship.

With regard to personality style, Brian's profile corresponds to a narcissistic personality disorder (P104), that is, a constant inflation or deflation of the self-esteem; affects of shame, contempt, or envy, a need to feel perfect, to feel OK; beliefs that others enjoy wealth, beauty, power, and fame, and the more I have of those, the better I feel; defences are idealisation and devaluation. He is in the depressed group (P104.2) described by the PDM as a "hypervigilant narcissist."

Moreover, Brian displays paranoid traits as illustrated in the PDM, namely a constant preoccupation of attacking (or being attacked) by humiliating others; affects of fear, rage, shame, and contempt; being dependant is dangerous; the world is full of potential attackers and users; extensive use of defences such as projection, projective identification, denial, and reaction formation.

Clearly the PDM-M axis matches nicely the DSM with regard to the paranoid colour of his personality constellation.

Profile of mental function—M axis

In this axis the categories cover diverse areas of mental capabilities which help the clinician capture the complexity of Brian's functioning.

In Brian's case, we find that the capacity for regulation, attention, and learning, which entails basic cognitive operations, has not improved over therapy. After the accident Brian suffered acute neurological problems which impaired his pre-morbid cognitive level. There was also interference from the heavy medication he was on. With regard to his capacity for relationships, Brian improved from a superficial, self-centreed style to a more caring and empathic stance towards significant others, in particular his life partner. His narcissistic personality traits made him somewhat manipulative. He could use people (e.g., his life partner) for his own means and disregard their needs in order to further his own success. Towards the end of therapy, Brian was more in touch with feelings of love towards significant others. However a harsh interactive style still marked his dealings with outsiders such as the SAAQ caseworker or employees at the gift shop. He would literally blow up in rage and lose control. Empathy and understanding with regard to his settlement or his gift shop employees' point of view were utterly absent.

Great improvement occurred in the quality of internal experience. At the onset of therapy, Brian felt very incomplete without his leg and because of the after-effects of the accident. He felt that he presented a pitiful sight to the outside world. Little by little, he learned to appreciate his interactions with friends and family and feel important again as a husband, father, and friend, etc. Towards the end, he basked in people's admiration for his golfing activities in spite of his being physically challenged. He also enjoyed sharing his experience with others who were preparing for similar amputations and so on. Brian also improved in the experience, comprehension, and expression of affect. At the beginning of therapy, Brian was highly suspicious of most people around him.

He was defiant and often interacted harshly with others. At the end he was starting to develop a capacity for deciphering interactional cues, but his style remained crude and in need of further improvement.

With regard to defensive patterns and capacities, Brian initially engaged in acting-out behaviour such as going on large-scale buying sprees to make himself feel good, for example, buying a boat or various goods on the spur of the moment. At the end of therapy he was able to use defences in a more rational fashion, mostly to deal with stressful emotions. He was more realistic and able to see that his acting-out did not soothe his inner suffering. Marked improvement also appeared with regard to Brian's capacity to form internal representations. He was extremely concrete in his representations throughout the therapy, engaging instead in acting-out behaviour. Towards the end, he started to use representations to shape the experience of his sense of self. Similarly, he started to develop a capacity for differentiation and integration of experiences of the self and non-self (others, fantasy, and reality, etc.). This progress was made along with an improved self-observing capacity (psychological-mindedness). Initially, Brian could reflect only concretely on his experiences. Afterwards, he developed a certain capacity for introspection, as long as he was not in a stressful situation. Finally he was also able to increase his capacity to construct or use internal standards and ideals. Initially, his values were based mostly on religious principles: "If I commit suicide I will not go to paradise." Brian continued to have some religious principles but they remained poorly integrated or poorly thought-out.

Structural analysis

In structural analysis, the focus is on the awareness-contact functions of the client. Of interest is the Contact-Dilemma, that is, early experiences which were simultaneously indispensable and intolerable for survival and which, through the primary introjective process and ensuing Unfinished Situation (US), yielded the Introjected Field (IF). The emphasis is on the dilemma as activated through present circumstances. These adaptive mechanisms come to light in the Functions of the Self.

The Id function

The Id function contains both physiological elements and Unfinished Situations readily accessible to consciousness as well as an unconscious and split part of the Self, which contains Unfinished Developmental Business: these elements of the Introjected Field consist of several Micro-fields (IM) which are slowly unveiled throughout the therapeutic process in its diverse experiential fields.

In Brian's case, deep feelings of despair and shame for his losses readily emerged from the Id from sessions one to nine elements. Rage and impulsivity came out at sessions ten and eleven. He was angry at the world. These feelings dominated until session thirty-eight at which time the SAAQ reached a decision for the financial settlement. Brian calmed down thereafter. He readily expressed his love and attachment for his family throughout the therapy. Obsessive thoughts about being rich came out strongly at around session ten and lingered on until session forty-six at which time he gave up riding a Harley again and reconsidered his options. Non-emergent feelings of vulnerability did not clearly appear before session seventeen when Brian returned to the scene of the accident and tears started flowing. Similarly, feelings of pleasure were non-emergent and appeared very progressively at session tenty-four and twenty-five (mid-therapy) during the summer. These feelings did not last long because of the stress engendered by the settlement and its aftermath. They reappeared at session forty-seven when Brian finally came to peace with the fact that he wouldn't ride a bike again.

During the first sessions, I was struck by the inflated (grandiose) description Brian made of his family status ("We are a very important family in the district!") and the make of bike ("If the Harley-Davidson had not existed, I would not have become a biker. Japanese bikes are a waste of my time.") This was in sharp contrast with his physically impaired appearance (cane, awkward gait with the artificial leg). Also Brian did not show his vulnerability as such, being extremely self-denigrating. He thought of himself as a pitiful sight, a worthless being. Although Brian reported feeling sad and desperate, he kept his tears and feelings of vulnerability in check. He boasted that he was the only one in the family with enough stamina to endure his ordeal. A contact dilemma could underlie these two contrasting stances.

We can speculate that Brian could not allow himself to show his more sensitive, fearful side to his cold and hard-working father. He has introjected (primary introjection) a field in which sensitiveness is to be disparaged. Better to be tough and hold back the tears. In the same vein he waited two years before being able to seek psychological help. Although feeling pitiful, he couldn't help but present a formidable self-image to the therapist. We hypothesise the following Contact Dilemma: it was both indispensable and intolerable to show a partial self (a tough side) to his distant father. In other words he could not express his vulnerable, tearful self, so as to be perceived and accepted in all his facets as a human being. In fact, his vulnerability and sensitivity were denied existence. Tears were the prerogative of the depressed mother, who could not see him either, because of those very tears. Brian was caught between a harsh, emotionless father and a highly emotive but powerless mother. He adjusted to this life up until the time of his accident. He states that as a small boy he cried a lot like his mother and then learned "to hide my tears and laugh on the other side of my face."

The Ego function

The Ego function connects the Self with the environment in such a way as to reproduce situations which will maintain the Internalized Field (IF) intact. It is an adaptive and defensive function.

Brian introjects compliments on his good looks, his inner strength, and stamina, or his abilities as a shrewd businessman. He retroflects his vulnerability, his tears, his overall sensitivity: " I often feel like crying but tears don't come out!" He deflects any expression of compassion or pity stemming from his family and friends: "They just pity me!" He also deflects any life choice that seems less glamorous that his initial choices, that is, his work as one of the best plumbers in the region, striking it rich, riding a Harley. He projects his harshness and cunning ways on to others such as the gift shop employees or the staff at the SAAQ (including the medical experts): "I have to watch out for my interests otherwise they'll trick me!"

These reproductions of the initial Unfinished Situation (US) consist of portraying himself as a tough and proud (although secretly scared and tearful) contender facing a harsh and pitiless Other (in some ways, he reproduces this at the first encounter with the therapist). The defensive functions aim at maintaining this conservative adjustment. Introjection and projection maintain the perception of a tough, much admired Self confronted with a cold and ruthless Other, quick to make a mockery of him if given the slightest chance. Retroflexion does not allow others to perceive Brian's need for help and comfort. The deflection of any sign of warmth or compassion from others helps maintain these perceptions and then confirms that others are insensitive and indifferent. His stance does not allow for warm relationships with the outside world (except for a few close ones) and confirms his outlook on the external world as illustrated in the Personality functions below.

The Personality function

This is the last element of the structural analysis, referring to the way the individual sees himself and perceives others in his life. It consists of a Matrix of Field Representation (MFR) which is readily accessible to the Self, and draws a map of the elements of the Field. It contains residues of past contact cycles contaminated by various representations of oneself and the Other. Brian's Matrix of Field Representation MFR appears in the table below:

Table 1. Matrix of Field Representation (MFR).

	Organism-Self	Organism-Other
Positive	I am resourceful.	My life partner is a good person.
	I am a good guy.	My parents are good people.
	I am hard working.	You are a good therapist.
	I have a lot of charm.	My brother is smart and hard-working.
	I know how to talk to People.	My son is a good boy.
	I have been bad, but I redeemed myself.	
	I am strong, I am a fighter.	
	I am a good looking man.	
	I am special.	
	I do special things (Harley, plumber).	
	I am a good son.	
	I am a good husband.	

(*Continued*)

Table 1. (*Continued*).

Negative	When a boy, I was a wimp like my mother.	My brother lacks social skills.
	I am only the shadow of the man I was since my accident.	My life partner does not know how to manage her business well.
	I am pitiful.	My son is not as clever as I am.
	I am finished.	My employees are all treacherous.
		People try to take me in (SAAQ, medical experts).

This configuration maintains a self-image of grandeur along with a very disparaging self-image since the accident. Significant Others, even if perceived positively, are generally not on a par with Brian in terms of ability. Others who are not closely related are out to do him wrong one way or another.

Unfolding of the therapeutic process

The structural analysis drew a psychodynamic portrait of Brian based on the content of the therapeutic sessions. At first Brian was unable to show his softer self. He presented himself to me as someone strong and enviable (rich family, Harley). He had expressed his despair through his initial telephone call, but was unable to reproduce it on a face-to-face basis. He retroflected his pain and tears. Clearly, over the years, he had presented himself to the world as self-sufficient and grandiose. Brian bragged repeatedly that it was a good thing that none of his siblings had gone through the same ordeal as he had because according to him, they would not have survived it. He was the strong one. He also projected his mistrust of others on to the SAAQ employees and professionals. They were out to get him. In fact, I immediately felt that I risked being swindled myself. This initial counter-transference effect, which did not completely subside, reflects Brian's narcissistic personality with its paranoid undertones.

Although acting strong, Brian was at a loose end with himself and entertained suicidal thoughts. I did not have access to his vulnerable side. He therefore reproduced, in therapy, his familiar style in which toughness and hypervigilance push aside his feelings of vulnerability and sadness. Brian fully introjected my acknowledgement of his inner strength and stamina. He deflected my initial suggestion that he could participate in a support group. He slowly showed his vulnerable side to me much later in the therapeutic process. We had to develop a climate of trust and mutual respect before Brian could open himself to me in this fashion. I had to be trustworthy and meet his standards.

This wariness is a manifestation of US developed during Brian's childhood. It still permeates his coping style when confronted with a major stressful life event. The Ego functions make him project ill-intent on to others, deflect expressions of compassion towards himself, and retroflect his own vulnerability. This process maintains an MFR which confirms the existence of a harsh outside world and the importance of acting strong even if feeling incomplete inside. These defences are used to maintain a conservative adaptation and maintain his outlook on life (MFR) intact. He presents a strong self capable of surviving any adversity, constantly protecting himself against deficient or dangerous others.

These coping patterns were developed in the fourth Experiential Field which pertains to the client's past. We are confronted with an IM formed by a contact dilemma (need to be tough, to be valued while, at the same time, feeling incomplete) when he was a little boy and which repeats itself over the years. The adaptive functions of the Self, developed at the time, helped Brian through his childhood, allowing him to survive in an environment where emotions were downgraded and apparent toughness overvalued. But these same adaptive functions locked him into a rigid behaviour pattern: he lives in a prison of suspicion and cold personal interactions with people in general (except for familiar non-threatening close friends or family members).

Therapeutic alliance: sessions one to three

Brian presents the traumatic events he has gone through in the last few years. He now realises that he will not be able to cope with daily hardship on his own. He is in a deep depression related to his substantial losses (looks, biker, worker etc.). Somehow he will have to change his inner dynamic and outlook on the world to get on with his life. In other words, he must engage in a creative rather than conservative adaptation. He agrees to leave his gun (used for hunting purposes) in his brother's care until he feels better. He fears losing financial support from the SAAQ. His dream is to become somebody rich and important, and he still hopes to achieve this goal one day. He openly talks about his rowdy youth but insists these are bygone days. Brian expresses his love and attachment towards his life companion and their little boy, as well as for his parents. His feelings are less positive with regard to his siblings. He lights up when describing his "now defunct" Harley-Davidson. Brian felt proud riding the bike with his friends. He further states that with his leather coat and good looks, "people looked at me when I entered a bar!" His first words when recovering from amnesia were to enquire about the Harley. He hopes to ride a bike again someday. In expressing these ideas, Brian constantly observes the effect his statements seem to have on the therapist.

At the onset of therapy, Brian had already moved on from his youthful acting-out. Although becoming a responsible husband, father, and worker, he has nonetheless maintained his narcissistic stance in life. Owning a Harley-Davidson and being a businessman made him feel important. The mourning process following the accident was complicated because it attacked the very elements which maintained a positive image of the Self. Brian had to ask for psychological help (initially he felt that he had enough stamina to manage on his own). Nonetheless, he approaches the therapist in his typical narcissistic style and attempts to impress her. He reproduces his usual manner of making contact with outsiders, that is, projecting a strong, magnificent self (Harley, influential and rich family, plumbing and business skills). He verifies the impact he has on the therapist. He does not readily show his vulnerable, sensitive self. His way of entering therapy reproduces the contact dilemma, that is, it is both indispensable and intolerable to be seen as a strong person who keeps a stiff upper lip in front of adversity but who is not in contact with his pain and whose tears are kept in check. He somehow tries to hold on to his old self-image, but falls into despair because of the reality he confronts. He then denigrates his maimed Self which he perceives as valueless.

Inner despair: sessions four to nine

In the following sessions, Brian goes deeper into the losses incurred following the accident. He deplores tiring easily in social gatherings. Noise disturbs him. He finds it difficult to engage in physical activities with his boy. He would like to wake up and be like before, comparing his experience to exchanging a brand new car for a jalopy. He is angry. He would like to beat up the "lousy" drivers he encounters on the road. He idealises his life before the accident "when he was always happy!" He fears he will never be happy again. He is anxious and gets tired easily at family reunions. He regrets dearly not being able to go hunting with his pals because of his hearing difficulties (unable to determine where a given noise comes from) and obvious mobility limitations. He tries to do manual work in his shed as before but lacks the necessary concentration and hurts himself with an electric saw. His family start to worry. He still feels suicidal (in the sense that he does not care if he lives or dies) but has no specific plans in that respect. He confirms that his guns are out of reach. He is impatient and wonders when the therapy "will help him feel good about himself again." He rejects the possibility of going to a support group. He feels sorry for himself and valueless. He is of no use to society anymore and feels like a social outcast.

In this early stage of therapy, Brian has not integrated his losses. He holds on to the past with a very split perspective. He idealises the past and denigrates himself violently. Rather than giving up his grandiose Self, he chooses to be nothing. He is a cripple, useless to society. The narcissistic Self is deeply affected and split. It is all or nothing. He is still unable to contact the intolerable side of the dilemma, that is, allowing himself to expose his vulnerable self.

Rage and paranoia—old demons are revisited: sessions ten to eleven

Brian gets angry and paranoid. He reproaches his common-law wife, Sheila, for having poor business skills and spending too much money on the business she runs. He fears she'll go bankrupt. He wants to become a rich man no matter what. He emphasises that he himself comes from a rich family. His father drives big cars, owns a small plane, and is a well-respected businessman in his community. He wonders if eventually his son would like to ride a Harley like he did. He fumes against the SAAQ because of the overly slow settlement process, and plans to complain to his local deputy. He wants to get his money and get rich. He gets impatient with therapy because it takes too much time and he has not reached happiness yet.

Brian reproduces his usual angry and impulsive acting-out style. The settlement and the therapy take too long. His wife and son become narcissistic extensions of himself. The anger and impulsiveness also permit him to avoid contact with inner suffering, as he has done all his life, show the extent of his losses, and reawaken old demons of constant appreciation and depreciation of himself in relation to others. No matter what, he aims at reaching the social position he has always aspired to have one day.

Facing the underlying suffering and reorganization of the self: sessions twelve to twenty-three

A shift in perspective is occurring slowly for Brian. He slowly realises that he is using Sheila to reach his goal of "striking it rich." He also slowly recognises the ephemeral quality of happiness derived from the impulsive acquisition of material goods. Nonetheless, he hopes to get rich through financial investments (with money from the SAAQ) and be an important man no matter what. He rambles on about being rich session after session, and worries about his financial investments. Although he still idealises his life before the accident, he realises that it had its ups and downs. Family members verify that he was not always happy. He wants to ride his bike again one day. Then on his own volition he decides to go back to the accident site. There are still marks of the impact on the pavement. It makes him break down and cry. At the following session, he brings pictures of his bike after the accident. He shares his pain with the therapist and starts to really show his tender side. He now feels more at ease doing this. This is all new to him: he does not have to act strong to be accepted and respected. In contacting his vulnerable side, he compares himself to a bulldozer without the tracks. The therapist is touched and expresses her empathic feelings. She also takes care to value her client's stamina throughout his ordeal. In return, Brian realizes that he had greatly invested in his bike and that it was a way to attract people's attention. He now has to rebuild his life differently.

While still reproducing narcissistic tendencies (being rich and important) Brian's Self is not as split as before. He enters the acknowledgement phase of the therapy through the hermeneutic dialogue, recognising that material goods are not a direct route to happiness: his wife and son cannot be manipulated to make him feel good about himself. Life prior to the accident was not always idyllic. The return to the scene of the accident was a turning point. Brian breaks down and contacts his vulnerability, allowing himself to share his pain with me rather than deal with it on his own as he had always done in the past. Being vulnerable does not sever the therapeutic tie between us, as it did with his distant father. Being seen in his vulnerability and being received by the Other (the therapist), rather than rejected, is a reparation of the initial Unfinished Situation. Our interaction has changed. Brian has mellowed: he is more open and in touch with his feelings. He introjects the empathic feelings of the therapist, and, as a result, I feel a closeness between us that was inexistent before.

Rediscovery of simple pleasures and ongoing reorganisation of the self: sessions twenty-four to twenty-five

During the summer Brian goes on a boat trip with his wife, her sister, and brother in law. He drinks a little. He has fun. He enjoys little moments of happiness like being with friends or family members, especially his young son. He even wonders if he could seduce a woman again, although he would not commit adultery and "would stop at the bedroom door." He fears that others consider him to be a pitiful sight: "That's the way I would have considered someone like me before I had the accident." He shows me his stump; he might have to be operated on again because of feelings of discomfort with the prosthesis. He gets less angry and realises little by little that he will have to integrate his losses to be happy again. His definition of happiness is shifting. He becomes more realistic about it.

Brian battles with issues of self-esteem. Could the new me be attractive sexually? He now goes a step further and dares exposing his wounded physical self to the therapist. He becomes conscious that in spite of his loss, he can still enjoy moments of happiness. He redefines what happiness means.

Financial settlement with the SAAQ and reactivation of the Contact Dilemma: sessions twenty-six to thirty-nine

Brian spends the next ten months undergoing numerous medical evaluations (neuropsychological, psychiatric, orthopaedic) required by the SAAQ before reaching a decision. These interviews prompt him to question himself: is he still capable of some kind of work? If so, for how long? What kind of work? Brian has mixed feelings. He is terrified to be told that he can work and terrified also to be told that he cannot. He struggles with feelings of not being able to resume some kind of activity anymore and what it means, for his self-image, to be officially branded as a cripple. He also expresses fear of getting a raw deal with the SAAQ but is determined to fight for his fair share. He consults a lawyer. His temper flares up again. He is enraged because one of the experts estimates that he may possibly work a fourteen-hour week. This means that Brian would lose his disability pension: "I felt like jumping over his desk to beat-him up!" He blasts the SAAQ case-worker. He describes himself as unhappy: "I feel sorry for myself, it is just too bad what happened to me!" He does not cry anymore: "If I cry it means that I have something to cry about!" Although Brian does not ask directly for support he mentions that it does him good "to ventilate". I attempt to regulate his affect, to get him to take things in stride. When the financial settlement arrives, Brian instantly calms down.

Stressful circumstances trigger a regression: he returns to the reproduction of patterns of uncontrolled anger, paranoia, and self-doubt. Acting "tough", he chokes back his vulnerable, scared Self. We suspect a re-enactment of the original dead-end: confronted with the father's stern outlook on life (only hard work and seriousness are valued) and not allowing oneself to express one's sensitive side, while crying inside like the tearful, depressive mother who does not see her little boy through her tears. A similar scenario appears in the current interaction between Brian and the SAAQ expert. It is intolerable to be seen as unable to go to work, but at the same time one feels unable to do so and cries inside.

Anticlimax after the settlement: sessions forty to forty-six

Shortly after the settlement, deep feelings of emptiness emerge and suicidal ideation reappears. Brian suddenly decides to stop his antidepressant medication "cold turkey" but then, at the therapist's insistence, agrees to resume taking it and consult with his doctor. He seems at a loss as to what to do next. He wants to invest his financial compensation wisely rather than spend it foolishly, as he did previously (he bought a second boat and a new car). Pondering now if having a bigger boat could ever bring lasting happiness, he comes to grips with the concept of inner happiness, as an alternative to short-term consumer satisfaction.

At this stage, the intensity of stress eases off. Brian reproduces some acting-out patterns (medication) but rather rapidly resumes his inner journey of Self healing. He has changed. He contemplates a form of happiness without numerous material goods. He wants to invest wisely. He contacts his feelings of solitude.

A major turning point in the journey with a sudden repairing event: sessions forty-seven to fifty-two

A very meaningful and striking event changes the course of the therapy drastically. Brian attempts to bring home a friend's Harley. He is really proud to be able to ride it in town in spite of his handicap but also feels fearful on the highway, and fully realises, finally, that his biking days are over. He still likes riding but does not feel diminished because he cannot do it anymore. After that, his mood improves steadily. He subsequently takes up golf in spite of his handicap. He is proud of his score. He feels that people admire him for what he has achieved. He wins a golf trip with his son to Florida. He eases up on his ruminations about moneymaking, making plans for the future such as marrying his life partner Sheila—"it would make her happy"—without worrying that she might be out to get his money. He wants to travel, do volunteer work, invest wisely. He feels that he is still young, with hope for the future. At the termination of therapy, Brian embraces me rather ceremoniously. He states that he will never forget me: "You have saved my life!" He is very proud to have gone through two years of therapy and has no regrets.

The biking episode seems to have been a major repairing event in Brian's therapeutic journey of reconstruction of the Self. It allowed him to turn the page on his biking days. He was able to allow his vulnerable Self to appear without forfeiting the strong Self developed over the years and much needed in the present circumstances. It brought closure to the mourning process. It allowed him to move on with his life. He still needs to be admired (playing golf or riding a Harley in spite of his handicap) but is now able to feel good about himself in spite of his physical handicap.

Conclusion

This therapy was principally aimed at resolving a complex mourning process. The first goal was to reduce the symptoms described by the DSM and PDM analytic grids. We made sure he would not engage in impulsive acting out that would endanger his life. We attempted to make him aware of his contact-regulation modalities and his paranoid projections concerning others (especially outsiders) in the MFR. We achieved a reconfiguration of his perspective on others and himself. He is now able to show his vulnerable Self more readily. Rather than identifying with emerging paranoid elements Brian is better able to be more attuned to the Field. He is less quick to act out and is generally more benevolent towards himself and others. He is able to value himself again in spite of his new physical challenge and life-long status as a disabled person. He is now able to find alternative responses to potentially humiliating situation, for example, playing golf with an adapted club, engaging in volunteer work with accident victims.

The therapy allowed a reorganisation of the self. Brian was able to integrate (unify) the split parts of the self, that is, the sensitive, vulnerable side with the strong, powerful other side of the self. Naturally, we could have pursued the transformation further with Brian, working through the IMs that emerge in the Id, and helping the client re-metabolise them. This was beyond the goal of the therapy. We concentrated instead on a reconfiguration of the MFR and re-education of the Ego to help Brian get on with his life. At the end, he felt satisfied that he had reached his goal of "feeling better about myself". In retrospect we feel that it was a good point in time to terminate the therapy, considering the intense suffering he had endured since his accident. Brian is reconstructing his self differently. He is reorganizing his lifestyle, making plans for the future. On the other hand, the termination could be seen as premature and a defensive manoeuvre on Brian's part. The therapy stops at a period of his life where he is "seen" and much admired by his friends and acquaintances (playing golf in spite of his handicap, providing emotional support to others in similar situations).

On a reflexive level, several authors could be cited, such as: Kohut's (1977) treatment of narcissistic disorders, that is, self-object and mirroring or subsequent idealisation transfer; Klein's (1946) passage from the paranoid-schizoid to the depressive position, that is, the earlier phase, governed by a split-self, is succeeded by the capacity to perceive the other as good and bad simultaneously, and brings a corresponding integration of the self; Freud's (1917) concept of mourning in which the self can be restored as compared to melancholia with a self beyond repair; Schore's (2003) view on the regulation of the self, that is, the client's hyperactivation of anger and impulsive emotional outbursts de-escalates eventually.

On an affective level, the empathic and therapeutic use of the countertransference allowed us to further grasp Brian's intrapsychic dynamic. Our projective identification with his feisty and imperious style motivated us to help him overcome his difficulties no matter what. At the same time, our perception of a potential manipulativeness in Brian could have made us overly careful. This latter aspect did not last very long and therefore did not interfere in the overall therapeutic exchange. Finally, the combination of the reflexive and affective levels allowed us to modulate our interactions with Brian throughout all three phases (reproduction, acknowledgment and reparation) of the therapeutic process.

Notes

1. Guilhème Pérodeau, Ph.D. is a full professor of psychology at the university of Quebec in Outaouais, in Quebec (Canada). She was trained as an ORGT clinician at the CIG. She would like to thank Line Girard, M.Ps, Nadine Delbeke, M.Psy., and Kieron O'Connor, Ph.D., for their most insightful and incisive clinical comments on this case-study presentation.
2. American Psychiatric Association (1994, 2000). *Diagnostic and Statistical Manual of Mental Disorders (DSM-IV-TR)*, Fourth Edition. Washington DC: American Psychiatric Association.
3. PDM Task Force (2006). *Psychodynamic Diagnostic Manual*. Silver Spring, MD: Alliance of Psychoanalytic Organizations.

CHAPTER THIRTEEN

Jade

A case study presented by Dorothy Scicluna[1]

Jade came to psychotherapy unaware of her non-embodied self. Throughout her journey she retrieved most aspects of herself, became aware of her views of Self and Others, and has figured out that she deserves to be happy.

Anamnesis

Jade calls for an appointment. She says that she was referred by an ex-client of mine. This is October 2008. I see her in private practice. She comes for her first session and she reminds me of a diligent school girl. Dark curly brown hair pulled back in a pony tail, no trace of makeup, rosy freckled cheeks, fair skin, small features, and dark blue eyes. She wears dark clothes. She will keep regular Friday appointments. She is a teacher in a secondary school reputed to be a difficult school. She says she has no trouble controlling the students.

The first session will feel like a warm session and that will be the last of its kind before a long time. At the time of writing this part of the report it is August 2009 and some warm sessions have reoccurred. I must admit, holding Jade during her therapeutic journey was a struggle.

Jade says that she opted for therapy because she was experiencing a sense of 'dizziness' and 'fear of people'. She needs to tell me what recently happened to her and her husband. At the word 'husband' I feel I need to verify her age. To me she kept appearing like a diligent first year university student. She had a way of coming to the session holding a file and she often utilised the words "learn", referring to parts of our session. Jade needs to justify the reason for which she is teaching at a secondary school. She explains to me how she gave up her post at junior college in order to give it to a dear colleague of hers who is also a teacher and who at that time was experiencing some family difficulties. It is important to note that in Malta teaching posts at the junior college are rare. Womanhood seemed totally missing.

She tells me that two weeks prior to this session she was strolling along a local promenade with her husband and another couple when a gang of young boys unexpectedly attack her friends' husband and beat him up. Her husband tries to help his friend and fortunately, unlike the other guy, is not injured. They are all taken to hospital to be treated for shock since these are not episodes that generally happen in Malta; rather, they are quite unheard of. In fact, word of this episode had spread around.

During our first and second sessions I felt that her current anxiety was plausible. I imagined she was momentarily reacting to the shock. She recounted the episode in great detail and was barely referring to her presenting symptom, the anxiety. I remember telling myself, "She must be a very sensitive person."

Eventually I asked her to speak to me about her dizziness and cloudy head and how and when she would experience such symptoms. She insisted on giving me detail and all I could see was barren space; a cold, barren space. I could not grasp a single emotion. I often let images guide me, so at this stage I decided to stay with this image of "the cold room". She describes herself as a pillar of strength and seemed annoyed at the uncontrollable feeling of anxiety.

The other image was that of the diligent, obedient school girl who needed to succeed in therapy just like she succeeded at school. In summary, our initial sessions consisted of detailed episodes of the attack and minor references to the anxiety. At my end, I felt like I was hearing her but not feeling her. She seemed to reside inside a vacuum. Eventually

Jade will decide to describe her anxious symptoms in great detail. Here I figured out that her symptoms, mainly physical, were typical of the anxious person: dizziness, cloudy head, shortness of breath, and apprehension. I usually explain to overwhelmed clients how catastrophic thinking can provoke anxious feelings. Generally I notice that clients are relieved to understand that what they feel is normal and that they are not physically unwell. Instead, Jade asked me not to give her any physical detail otherwise she would feel those same symptoms over her body.

This is how our first session ended. I remember being overwhelmed by a sense of needing to be exact and precise around this person and a sense of having to get it right. Why did it feel like being at school? I remember that it seemed like she had instilled the sense of seriousness in me. It felt like she had handed over to me some huge assignment to complete. I decided to wait until the following sessions. I also remember thinking how well she covered her anxiety.

I immediately felt this was going to be challenging work.

Jade books regular weekly appointments. There were times when she even asked for two sessions a week because she felt her pain was unbearable. Yet I could not see any trace of this pain. I could not feel it anywhere. Our sessions carried on being scholarly-like and I never seemed to manage to move the session towards emotions. She would redirect it towards cognitions. She had not as yet figured out the client role; she needed to be in control. Jade came to lessons, not to psychotherapy sessions. Trust, this is what I needed to work on. "I wonder what makes it so difficult for you to trust me" were the words that reverberated in my head.

From this session onwards she will look at me with very piercing eyes as if she wants to see through me. At times this created discomfort in me; however, I took this to be one of her ways of contacting the world. She needs to see through before she treads into a new place. Where is all this diffidence stemming from? At times she attempted to revert roles. She would use phrases like "I can see your pain" and "I can see the pain when I look beyond and see through your eyes." I admit that at these times I felt scared and I started to doubt my initial diagnosis. She had once added, "Who takes care of you?" and "You are in here all alone." The time she said these words I was in fact going through a rough time and I thought that she could maybe be seeing that, but rarely do clients point it out or worry about me. For instance, I remember once seeing my supervisor looking shattered but I opted not to comment about. Instead Jade did.

It felt like she needed to know me, win me, and befriend me. Control me? At this stage I reassured her that I had support and that I enjoyed the quiet afternoons at the clinic. I often wondered what psychotherapy meant to her. Gradually these comments stopped and I noticed that she was learning to trust me and the therapy sessions.

Up until now I had still been battling with a diagnosis. Many ideas were going through my head but none of them fitted the picture clearly. I was only sure of her precise nature, her fear of physical symptoms, and her ability to totally dissociate from her emotions. Moreover, she also recounted that some months prior to our initial sessions she had been experiencing signs of a high body temperature, that is, unexplained bouts of fever, and, despite several tests, no doctor had managed to understand from where this could be stemming. She also explained that she hated clinics and feared hospitals and every time she needed to visit one her heart would race abnormally. Could the high body temperature be related to anxiety and high blood pressure? Later on I would discover that her father and sister faint at the idea of sickness and doctors, and that her mother seemed to suffer from fear of contamination. She laughs at how her father is obsessed with scientific matters, and at how he fears the common flu, and at how he needs to park precisely within the lines. Her sister is defined as a genius and her mother presents with hugely strict moral values. This is the world Jade knows.

She is the daughter of a teacher and is a teacher herself. For this reason she needed to make sure to never stepped out of line, and this she had done since she had been a very little girl.

During our second session she told me that, while relating a childhood episode to some friends, she had suddenly remembered that as a child, as a five year old, she had been abused by a man while hospitalised. This man and Jade were both hospitalised at what is today a skin cancer and convalescence hospital. Jade was quarantined because the doctors feared that she was suffering from scarlet fever. She says that it all started when she innocently told her friend, "This man used to hold me on his lap." Apparently this is when she remembered what this man used to do to her while nobody was around. She said the nurses were not too happy handling her so she spent quite some time alone in her room.

At this stage I am truly puzzled. I have heard other recounts of abuse and when they were ugly the client found it hard to give details. They would generally cry. Instead Jade was clinical. She would tell me: "I remembered something else", and she would look as if she was in a trance, giving me very precise details of what her abuser used to do to her. The descriptions she gave were atrocious. This man tied her to the bed, inserted crumpled paper and rosary beads up her vagina, forced fellatio, pushed her to rock against the corner of a chair, and other similar episodes. I started to wonder if these were false memories. Could her parents, being so overprotective, not realise that their child was bruised? Could not the nurses notice any of these signs? She described that, as an adult, she often felt the presence of someone cruel, a pair of harsh eyes following her especially when she tried being intimate with her husband.

This spectre became the abuser to Jade. She resolved the puzzle. I kept in mind that this girl spent considerable time alone and had no life really. She had few friends, who she rarely met socially. Her husband was described as not affective and unloving. Her only way of going out was to visit her parents. She also found refuge in binge eating.

It is now January 2009 and in Malta there is the trial of a murderer going on. This man had stabbed his partner to death and there was enough proof to show that he had done this cold-bloodedly. It so happened that Jade's husband and this man had the same surname. Apparently Jade's husband often tried to play "macho" at home and he referred to this coincidence of the surname as some sign of physical prowess.

At this stage Jade abandoned the abuser story and became absorbed with the victim of this tragic episode. She needed to tell me how she identified with the victim, how she feared the same would happen to her, and how she felt the presence of this woman at times. During the session she would concentrate hard and follow imagery in her head; as if she was watching an internal movie; as if she was on stage. She had nice messages from this lady. At this stage, after consulting with my supervisor, I decided to stop trying to verify whether these episodes were true or not. It was suggested I wait a little bit longer to see if she reverted back to the abuse fantasies. These memories did not seem to be impairing her daily functioning, except for the staring eyes, and she was in complete touch with reality.

Jade needed to be listened to. I listened to her. However, I also figured out that this woman needed to be more in the world. Only the outside world could save her.

It was a time when I was about to start holding a long-term group psychotherapy programme for binge eating disorder and I asked her if she would be interested in joining. Luckily she accepted. Group therapy consisted of experiential therapy and it involved different professionals, including a dancer and a chef. Apart from psychotherapy, it included discovering nice walks around Malta while discovering Maltese history, dancing, painting, slow cooking, and more. This group would take her out to the world. It did.

The bingeing stopped immediately prior to group therapy. It stopped because she promised me she would not do it. Diligence is once again at play. Also around the beginning of our therapeutic journey Jade gave me a gift. It was a concave glass frame with silver left and right edges, and inside was the picture of a little child sleeping with an angel guarding over him. Jade said I was like that angel. This is when I felt trust had started to grow.

She was taking antidepressants and anxiolytics prescribed by her family doctor. This somehow reassured me, in the sense that I didn't feel I was handling this case on my own.

At this stage she stopped mentioning her anxiety. The episodes relating to the abuse and to the victim of the atrocious crime stopped. She would mention anxiety sometimes when the dizziness occurred at school. The sessions prior to this moment felt very much like a tidal wave that needed to sweep several issues away; the aftermath was a lonely, quiet, and somehow serene place; a little bit like a barren beach after the storm, where I felt allowed to explore.

The barren beach became a creative void; from this place I was allowed to explore and every so often she would come and help me explore. I would upturn shells, listen to the waves, follow footsteps on the sand; one day Jade joined me and became curious about this game. She was mesmerised by the beauty of the world and would, on her own, go and explore different places and look and find meaning in leaves, bastions, cemeteries, and the sea. This adventure she called Life.

This was also the time she felt more comfortable mentioning her husband and his attitude towards her. She described him as easy to anger and having a world of his own. She always made sure not to contradict him. This is how she survived living around him, she explained. Where did she learn to endure in silence?

I asked whether I could meet her husband when she started revealing more information about her marital life. (Jade's husband will be referred to as M. in the following report.) M. accepted the invitation and came for a session along with Jade. He seemed dejected and oozed a sense of helplessness; a rather tall guy who appeared sad. He recounted that some time prior to this appointment, possibly some weeks before, Jade had asked him to accompany her to the gynaecologist due to a recurrent pain in her groin. When the visit was over the gynaecologist called M. and she told him that there was nothing physically wrong with his wife. The pain was all psychological and she gave him three possible hypotheses. Jade could have been physically abused, traumatised in some way, or else had had a very rigid upbringing.

M. revealed this information to his wife for the first time during our session together. During the session he repeated himself as though he needed me to empathise with him and also confirm that he was right, that is, he wanted me to agree that not being intimate with his partner for a whole ten years could lead to the depression. M. followed up with individual sessions with me and during every session he needed to repeat his story from the very beginning. He attended ten sessions and during the final ones he admitted he no longer felt attracted to his wife and that he was off women completely. I had also referred him to a psychiatrist, since his depressive symptoms seemed to be increasing and he would not engage in therapy. He was becoming increasingly impulsive and, for instance, crashed twice over four weeks. The psychiatrist felt the way I did. He was waiting for us to confirm that he could go on with filing for an annulment and that he was not to blame.

M. blamed Jade's lack of interest in sex on her upbringing, which he defines as uptight, very strict, and highly intellectual. He discounted the abuse episode and refused to admit that he was aggressive in any way. During the session he explained that Jade never showed any interest in sex. She used to appear scared and often pushed him away when he tried to approach her physically. She used to tell him that they would be intimate after marriage. She even refused kissing. Their courtship lasted for six years. He says that she found kissing disgusting.

During one of our individual sessions I enquired of Jade with regard to her libido. Did she remember any teenage crushes? Did she ever feel physical attraction during the time she was still dating her husband?

Her answers were in the negative. She explained that she could not afford to get pregnant because she was a teacher (and the daughter of a teacher). In Malta, despite the fact that several pregnancies happen out of wedlock, it is shameful to be a teacher and be pregnant. Students usually pick on those teachers, especially in secondary schools, since this goes against the school's teaching.

My suspicion, and that of the psychiatrist, was that, apart from the rigid upbringing which was conducive of this behaviour, there was also a fear of contamination which manifested itself in several of her behaviours. As I shall further explain, Jade challenged all these fears and acknowledged they were learnt behaviours.

M. described Jade as extremely precise, like both her parents and her sister. The latter seem to be very rigid people who value strict rules over spontaneity, whereas M. was the total opposite. He had endured this behaviour because Jade had promised that everything would be different after marriage. There are still some couples in Malta who refrain from complete sex in the name of religion. However, he explained that she never allowed him to touch her. She even refused to kiss him. According to him, Jade seemed totally devoted to her parents. She enjoyed being a good girl, who functioned according to their rules.

Further investigation revealed that Jade's father presents with severe health anxiety, to the extent of fainting at the mention of illness, and that her mother suffers from fear of contamination. Her older sister seems to have followed suit. For instance, Jade laughed at how they go to restaurants and spray disinfectant over the cutlery or drinking glasses especially around the time of the N1H1 virus outbreak. The sister seems to show some traits of Asperger syndrome, though this could not, of course, be verified.

Whilst acknowledging her fears, Jade blamed her husband for the lack of intimacy. She states that he stormed out of the room on the first night of their honeymoon. She had never experienced sexual desire, or so she says. However, she recalls that as a child, after the said abuse, she used to engage in masturbation and her mother used to scold her. This could also be one of the reasons behind her refusal to engage in or initiate sexual behaviour. M. explained that she was so meticulous during their intimacy that he used to feel frustrated. For instance, she fussed over the proper use of condoms and the washing of her partner's hands. Having said all this, I believe that M. was a little bit too hasty—he had only one previous experience with a non-Maltese girl at the age of eighteen. He described her as easy and he possibly imagined that Jade would behave in a similar fashion. Instead, only gentle touch and enormous patience would have helped Jade out of her fear. This was the work of psychotherapy.

This is where our therapeutic journey started off from.

Multiaxial Diagnosis

Axis I—Clinical Disorders, most V-Codes, and conditions that need clinical attention

- Anxiety Disorder:

    a. Specific Phobia—Health anxiety and fear of contamination and, to a certain extent, social phobia (300.29)
    b. Generalized Anxiety Disorder (300.02)

- Eating Disorder—Eating Disorder Not Otherwise Specified (307.5)

    a. Binge Eating Disorder

- Sexual Dysfunction:

    a. Hypoactive Sexual Desire Disorder (302.71)

Axis II—Personality Disorders and Mental Retardation

- Obsessive Compulsive Personality Disorder (301.4)

I would think that Jade presents with a mild degree of this personality pattern. She is known for her sense of perfectionism in several areas of her life and for her ability to be highly organised. She is excessively devoted to work and has only recently challenged some of her deeply ingrained moral values. She can be stubborn when corrected or contradicted. These traits have softened during the course of therapy.

Definition as per DSM-IV-TR criteria:

> Obsessive-Compulsive Personality Disorder is characterized by perfectionism and inflexibility. A person with an Obsessive-Compulsive Personality becomes preoccupied with uncontrollable patterns of thought and action. Symptoms may cause extreme distress and interfere with a person's occupational and social functioning.

Diagnostic Criteria (DSM-IV™) made easy

(From http://psyweb.com/Mdisord/DSM_IV/jsp/dsm_iv.jsp)

Marked inflexibility and preoccupation with orderliness, perfectionism, and mental/interpersonal control, as indicated by at least four of the following:

1. Marked preoccupation with details, lists, order, organisation, rules, or schedules.
2. Marked perfectionism that interferes with the completion of the task.
3. Excessive devotion to work.
4. Excessive devotion, and inflexible when it comes to ethics, morals, or values.
5. Cannot throw out worn-out, useless, or worthless objects, with no sentimental value.
6. Insist others work or do task exactly as they would.
7. View money as something to be hoarded.
8. Stubborn and rigid.

I have also referred to the description given by Frances et al. (1995, p. 378) who describe individuals with OCPD as follows:

- perfectionist, constricted, and excessively disciplined
- behaviourally rigid, formal, cool, distant, intellectualized, and detailed
- aggressive, competitive, and impatient
- driven with a chronic sense of time pressure and an inability to relax
- controlling of themselves, others, and situations
- indirect in their expression of anger although an apparent undercurrent of hostility is often present
- often inclined to hoard money and other possessions
- preoccupied with orderliness, neatness, and cleanliness
- inflexible and stubborn in relationships.

Axis III

None

Axis IV—Psychosocial or environmental problems

a. Other psychosocial or environmental problems. Jade comes from a highly rigid family background which continuously stunts her emotional growth and punishes her for marrying the man she did. On the other hand her husband does not relate to her, does not show signs of affection, shows signs of depression, and is rarely at home. Jade spends most of her time alone which further reinforces her need to focus on work.

Axis V—Global Assessment of Functioning Scale

GAF—71-80

V Codes

V62.81

Structural classification: Structural analysis of the Self

Structure of the Self

What Jade's contact functions reveal about the Introjected Microfields, or rather, about the presenting contact dilemmas.

"Personality Disorders may be defined as a constellation of conservative behaviours and attitudes whose function is to preserve the Introjected Field (IF) by seeking out and generating in various experiential fields, contact and relational configurations capable of maintaining dynamic links with Unfinished Situations (USs)" (Delisle, 1998, p. 275).

Jade's contact functions reveal this kind of conservative adjustment.

Jade's eye contact is usually focused, piercing, and rather continuous, as if she is scanning information. As a matter of fact she will later on say: "I capture what is going on in the environment. I don't miss anything." It creates, at times, a sense of uneasiness; it is not warm and it is void of contact. It is inquisitive. Her speech often takes an informative tone and makes sure she does not leave out any detail when relating an episode. She often rejects what is proposed to her in terms of empathy by using phrases such as, "No, it is not quite that." The initial sessions were void of feeling. She was unable to convey emotions; she was unaware of feelings occurring in her body. She could not embody her body.

After joining group therapy Jade altered the way she contacted the world. She became softer. For instance, nowadays she often carries a smile; she can convey a sense of glee and is ready to speak her emotions. She plays the battle of the most intelligent much less. Her eye contact has normalised and I rarely feel her scanning me except for when she tries to figure out which therapeutic technique I am using. Jade is highly interested in psychotherapy and I feel she might soon join some course. She still behaves very much like a student during group therapy and has the ability to write down everything I say. She shifts to client role when necessary.

The Id

What emerges most easily at first glance

What emerges most easily is a contained self, a composed self. A person who behaves according to what is right but who is incapable of spontaneity. A non-embodied body. She is someone with very little life experience and who is unaware of life's nuances. Jade is a correct, honest, and diligent individual who strives for perfection. She needs to portray a strong front and she comes across as someone who needs to stress that she is always the best.

I see lack of femininity. There seems to be a lack of experienced womanliness. I see a diligent student who believes life is about getting it right. The monotone dialogues are also rather apparent, especially in the way they lack tone or lustre.

What emerges least easily

At a deeper glance I notice the splitting characteristic of the loss of unity of the Self present in most personality disorders. I notice the strong IMs lurking in the background and how these often contaminated Jade's perceptual processes. I often became someone she needed to harm; someone she was angry at; someone who, for a very long time, corrected her behaviour. Jade had to shelf her "lifefulness" in order to maintain peace at home. Playing up and playing Cowboys and Indians, a game she loved, was inappropriate. Jade gave up and followed on the sombre brick road laid out for her by her father. Her sister enjoyed this route and received all the applause. Jade ended up believing that her wishes were wrong and that she was therefore a bad little girl and, worse still, that the way to be in life was the way her father dictated and the way her sister behaved. She surrendered, and moulded herself into little Miss Perfect. She shelved her "lifefulness".

These IMs contaminated JADE's perceptual reality and she mistook them for her reality.

The Ego function

In the case of *pathology* the Ego Function seeks mainly to repeat the type of situation that led to the US and at times, but only incidentally, to change it.

> Thus the Ego Function *eliminates* opportunity for change in order to maintain the integrity of the IF and ensures that the elements of the field that might invalidate an IM stay in the background, while those liable to confirm it come into the foreground." (Delisle, 2009, in press)

Jade experienced a rigid upbringing whereby she needed to fight, struggle, and hope in order to obtain acknowledgement and emotional holding. As an adult she seeks and recreates the same scenarios. She is known for saving people from difficult situations. She relates that prior to the marriage people had pointed out that her husband was a difficult character. However she reasoned that she would not abandon him or give up on him like the rest of the world had done. She imagined that she could save him from his plight. Her husband is incapable of emotional holding; he is short-tempered and often bursts into rage.

Moreover her Id is contaminated by strict moral values through which she will function as an adult. She will swipe away her needs and put her emotions into the background, will detach from her body in order not to experience any needs and, thus, not to hurt. She will become the stoic person I met during our first therapy sessions. She is apt at dissociating from her body.

Jade becomes the injured narcissist made of marble, and only warm, gentle contact can soften the statuesque sense of self. This will require building trust and therefore learning intimacy which has been defined as "the process of making my inner world known and getting to know the inner world of the other" (Wheeler, 1998). This is inside knowing, which happens in a world which is intersubjective, which is to say, in a bonded relationship, "with another person, who presents as a self, who models, who exposes her/his own self-process in some way and who relates to us as a subjective being with an active self-process like his/her own" and "[o]nly to the extent that the relational field is a field of intimacy does a full experience of subjectivity arise" (ibid.).

Jade once told me:"I believe in myself; I don't have a low self-esteem like you imagine." She had to construct a huge, strong, sense of self; a self that would take care of the little injured Jade that existed within the statuesque sense of self; therefore she had to be strong and in control and defended.

Her home background reinforced "in-control" behaviour and she grew stronger in this way of being. The more precise she was, the more she was applauded. The harder she studied, the more satisfied her parents appeared. The more she behaved according to family morals, the better she became in their eyes and consequently in hers. Her choice of not engaging in any intimate behaviour with her husband was also partly a result of her strict moral values which said: "No sex before marriage". Besides, she had experienced sexual abuse which possibly made her shun physical contact. She knew a strict father and a male adult who had harmed her. As a child she remembers repeating the words, "You shall never harm me again." Eventually she will try to save people from their plights; she will not allow anyone to experience pain. She will also marry a man who appears unemotional.

Jade did not know the world of pleasure. For instance, at home they were not allowed sweets and they had to study throughout the whole summer, which in Malta is nearly three months long. They were not allowed to play outside with the neighbours. Growing up around strict moral values and very high standards made little Jade feel that her behaviour or her achievements were never good enough. Besides, through the abuse, she ended up believing that she was a bad person. Therefore she tried hard to achieve perfection. The harder she tried the more she was applauded but, yet again, at home she was never as good as her sister. This trying escalated into the perfectionist and OCPD traits observed today. I would say that presently, February 2010, the degree of her perfectionism (OCPD) has toned down greatly. Jade is today an average perfectionist.

Besides she has also possibly inherited, or acquired, a fear of contamination. This would possibly explain why she found kissing disgusting.

I remember that once during a group session we had apples placed next to each notepad and she fretted and panicked at the idea of eating the apple without making sure it was properly washed. This apple served to challenge one of her fears and she managed to eat it without re washing it. This behaviour was also indicative of the emergence of trust.

Jade once recounted how her family behaves when they eat out. They disinfect glasses with spray or wipe cutlery and glasses thoroughly. During the time of the swine flu she challenged them while at a restaurant and refrained from engaging in any of their rituals.

At home she was often compared to her intellectual sister. Deep down this will hurt and will generate anger towards her father which she represses and turns towards herself. As an adult she challenges people intellectually and insists on proving that she is better than them. For instance, during therapy she once told me that 'this is the battle of the most intelligent.' During the initial phases of group therapy she tried to beat everyone, whether it was exercise, correcting eating habits, or learning new techniques. Today she queries 'Why do I battle you?' The therapeutic process will be outlined further on in the report.

She used to constantly recreate the same scenario; spaces are transformed into classrooms where she is either learning or teaching. The learning process would last very little and she would shift to professor and would then challenge any speaker. This is the underlying IM at work being transferred on to people in authority: "I am as good as my sister and you will not tell me what to do." This behaviour generally attracted praise and she would thus feel acknowledged. Meanwhile she allowed nobody to come close to her safe space. She was surrounded by a bastion.

With peers she is a helper, a Mother Theresa. The underlying mechanism at play is the same one: "I can take care of you. I can see to your needs." This put her in an advantageous position which would once again reinforce her need to be acknowledged. For instance, once we had a scheduled nutrition session as part of the group therapy and it needed to be shifted while I was abroad. Jade took it upon herself to organise this. I received emails from her explaining what trouble she was going through while she jokingly complained regarding the other group members' absent- mindedness. Once again this put her in a superior position. "I am better than all of them." I am good—they are bad (the overt MFR). In this way she recreated her own solitary space—the space she knew as a child; the space she unconsciously believed she deserved. Moreover, she was unable to express her anger at their behaviour. Instead she retroflects it.

Only genuine warmth and contact could melt her pain and thus invite her to develop trust.

"The Ego Function uses five means to regulate exchanges between the self and the environment and between the inner and the outer" (Delisle, 2009); these being confluence, introjection, projection, retroflection, and deflection.

Jade's Ego Function sought mainly to repeat the type of situation that led to her US. She often became confluent with other people's stories irrespective of these being positive or negative. She could easily get carried away with her imagination and identify with other people's stories. She would, for instance, tell me or others that she could see our pain during times when we would not particularly be experiencing difficulties. Her pain was projected on to others. Nowadays she finds it easy, at least with me, to admit that she is terribly sad. Moreover Jade fully introjected her parents' belief systems and believed the world functioned in this manner. She also introjected society's values and would not alter them in any way. Her anger towards her father and the abuser was thwarted inwards (retroflected) and at times she engaged in minor self-harm and binge eating as a form of destructive behaviour. Jade will often talk of being dissociated from her body as though her body did not belong to her. She will find it hard to link inner with outer. Jade dissociated from her feelings. The abuser abused her of her innocent self and he hurt her, and for this reason she dissociated from her feelings and her body. As a consequence she believed she was a bad person. She further believed she was a bad person.

Jade grew up with an oppressive, easy to anger, and anxious father and with a mother who tried to keep the peace. This dynamic was "poisonous" to sensitive Jade who hurt because these parents did not understand her reality. She had no choice but to obey, and suppress her lively wishes. She was being coerced to be who she did not wish to be. Presently she admits: "I never chose what I wanted. I always chose according to my father's wishes." She had to adapt and find a way through which she would not experience pain. She transformed herself into a marble statue that could no longer experience emotions. The anger would surface at times but she was not allowed to voice it so she turned it inwards. Prior to the final stages of therapy she could not blame her father but she could blame the abuser.

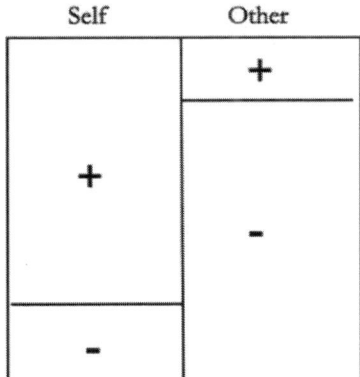
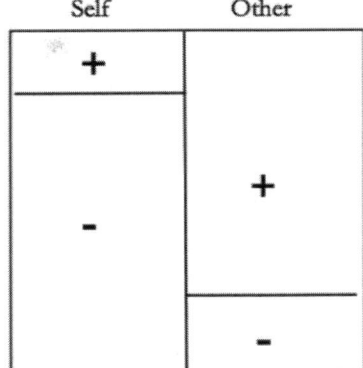

Figure 1. Overt MFR. Figure 2. Covert MFR.

How, then, did Jade consciously represent the field, that is, what does Jade's Matrix of Field Representations look like?

The MFR is the conscious residue of contact experiences in which Self and Other are represented.

I would think that JADE presents with two MFRs: an overt one and a covert one:

The Overt MFR is Jade's quotidian representation of Self and Others. She is better than the Other. The Other is worse than her. Throughout the course of psychotherapy I managed to understand that Jade was aware that at times, deep down, she felt worse than the intellectual Other. This is what I termed the Covert MFR. The aim of psychotherapy was to reach a balance between the two and obtain an MFR configuration closer to the one numbered seven in ORGT.

Inferences concerning the IF

The observation of the client's behaviour in and outside of therapy seems hugely indicative of her IMs lurking in the Id's background. The hypotheses are the following:

1. Jade grew up in a very rigid and anxious environment. Her father would show signs of anger at Jade's playfulness. For instance, once he hit her because she removed his cap at the beach. She was not allowed to play mischievously. Her father presents with severe health

anxiety to the extent of fainting at the idea of common sickness. He is a teacher by profession. Her mother suffers from fear of contamination and makes sure to keep the father's irritability and anxiety at bay by correcting the children. Jade's sister was the parents' ideal because she happened to also be an intellectual and could already correct the teacher at a very young age. She was often bullied and Jade felt she needed to protect her.

2. Jade was unhappy during her childhood because the parents were not tuning in to her reality. She was scolded when she tried being an average child. The childhood fantasy said: "I can only be loved like my sister is if I do what my parents say." For this reason she had to bury most of her needs and obey and mostly do what pleased her father. She became an excellent pianist and scholar but she would instead have preferred to play basketball or netball. She wanted to sing and dance; instead she sat down and dreamt and lived a colourful life through her books.

3. She thought that expressing emotions was uncalled for. Showing anger towards her parents would have cost her a huge price, therefore she learnt to suppress it and turn it inwards to the extent of self-harm and feeling dizzy.

4. Linked to the above was the belief that having pleasure is wrong. Cakes are not to be enjoyed. They are not delicious, they are noxious. Messy play as children was not dreamt of; they had to look clean and proper, after all they were the teacher's children. Trying alcohol or going to parties as teenagers was to be looked down upon. She never tried any. Feeling physical attraction was also sinful and so was any discussion related to sexual behaviour. The consequence was the absence of libido. Life was to be lived in its purest form. They were good children and daddy was happy.

5. Moreover, when Jade was about eight years old her father hurt himself badly while working in his workshop. He nearly cut through a main artery. The family found him on the floor bleeding. Jade plucked up courage and went in to see what had happened. At this time her father told her that she now had to take care of her mother and sister. He survived the accident but spent several weeks in hospital. This belief remained in Jade's head.

6. At around age five Jade experienced sexual abuse through which she learnt to dissociate from physical pain and from her body and through which she concluded that she was a bad girl.

7. The above points explain how Jade developed excellent cognitive skills, a florid fantasy, and poor recognition of personal needs and emotions.
8. Her overt MFR configuration led her to choose a husband who could not see to her emotional needs. The cycle is once again repeated.

The above experiences constitute, according to me, the relational configuration whereby "the experience was both indispensable and intolerable" and have thus possibly ended in a US, leading to the development of the IMs and consequent IF.

Her conservative adjustment is about constantly appearing stronger or superior to others. Jade is continuously trying to prove to the world (and her own self) that she is as good as her sister. She is constantly guarding herself and making sure she will not hurt. She is also constantly taking care of other people. Whilst wishing for love and contact she unconsciously rejects it by appearing strong and extremely self-sufficient. This way she unconsciously relives her childhood experience where she suppressed her needs and abided by the law. Presently, within her marriage, she suppresses her needs and endures in sadness. In life she admits that she has always suppressed her wishes and followed her father's instead, including her career choice. She is convinced that she is not good enough, she is bad, and no matter how hard she tries she cannot seem to reach the epitome of perfection—hence her need for detail and perfection.

She defends her conservative adjustment by distrusting people. She keeps them at arms' length and will socialise mainly with her parents and sister and sometimes with two colleagues. This defensive behaviour is the result of her conscious MFR whereby others are classified as bad. Prior to therapy she engaged in no social activity, except for the odd wedding or a stroll with one of her two friends. For instance, prior to the group therapy experience she had never visited the Three Cities in Malta since these are considered by some to be shallow places. The beauty of these magical cities allowed her to challenge one of her introjects passed on to her by her parents. Through group therapy she learnt how other women contact the world; she learnt that some other people hurt and that they achieve healing through narrating their tales. She figured out that fun and pain can co-exist; she dared to dance and act and bake. She also accepted that she can be corrected and yet remain a unitary whole, an adult. She achieved reparation of the Self.

Treating personality disorders through experiential dialogue

The above experiential processes brought about changes in Jade's affective, cognitive, and behavioural ways of being in life. Group therapy saved Jade. I invited her to join the group since I believed this would offer her a window on to the world. It did. She is adjusting in the most creative way possible.

Following is a brief description of the long-term group psychotherapy programme for eating disorders that Jade joined. It consists of eight consecutive weekly two-hour sessions with the inclusion of two or three workshops throughout the eight weeks. The workshops vary and they have so far included nutrition, slow cooking, walks around the Three Cities of Malta, physiopilates and jazz dance, expressive arts, pole fitness, swimming and dance therapy, to mention but a few. The experiential part of the therapy group allows the participants to express themselves in different ways and it enables them to experience their selves as whole, as all- rounded people. Contact is healing.

Since Jade joined the group she has lost over twenty kgs (although weight is not the main issue within group therapy), has made friends, attends a gym regularly, has taken up walking and swimming, and attends yoga with a friend. She laughs more often and is not scared of telling us that she is sad while she is at home alone. Whilst the other group members told their tales she was indirectly figuring out that people open up, that people make mistakes, and they make fools out of themselves, that they feel sad and lonely and that they also binge when sad or angry. She also figured out that engaging in sexual behaviour or being intimate seems to be a basic need and has also admitted that she would be willing to melt into this experience. Unfortunately her husband could not latch on to Jade's growth in this area. He feels he has now reached beyond breaking point. Moreover he expects Jade to abide by his rules: "Expressing yourself during intimacy is unnecessary," he retorts.

At this stage of therapy Jade knows that her husband is depressed and that he is not willing to work on the relationship. He says that he leaves it up to her and that if she wants to she can file for an annulment. Jade is not in a rush. She observes her relationship, learns how to handle her pain without harming herself, understands that she deserves to be loved and cared for, pities her husband's state, and considers separation.

During therapy we often used the metaphor of the little boat sailing along the seas of Life. This is how Jade was learning to trust Life while the dialogic therapeutic relationship, as she says, "offers support towards the favourable winds." In our personal therapy we have used several phrases from Paolo Coehlo.

Therapeutic goals

Psychotherapy with Jade has been a beautiful and enriching journey based on Dia-Logos within a phenomenological context which allowed for the repetition of impasses with a response to these impasses that was different from the habitual, that is, "not in the way people always have responded."

Although right now I might refer to various levels of objectives in the psychotherapeutic journey these levels were not followed in a hierarchic fashion. We danced to and fro each time with more awareness and deeper trust.

Initially I listened to Jade tell her tale. I did not challenge or contradict her since I noticed that this brought upon her defensive nature, whereby she would try to become more clever than me and then re-enact the scene of "I am more intelligent than you and you shall not tell me what to do." I offered empathic understanding and warmth and hoped that Jade would see that some people out there can be trusted.

I listened to her stories of abuse and of anxiety. I heard what she needed to say about her husband, sister, friends, and parents and I offered support with her sad moments. When the session became a lesson I let her know that it was not necessary that she remember everything we said; that in a therapy session, unlike a school session, clients had the luxury of forgetting; the brain would do the job. She struggled for a long time before she could understand what I meant and kept coming to the session as if it was a lesson. At times she also tried to become a teacher to me and I listened, but gently, and let her know that sometimes with her I did not need to work because she did the job. Then I wondered, along with her, how that must have felt for her. She replied: "I'm used to that." Therefore, while addressing DSM symptoms, I was already referring to her ways of creating conservative adjustments.

Jade carried on mistrusting me until December 2008, just before Christmas. This was the time she was giving me the story of the abuse. She would give me more and more detailed pictures of what happened while she had been left alone in hospital. She always thanked me for believing her story. It was when she still reverted to food as a means of support and when she still spent endless hours locked at home.

One day, while I was Christmas shopping, something told me that I should get her small gift. She had already given me the glass frame with the angel and she had made sure to show me that it was precious. I could not quite explain why I felt I needed to make her happy at around this time of the year. It felt like I needed to tell her that she was not going to be alone. I let myself be guided by my intuition and I bought Jade a Chinese tea cup, where the cup serves as a lid to the pot. I saw it and thought "Ok, this could do", although I did not associate any meaning to my choice of gift. It had to be just that—a gift.

When I gave it to her it all made sense. She needed to take time to reflect. Using this tea cup required brewing tea; besides, this tea pot/cup could be carried around. She could for instance take the pot to her desk and slowly sip and savour the tea instead of bingeing. When Jade received the gift she went bright red and could not contain her glee. The transformation had happened. The MFR configuration was starting to shift: not everyone out there is a monster who is ready to criticise me or tell me what to do. Some people are nice and they actually care. The natural phrase that came to me on this particular occasion was: "You deserve a lot of this."

Psychotherapy had started. The marble statue was starting to melt. The overt MFR was shifting in the following manner: "At school and outside school some people meant no harm." She was also unknowingly challenging her social phobia. She understood that her dizziness was related to her anxious thoughts and that this was common. Catastrophising her thinking could only make it worse. At one point she came slightly late for a session and was not upset about it. She was undoing her projections in connection with the representation of the Other in the MFR.

The Other was not always cruel, ready to pounce on her and harm her. Out there people were not all bad. The Ego function was being re-educated. She started to realise that, compared to the other group members, she was a bit too rigid. Jade also questioned why I had remarked that during her session I felt we became teacher—student and she understood. "I always think I have to learn and get it right"; then she smiled. At that point I knew she was ready to lie back and be a client for a while.

During the initial stages of therapy Jade was preoccupied about my well being.

Jade: I think about how you spend time in here all alone. There is no one. Who takes care of you? At times I see pain when I look into your eyes.

Myself thinking: *She seems to be projecting her sadness on to me and at the same time her IM is emerging through the Id. She spent a lifetime taking care of people.*

Myself: Thank you for thinking about my well-being. It can get a bit lonely in here sometimes, however this is a job I enjoy doing and I do like the silence. Then when I go home I also make sure I'm taken care of. It feels nice to have someone think about your well-being so I want to thank you once again for thinking about me.
Jade passed this comment at the very end of a session, actually when it was over and I was walking her to the door.

This comment will give me the opportunity to work on the IMs. Theoretically speaking this work would be equivalent to Levels 2 and 3 of the continuum of objectives. Jade is a very bright and alert client and spends time analysing what we say. I knew that she would think about my comment and also wonder why she needed to take care of me. At my end I also made sure that during my next session I would pass a comment like "Hope you had a nice weekend", which would possibly trigger some information as to how I spent time in play mode (we had referred to the "All work and no play" expression). Here I am keeping in mind that Jade needs to understand that people do on average, spend all their days working and that usually they are surrounded by people who are looking forward to being with them. Remember that Jade lives with a non-existent, rather depressed, husband and goes to parents who are incapable of lightness.

Sure enough my comment above triggered a sad look in Jade. She would look down and sit in silence.

Jade: Inside there is a lot of pain. I can hide it. I have learnt to endure. I wish to cry but I cannot in front of you. It doesn't happen. I don't want to hurt you.

Myself: It is ok if you cry. I would be glad to help with this pain and I would also like to hear about it.

Jade: But you say that because it is your job to say so.

Myself: Yes my job does involve helping people through their pain and I am genuinely interested in supporting you through it. I am sure that together we can figure out what this pain is about.

Trust was becoming stronger. Jade was slowly coming off her pedestal and for half a session she would join the rest of the common mortals and accept that feeling pain and expressing it is plausible.

This phrase is loaded with material for growth. Jade was reconstructing her Self. To start with she acknowledged and admitted an intense emotion happening within her in front of someone. Remember, Jade could only repress "what is unacceptable". She says that she has learnt to hide and endure the pain. This is the IM emerging and Jade was identifying with this emergence. She was re-enacting what she had learnt as a child. "I do not cause trouble. When I do daddy is upset and so is mummy, then I become a bad person."

I was hoping that my phrase would help her focus on what was happening in the phenomenology of the current field, in the here and now. Simultaneously I was hoping that she would start correcting the covert MFR where she feels she is a bad person.

I remember that my phrase gave her the opportunity to talk about what was making her sad. She still recounted the events with very little emotion attached to them. Afterwards she also queried what she was to do with the pain.

Jade: What do I do with my anxiety and sadness?

Myself: Sadness is sometimes referred to as the wise old man and together we shall see what this wise old man is trying to tell you. Sadness is very often a vehicle for growth. There is no need to fear it.

Therapeutically we are in Experiential Fields 1 and 2 (on both an external and internal level) and very much approaching Fields 3 and 4. At this present stage of therapy Jade is starting to feel comfortable talking about her childhood experiences and how these could have shaped her current modes of thinking, feeling, and behaving.

Treating the cycle of repetition of contact impasses

> The therapeutic process implies retracing, through the client's experience, the contact cycles that bear mark of the IF, making sense of them, and completing the unfinished experience. This process is based on joint, interactive, dialogic attention on the part of the client and therapist. It involves the whole person in the cognitive, affective, and sensorimotor spheres. (Delisle, 2009)

At this stage of therapy Jade could tell when she was behaving in ways similar to her childhood experiences. She could understand when, for instance, she was battling me (using her terminology) but she could not always understand the reason behind her behaviour.

Experiential fields: from here and now to there and then

Jade started to attend group therapy, along with individual therapy, around the fifth/sixth month of her therapeutic journey. The initial two phases of the programme involved regular physical activity that often followed the two hour psychotherapy session. The programme was being held at a spa resort. Several forms of physical activities were introduced in order to give the clients the opportunity to choose which one, in the long term, they wanted to engage inm.

Jade was on a mission. She wanted to beat everyone at everything and, although she complained along with the others about the fatigue felt after exercising, when alone she engaged in further exercise to the point of exhaustion and in the name of precision. She wanted to learn the perfect swimming technique and the precise ways of squatting or running.

She came to an individual session and she made sure to tell me how she was excelling, how she was over-exercising to the point of hurting herself. I knew that she was defying me. We had previously discussed the risks of over-exercising combined with under eating, both of which she was engaging in. She was misbehaving and trying me out, possibly like she did with her father when he imposed strict rules on her.

E2-E1—During this session Jade was describing an immediate, observable, past event which was also happening in the here-and-now. At the gym she was competing with her peers; during therapy she was battling me. The feeling in me was disappointment and anger because she was "misbehaving". I refrained from using a reproachful tone since this would do to Jade what her father used to do to her when she stepped out of line. Instead I gently told her that her body didn't deserve that.

Jade appeared angry (retroflection) and said: "Yes I can harm my body. I can do to it what the abuser did to me." I could see that she was becoming confluent with the emergence of the IM. In the past (E4) she was not allowed to play and jump and dance, and she harboured extreme anger at her father—anger of which she was not, as yet, aware.

I was tempted to ask whether I had contributed in any way to the emergence of this behaviour in the here-and-now (E2). However at that time I feared that this question could further trigger the feeling for Jade that I know better than her, with the consequence of having her battle me more. Then we would create "the battle of who is the most intelligent", as she once called it. I kept E2, E4, and I4 in mind. Appearing knowledgeable would have created an immediate Repetition. I was gradually after Recognition and Reparation.

I kept asking myself: "What is it that she is trying to tell me?" The MFR was in action: "'You are bad because you force me but I will fight you" and "I am bad because I misbehave and then I hurt because I disappoint you."

The identification with the idea of power and grandiosity was also huge, so I even had to think about a way for her to understand that not succeeding at being the best is also fine. Theoretically I was thinking about E1—I2; however, in practise this would have qualified as a premature intervention.

The scenario is in E1 and E2, the here-and-now and the here-and-then, which slowly moves towards I1 and I2, which is the internal representation of the therapeutic relationship in the here-and-now and in the here-and-then. At this stage we are at little Jade defying strict father and protecting herself from the abuser. The more the father will tell her not to do it, the more her peers will tell her that she is exaggerating, the more she will feel satisfied at having fought the father. The more she would prove to him that she is as good as her sister, and that she is not the bad little girl. Therefore, Jade needs acknowledgement.

I remember, however, that I needed to tell her how I felt every time she rejected what I had to say; every time she battled me. "When you reject my words in this way I feel like you don't need me, that I am not important to you. This is quite sad because then we end up both alone." I was hoping that this phrase would further help her correct the configuration of self and others into something like: "There are others who care. Not all adults are trying to hurt me or impose truths on me."

She felt sorry about her behaviour and I knew that she would give this exchange a good deal of thought. I was hopeful; I could see the emergence of a unified Self.

Regarding the anger and the need to instil pain on to herself, I intervened as follows: "You seem very angry. Do you remember yourself being angry in this way at some other point in your life?" Here I was slowly trying to explore I3 and I4. Jade immediately referred to her current situation with her husband, replying that he was the one to make her angry and yet her anger could not be expressed because he is quickly irritated and does not want to risk accidents of any kind. She also referred to being angry at her mother who constantly points out how M. does not respect her. Yet she cannot tell her mother how she feels, that her words hurt her.

Here I could see Jade's repetitions. From a strict father and a heartless abuser she moved on to an insensitive and angry husband where once again she is not allowed to live her life freely. She says: "In my past I had the abuser; in the present I have my husband." I pointed out that the good news is that our present can be edited with enough good work, awareness, and some practise.

Jade is as yet not aware of I3 → I1 process, that is, "Does whatever is going on in the client's internal field with regards to the therapeutic relationship look like or feel like her internal experience and or representations of some current relationship in her life?", nor of the I4 → I1, which translates as "Does whatever is going on in the client's internal field with regard to the therapeutic relationship look like or feel like his internal experience and or representations of some significant relationship in her developmental past?"

Later on in therapy, when Jade has also heard the other group members open up freely about their childhood experiences, she will start to link her internal experience of the here-and-now with her own internal representations. Our session regarding the battle with me in the here-and-now evolved and proceeded as follows.

Jade: I know I battle you. I promise I won't do it anymore.
Myself: Is there anything that happens between us that makes you feel you want to fight me? Is it anything that I do or say?
Jade: I don't know. It happens.
Myself: Do you catch yourself doing this elsewhere, with other people?
Jade: Lately since I discovered Life, I know I am angry at my father. He was very strict and never allowed me to play. I liked playing with a toy gun and he despised this. I had no one to play with because my sister was just into books. My father didn't like it when I teased him. We were not allowed out with the other children.
Jade started to see the connection between the external and the internal. She was starting to understand that she was merging the two internal fields.
Myself: I wish I could come next to little JADE and tell her that playing is in fact ok, that she could do it. I would also tell her that daddy doesn't know otherwise. He thinks that school is better than play. I would tell her that she can do both and that teasing daddy sometimes is also ok.
That would have been nice.

Jade came for therapy because of a current issue presenting in the observable Field 3, the there-and-now. This was the episode of the attack on the couple and friends while they were strolling along the promenade. This observable Field 3 brought information in the observable Field 1, the here-and-now, where I felt the sessions were frozen and void of meaning. Jade was like a marble statue. The here-and-now proceeded into several here-and-then (Field 2) which also shed light on Jade's MFR configuration. Meanwhile the immediate there-and-now (Field 3) led to a further observable there-and-now, JADE's marital situation which gradually proceeded to the external there-and-then (Field 4). Figuratively this would look as follows.

Field 3

↕

Field 1 ↔ Field 2 ↔   further Field 3   ↔ Field 4

The above is paralleled by similar Fields happening on the internal level.

The above external observable fields were gradually shedding light on their parallel internal fields. The dynamics occurring on Field E1 and E2 were somehow explaining Jade's MFR configuration whereby the Other was a tyrant whom she had to challenge and to whom she had to show that she was better and invincible. Field E3 was revealing information regarding her IMs. At home with her husband she endured, she behaved like she behaved when she was at home with her father (Fields I3 and I4).

Jade has reached Recognition and is engaging in Reparation. Today she can see the totality of her own picture. She can link outer to inner and inner to outer. She has discovered a world that she loves, the world of psychotherapy and reads related material. Her body is now embodied with a woman who is in touch with her soul. The marble melts into flesh. She listens to others and understands that not everyone out there is ready to harm her. Finally she has also accepted that she tends to be an anxious type and that when her heart beats rapidly she does not need to panic or fret. She will need to remind herself that she will soon be fine. She is at a very nice place.

Note

1. Dr. Dorothy Scicluna is a Clinical Psychologist. She holds a doctorate in Clinical Psychology from the University of Padova, Italy. She is in private practice in Malta where she specializes in eating disorders and obesity.

Appendix

Structural analysis of the self (Based on the Revised theory of the Self. Delisle, 1995–1998)

A. Function/structure of the Self

Id: *Fluidity and relative strength of emergences What seems to emerge most easily and least easily?*

Ego-function: *Ability to correctly give voice to the Id and the MFR in relations with the current environment. What are the specific elements most often affected by each of the modes of regulation? What does the client project? Introject? Deflect? Retroflect? In which field configurations does the client seek confluence?*

Personality function: *Configuration of the MFR and nature of representations*

242 APPENDIX

Configuration of MFR

What seem to be the nature of Self- and Other-representations?

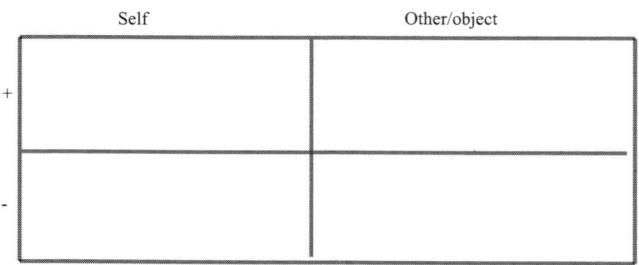

B. Inferences concerning the I.F.

Inferential hypotheses concerning the presence of Introjected Microfields in the background of the Id, taking into account your observations of the Ego function and the MFR.

1. *What dynamic does the client seem to be trying to set up (process of repetition of impasses) in the relationships he or she mentions and/or in the therapeutic relationship? Can you describe this process of "repetition" in terms of some unfinished developmental issue?*
2. *How are defensive operations used to maintain/reproduce this unfinished developmental issue?*
3. *What were the known risk factors and resiliency factors around this specific issue in client's developmental past?*

Reflections on therapeutic process (*adapted from Delisle, 1995–1998, CIG, Montréal*)

---

1. Essentially, what is my experience with this client?

---

2. Can I find some thematic affinities between my experience with the client and some of what he/she reports as occuring in field 3

---

3. Can I find some thematic affinities between my experience with the client and some of what he/she reports as having occured in field 4?

---

4. How could I express this construction of meaning in hermeneutic terms?
   a partial hypothesis ...
   that does not exhaust the entire meaning of the phenomenon ...
   that stimulates the clients' own constructive creativity ...
   and that keeps affect alive ...

---

5. Can I think of a restorative response that ...
   would be different than those that the client tends to evoke ...
   that I feel I could maintain with integrity over time ...

REFERENCES

Abend, S. M. (1988). Intrapsychic versus interpersonal. The wrong dilemma. *Psychoanalytic Inquiry, 8*: 497–504.
Abraham, R. E. (1993). The Developmental Profile: The Psychodynamic Diagnosis of Personality. *Journal of Personality Disorders, 7*: 105–115.
Alban, L. S. & Groman, W. D. (1975). Dreamwork in a Gestalt therapy context. *American Journal of Psychoanalysis. 35*: 147–156.
Allen, J. G. & Fonagy, P. (2006). *Handbook of mentalization-based treatment.* New York: Wiley.
Alpert, M., Cohen, N. L., Martz, M. & Robinson, C. (1980). Electroencephalographic analysis: a methodology for evaluating psychotherapeutic process. *Psychiatry Research, 2*: 323–329.
American Psychiatric Association (1980). *Diagnostic and Statistical Manual of Mental Disorders III.* Washington, DC: APA Press.
American Psychiatric Association (1987). *Diagnostic and Statistical Manual of Mental Disorders III* (Revised). Washington, DC: APA Press.
American Psychiatric Association (1994). *Diagnostic and Statistical Manual of Mental Disorders IV.* Washington, DC: APA Press.
American Psychiatric Association (1994). *Diagnostic and Statistical Manual of Mental Disorders* (4th Edition). Washington, DC: APA.
Amini, F., Lewis, T., Lannon, R., et al. (1996). Affect, attachment, memory: contributions towards psychobiologic integration. *Psychiatry, 59*: 213–239.

AQG (1993). Compte-rendu de la table ronde sur la Gestalt et la psychothérapie de long terme. *Revue Québécoise de Gestalt*, 1–2.

Aron, E. N. (1998a). *The Highly Sensitive Person: How to Thrive When the World Overwhelms You*. New York: First Broadway Books.

Bakan, D. (1967). *On Method: Toward a Reconstruction of Psychological Investigation*. San Francisco: Josey-Bass.

Barlow, D. H. (2008). *Clinical Handbook of Psychological disorders: A Step-by Step Treatment Manual* (Fourth edition). New York: The Guilford Press.

Basch, Michael, F. (1987). The interpersonal and the intrapsychic: Conflict or harmony? Reply. *Contemporary Psychoanalysis*, 23: 410–414.

Becker, E. (1982). Growing up rugged: Fritz Perls and Gestalt therapy. *Revision*, 5: 6–14.

Bergin, A. E. & Garfield, S. L. (1991; 1994): *Handbook of Psychotherapy and Behavior Change*. New York: J. Wiley.

Besyner, J. K. (1985): Multimodal inpatient treatment of Vietnam combat veterans with post traumatic stress disorder. *Psychotherapy in Private Practice*, 3: 43–47.

Beutler, L. E. & Castonguay, L. -G. (2006). The task force on empirically based principles of therapeutic change. In L. -G. Castonguay & L. E. Beutler (Eds.), *Principles of Therapeutic Change that Work* (pp. 3–12). New York: Oxford University Press.

Bohart, A. C. & Greenberg, L. S. (1998). *Empathy reconsidered: New Directions in Psychotherapy*. Washington: APA.

Bouchard, M. A. (1985). L'arrière-fond intellectuel de la Gestalt thérapie. *Psychothérapies*.

Bouchard, M. A. (1990). *De la phénoménologie à la psychanalyse*. Bruxelles: Pierre Mardaga, Éditeur.

Bouchard, M. A. & Derome, G. (1987). La Gestalt thérapie et les autres écoles: complémentarité clinique et perspective de développement. In: C. Lecomte & L. G. Gastonguay, *Rapprochement et intégration en psychothérapie*. Montréal: Gaëtan Morin Éditeur.

Bouchard, M. A. & Guérette, L. (1991). Notes sur la composante herméneutique de la psychothérapie. *Revue québécoise de psychologie*, 12: 19–33.

Brandt, W. L. (1982). *Psychologists Caught: A Psycho-logic of Psychology*. Toronto: University of Toronto Press.

Breshgold, E. K. (1989). Resistance in Gestalt therapy. An historical theoretical perspective. *Gestalt Journal*, 12: 73–102.

Breshgold, E. K. & Zahm, S. (1992). A case for the integration of self psychology developmental theory into the practice of Gestalt therapy. *Gestalt Journal*, 15: 61–93.

Bruner, J. S. (1990). *Acts of Meaning*. Cambridge: Harvard University Press.

Buck, R. (1994). The neuropsychology of communication: Spontaneous and symbolic aspects. *Journal of Pragmatics, 22*: 265–278.
Buchbinder, J. (1986). Gestalt therapy and its application to alcoholism treatment. *Alcoholism Treatment Quarterly, 3*: 49–67.
Bugental, J. F. T. (1978). Existential-humanistic psychotherapy: Evoking the subjective potential. In: R. Herink (Ed.), *The Psychotherapy Handbook* (pp. 186–188). New York: Jason Aronson.
Bugental, J. F. T. (1987). *The Art of the Psychotherapist*. New York: Norton.
Bugental, J. F. T. & Bracke, P. E. (1992). The Future of existential-humanistic psychotherapy. *Psychotherapy, 29*.
Burgalières, R. (1992). La Gestalt thérapie et la théorie des relations d'objet. *La Revue Québécoise de Gestalt*. Montréal: Les Éditions du CIG.
Cadwallader, E. H. (1984). Values in Fritz Perls's Gestalt Therapy: On the dangers of half truths. *Counseling and Values, 28*: 192–201.
Cahalan, W. (1983). An elaboration of the Gestalt personality theory. The experience of self in social relations. *Gestalt Journal, 6*: 39–53.
Calarge, C., Andreasen, N. C. & O'Leary, D. S. (2003). Visualizing how one brain understands another: A PET study of theory of mind. *American Journal of Psychiatry, 2003; 160*: 1954–1964.
Cashdan, S. (1988). *Object Relations Therapy: "Using the Relationship"*. New York: W. W. Norton & Company.
Castonguay, L. G. & Beutler, L. E. (2006). *Principles of Therapeutic Change that Work*. New York: Oxford University Press.
Castonguay, L. -G., Goldfried, M. R., Wiser, S., Raue, P. J. & Hayes, A. M. (1996). Predicting the effect of cognitive therapy for depression: A study of unique and common factors. *Journal of Consulting and Clinical Psychology, 64*: 497–504.
Castonguay, L. -G., Reid, J. J., Halperin, G. S. & Goldfried, M. R. (2003). Psychotherapy integration. In: G. Stricker & T. A. Widiger (Eds.), *Handbook of Psychology* (8). New York: Wiley.
Ceci, S. & Bruch, M. (1993). Suggestibility of the child witness: a historical review and synthesis. *Psychological Bulletin, 113*: 403–439.
Chambless, D. L. & Hollon, S. D. (1998). Defining empirically supported therapies. *Journal of Consulting and Clinical Psychology, 66*: 7–18.
Civin, M. & Lombardi, K. L. (1990). The preconscious and potential space. Special Issue, Susan Deri An appreciation. *Psychoanalytic Review, 77*: 573–585.
Clarckson, P. & Mackewn, J. (1993). *Fritz Perls*. London: Sage.
Clarke, K. M. & Greenberg, L. S. (1986): Differential effects of the Gestalt two chair intervention and problem solving in resolving decisional conflict. *Journal of Counseling Psychology, 33*: 11–15.

Clarkin, J. F., Yoemans, F. E. & Kernberg, O. F. (1999). *Psychotherapy for Borderline Personality*. New York: Wiley.

Conoley, C. W., Conoley, J. C., McConnell, J. A. & Kimzey, C. E. (1983). The effect of the ABCs of Rational Emotive Therapy and the empty chair technique of Gestalt Therapy on anger reduction. *Psychotherapy Theory, Research and Practice, 20*: 112–117.

Corbeil, J. (1992). Histoire de la Gestalt au Québec. *Revue Québécoise de Gestalt, 1*: 1.

Cozolino, L. (2002). *The Neuroscience of Psychotherapy*. New York: Norton.

Critchfield, K. L. & Benjamin, L. S. (2006). Integration of therapeutic factors in treating personality disorders. In: L. -G. Castonguay & L. E. Beutler (Eds.), *Principles of Therapeutic Change that Work* (pp. 253–271). New York: Oxford University Press.

Crocker, S. F. (1983). Truth and foolishness in the "Gestalt Prayer." *Gestalt Journal, 6*: 4–15.

Crowell, J. A., Warters, E., Kring, A. & Riso, L. P. (1993). The psychosocial etiologies of personality disorders: What is the answer like? *Journal of Personality Disorders, 7* (supplement): 118–128.

Crump, L. D. (1984). Gestalt therapy in the treatment of Vietnam veterans experiencing PTSD symptomatology. *Journal of Contemporary Psychotherapy, 14*: 90–98.

Cuerrier, J. (1994). *L'Être Humain*. Montréal: Mc Graw-Hill.

Dahl, A. A. (1993). The personality disorders: A critical review of family, twin and adoption studies. *Journal of Personality Disorders, 7* (supplement): 86–99.

Dahl, A. A. & Bordhal, P. E. (1993). Obstetric complications as a risk for subsequent development of personality disorders. *Journal of Personality Disorders, 7*: 22–27.

Damasio, A. R. (1995). Toward a neurobiology of emotion and feeling: operational concepts and hypotheses. *The Neuroscientist, 1*: 19–15.

Damasio, A. R. (2000). *L'erreur de Descartes. La raison des émotions*. Paris: Odile Jacob.

Damasio, A. R. (2003). *Spinoza avait raison*. Paris: Odile Jacob.

Davidove, D. (1991). Loss of Ego functions, conflict, and resistance. *Gestalt Journal, 14*: 27–43.

Davis, R. & Millon, T. (1995). On the importance of theory to a taxonomy of personality disorders. In: W. J. Livesley (Ed.), *The DSM-IV Personality Disorders* (pp. 377–396). New York: The Guilford Press.

Delisle, G. (1990). Conférence d'ouverture du 2e Colloque annuel de l'Association Québécoise de Gestalt. Montréal.

Delisle, G. (1991). *Les troubles de la personnalité; perspective gestaltiste*. Montréal: Les Éditions du Reflet.

Delisle, G. (1992). De la relation clinique à la relation thérapeutique. *Revue québécoise de Gestalt, 1*: 53–77.
Delisle, G. (1993). La relation thérapeutique tri-dimensionnelle et l'identification projective . *Revue Québécoise de Gestalt, 1*.
Delisle, G. (1993). *Les troubles de la personnalité; perspective gestaltiste* (Troisième Édition). Montréal: Les Éditions du Reflet.
Delisle, G. (1998). *La relation d'objet en Gestalt thérapie*. Montréal: Les Éditions du Reflet.
Delisle, G. (1998). *La relation d'objet en Gestalt thérapie*. Montréal: Les Éditions du CIG.
Delisle, G. (2000). *Vers une psychothérapie du lien*. Montréal: Les Éditions du CIG.
Delisle, G. (2001). Le dialogue herméneutique en psychothérapie. Conférence à l'Hôpital de Tourcoing, Lille. *Actes du colloque de Champ-G*.
Delisle, G. (2001). *Vers une psychothérapie du lien*. Montréal: Les Éditions du Reflet.
Delisle, G. (2004). *Les pathologies de la personnalité; perspectives développementales*. Montréal: Les Éditions du Reflet.
Delisle, G. (2008). Attachement et relations d'objet; aspects neurodéveloppementaux et implication pour la psychothérapie. Conférence présentée à Montreal.
Delisle, G. (2009, in press). *Object Relations in Gestalt Therapy: Towards an Integrated Approach to the Treatment of Personality Disorders*.
Dollard, J. & Miller, J. E. (1950). *Personality and Psychotherapy*. New York: McGraw-Hill.
Dolliver, R. H. (1981). Some limitations in Perls' Gestalt therapy. *Psychotherapy Theory, Research and Practice, 18*: 38–45.
Drapela, V. J. (1987). *A Review of Personality Theories*. Springfield, IL: Charles C. Thomas.
Driessen, M., Herrmann, J., Stahl, K., Zwaan, M., Meier, S., Hill, A., Osterheider, M. & Petersen, D. (2000). Magnetic resonance imaging volumes of the hippocampus and the amygdale in women with borberline personality disorder and early traumatization. *Archives of General Psychiatry, 57*: 1115–1122.
Drouin, M. -S. (2003). L'empathie en Gestalt Thérapie: quelques considérations cliniques et éthiques. *Revue Québécoise de Gestalt, 6*: 85–105.
Dublin, J. E. (1973). Gestalting psychotic persons. *Psychotherapy Theory, Research and Practice, 10*: 149–152.
Dublin, J. E. (1976). Beyond Gestalt. Toward integrating some systems of psychotherapy. *Psychotherapy Theory, Research and Practice, 13*: 225–231.
Elliott, R. (2002). The effectiveness of humanistic therapies: a meta analysis. In: D. J. Cain & J. Seeman (Eds.), *Humanistic Psychotherapies: Handbook of*

Research and Practice (pp. 57–82). Washington: American Psychological Association.

Ellman, S. J. (1991). *Freud's Technique Papers: A Contemporary Perspective.* New York: Jason Aronson.

Endler, N. E. (1984). To know or not to know: That is the method. *Department of Psychology Report* No. 142. (North York: York University.)

Enns, C. Z. (1987). Gestalt therapy and feminist therapy. A proposed integration. *Journal of Counselling and Development, 66*: 93–95.

Eysenck, H. J. (1952). The effects of psychotherapy: an evaluation. *Journal of Consulting Psychology. 16*: 319–324. Fairbairn, W. R. D. (1943). Repression and return of the Bad Object (with special reference to the war neurosis). In: *An Object Relations Theory Of Personality.* New York: Basic Books, 1952.

Fairbairn, W. R. D. (1951). A synopsis of the author's views regarding the structure of the personality. In: *An Object Relations Theory Of Personality.* New York: Routledge, 1952.

Fairbairn, W. R. D. (1954). *Psychoanalytic Studies of the Personality.* New York: Basic Books.

Fairbairn, W. R. D. (1958). On the nature and aim of psycho-analytical treatment. *International Journal of Psycho-Analysis, 44*: 224–225.

Fairbairn, W. R. D. (1963). Synopsis of an Object-Relations theory of the personality. In: *Fairbairn and the Origins of Object Relations.* New York: The Guilford Press, 1994.

Feder, B. (1978). Responsibility and the Gestalt therapist. *Gestalt Journal, 1*: 83–87.

Fensterheim, H. (1983). Introduction to behavioural psychotherapy. In: H. Fensterheim & H. I. Glazer (Eds.), *Behavioral Psychotherapy: Basic Principles and Case Studies.* New York: Brunner/Mazel.

Feyerabend, P. K. (1975). *Against Method.* London: Verso.

Fondation canadienne de la recherche sur les service de santé (mai 2005). Conceptualiser et regrouper les données probantes pour guider le système de santé. Extrait du 16 octobre 2006 (www.fcrss.ca).

Forge (1995). Lexique International de Gestalt Thérapie. Fédération Internationale des Organismes de Formation en Gestalt. Paris.

Fosshage, J. L. (1994). Toward reconceptualising transference: Theoretical and clinical considerations. *International Journal of Psycho-Analysis, 75*: 265–280.

Frances, A. J. (1987). *DSM-III Personality Disorders: Diagnosis and Treatment.* New York: BMA Audio Cassettes, The Guilford Press.

Frances, A. M.D., First, M. B. M.D. & Pincus, H. A. M.D. (1995). *DSM-IV Guidebook.* Washington, DC: American Psychiatric Press, Inc.

Frankl, A. J. (1984). *Four Therapies Integrated.* New Jersey: Prentice-Hall.

Franks, C. M. & Wilson, G. T. (1979). Behavior change: An overview. In: C. M. Franks & G. T. Wilson (Eds.), *Annual Review of Behavior Therapy*. New York: Brunner/Mazel.

Franks, C. M. (1984). On conceptual and technical integrity in psychoanalysis and behavior therapy: Two fundamentally incompatible systems. In: H. Arkowitz & S. B. Messer (Eds.), *Psychoanalytic Therapy and Behavior Therapy: Is Integration Possible?* New York: Plenum. Freedman, N. & Lavender, J. (1997). On receiving the patient's transference: the symbolizing and desymbolizing countertransference. *Journal of the American Psychoanalytic Association*, 45: 79–103.

Freud, S. (1917). Mourning and melancholia. 14th edition. London: Vintage.

Friedman, L. J. (1975). Current psychoanalytic object relations theory and its clinical implications. *International Journal of Psycho Analysis*, 56: 137–146.

Fries, P. (2005). A mechanism for cognitive dynamics: neuronal communication through neuronal coherence. *Trends in Cognitive Science*, 10: 474–480.

Frijda, N. H. (1994). The structure of subjective emotional intensity. *Cognition and Emotion*, 8: 329–350.

From, I. (1980). *Notes inédites d'un stage sur la théorie du Self de Perls et al.* Montréal.

From, I. (1984). Reflections on Gestalt therapy after thirty-two years of practice: A requiem for gestalt. *The Gestalt Journal*, 7: 4–12.

Gabbard, G. O. (1994). Mind and brain in psychiatric treatment. *Bulletin of the Menninger Clinic*, 58: 427–446.

Gabbard, G. O. (2000). A neurobiologically informed perspective on psychotherapy. *The British Journal of Psychiatry*, 177: 117–122.

Gagnon, J. H. (1981). Gestalt therapy with the schizophrenic patient. *The Gestalt Journal*, IV-1: 29–47.

Gagnon, J. H. (1993). Compte-rendu de la table ronde sur la Gestalt et la psychothérapie de long terme. *Revue Québécoise de Gestalt*, 1–2.

Gedo, J. E. (1986). *Conceptual Issues in Psychoanalysis: Essays in History and Method*. Hillsdale, NJ: Analytic Press.

Gelso, C. J. & Carter, J. A. (1985). The relationship in counseling and psychotherapy: Components, consequences and theoretical antecedents. *The Counseling Psychologist*, 13: 155–243.

Gendlin, E. T. (1978). *Focusing*. New York: Everett House.

Gergen, K. (1982). *Toward a Transformation in Social Knowledge*. New York: Springer-Verlage.

Gergen, K. J. (1989). Social sychology and the wrong revolution. *European Journal of Social Psychology*, 19: 463–484.

Giesen-Bloo, et al. (2006). Outpatient psychotherapy for BPD. *Arch Gen Psychiatry*, 63: 649–658.

Gilbertson, M. W., Shenton, M. E., Ciszewski, A., et al. (2002). Smaller hippocampal volume predicts pathologic vulnerability to psychological trauma. *Nature Neuroscience, 5*: 1242–1247.
Ginger, S. (1984). L'imaginaire en Gestalt thérapie. *Etudes Psychotherapiques, 15*: 99–106.
Ginger, S. (1987). *La Gestalt. Une thérapie du contact*. Paris: Hommes et Groupes.
Ginger, S. (1992). Le corps en Gestalt: Corps interdits ou inter-dits? *Revue Québécoise de Gestalt, 1*: 79–90.
Goldfried, M. R. (1980). Toward the delineation of therapeutic change principles. *American Psychologist, 35*: 991–999.
Goldfried, M. R. (1982b). *Converging Themes in Psychotherapy*. New York: Springer.
Goldfried, M. R. (1987). Rapprochement en psychothérapie: historique, état de la situation et perspectives d'avenir. In: *Rapprochement et intégration en psychothérapie*. Chicoutimi: Gaétan Morin.
Goldstein, W. N. (1991). Clarification of Projective Identification. *American Journal of Psychiatry, 148*: 153–161.
Goodman, G. & Timko, M. G. (1976). Hot seats and aggressive behavior. *Academic Therapy, 11*: 447–448.
Goodman, P. (1945a). The political meaning of some recent revisions of Freud. In: *Nature heals: Psychological essays*. The Gestalt Journal Publications, 1977.
Goodman, P. (1945b). The father of the psychoanalytic movement. In: *Nature heals. Psychological essays*. The Gestalt Journal Publications, 1977.
Goodman, P. (1991). *Nature Heals: The psychological essays of Paul Goodman*. The Gestalt Journal Publications.
Gottfredson, L. S. (1983). Creating and criticizing theory. *Journal of Vocational Behavior, 23*: 203–212.
Granger, L. (1994). Les limites de la méthode expérimentale en psychologie sociale et clinique. *Psychologie Canadienne, 35*, No. 1: 1–10.
Greenberg, E. (1989). Healing the borderline. *Gestalt Journal, 12*: 11–55.
Greenberg, J. R. & Mitchell, S. A. (1983). *Object Relations in Psychoanalytic Theory*. Cambridge: Harvard University Press.
Greenberg, L. S. (1980). The intensive analysis of recurring events from the practice of Gestalt therapy. *Psychotherapy Theory, Research and Practice, 17*: 143–152.
Greenberg, L. S. (1983). Toward a task analysis of conflict resolution in Gestalt therapy. *Psychotherapy Theory, Research and Practice, 20*: 190–201.
Greenberg, L. S. & Higgins, H. M. (1980). Effects of two chair dialogue and focusing on conflict resolution. *Journal of Counseling Psychology, 27*: 221–224.

Greenberg, L. S. & Kahn, S. E. (1978). Experimentation: A Gestalt approach to counselling. *Canadian Counsellor, 13*(1).

Grotstein, J. S. (1991). An American view of the British psychoanalytic experience III: The British object relations school. *Journal of Melanie Klein and Object Relations, 9*: 34–62.

Grotstein, J. S. (1994). Notes on Fairbairn's metapsychology. In: *Fairbairn and the Origins of Object Relations*. New York: The Guilford Press.

Grotstein, J. S. & Rinsley, D. B. (1994). *Fairbairn and the Origins of Object Relations*. New York: The Guilford Press. Guntrip, H. (1971). *Psychoanalytic Theory, Therapy and the Self*. New York: Basic Books.

Gurvits, T. V., Shenton, M. E., Hokama, H., et al. (1996). Magnetic resonance imaging study of hippocampal volume in chronic, combat-related post-traumatic stress disorder. *Biological Psychiatry, 40*: 1091–1099.

Hall, C. S. & Lindszey, G. (1957; 1970; 1985). *Theories of Personality*. New York: John Wiley.

Hebb, D. O. (1949). *Organization and Behavior*. New York: John Wiley.

Heinen, J. R. K. (1985). A primer on psychological theory. *The Journal of Psychology, 119*: 413–421.

Henle, M. (1978). Gestalt psychology and Gestalt therapy. *Journal of History of the Behavioral Sciences, 14*: 23–32.

Hietanen, J. K., Surrakka, V. & Linnankoski, I. (1998). Facial electromyographic responses to vocal affect expressions. *Psychophysiology, 35*: 530–536.

Himelstein, P. (1984). Dream symbol or dream process? *Psychology: A Quarterly Journal of Human Behavior, 21*: 1–9.

Howard, K. I., Moras, K., Brill, P. L., Martinovich, Z. & Lutz, W. (1996). Evaluation of psychotherapy: Efficacy, effectiveness, and patient progress. *American Psychologist, 51*: 1059–1064.

Hycner, R. (1985). An Interview with Erving and Miriam Polster. *Gestalt Journal, 10*: 27–66.

Jacoby, R. (1975). *Social Amnesia*. Boston: Beacon Press.

Juston, D. (1990). *Le transfert en psychanalyse et en Gestalt thérapie*. Lille: La boîte de Pandore. Kandel, E. R. (1979). Psychotherapy and the single synapse. *New England Journal of Medicine, 301*: 1028–1037.

Kandel, E. R. (1998). A new intellectual framework for psychiatry. *American Journal of Psychiatry, 155*: 457–469.

Kupfer, D. J., First, M. B. & Regier, D. A. (2002). *A Research Agenda for DSM-V*. New York: APA Press.

Kaplan, N. R. & Kaplan, M. L. (1978). The Gestalt approach to stuttering. *Journal of Communications Disorders, 11*: 1–9.

Katzeff, M. (1983). La Gestalt: Une thérapie par l'expérimentation et la mise en action. In: Actes du 1er Colloque de la SFG. Paris.

Kernberg, O. F. (1994). Fairbairn's theory and challenge. In: *Fairbairn and the Origins of Object Relations*. New York: The Guilford Press.
Klein, M. (1946): Notes on some schizoid mechanisms. *International Journal of Psychoanalysis, 33*: 433–438.
Klein, M. (1946). Notes on some schizoid mechanisms. *International Journal of Psychoanalysis, 27*: 99–110.
Klein, M. (1959). Our adult world and its roots in iInfancy. In: *Envy and Gratitude*. London: The Hogarth Press and The Institute of Psycho-Analysis.
Kohut, H. (1977). *The Restoration of the Self*. New York: International Universities Press.
Kohut, H. & Wolf, E. S. (1978). The Disorders of the Self and their Treatment: an Outline. *International Journal of Psychoanalysis, 59*: 413–425.
Kovel, J. (1976; 1991). *A Complete Guide to Therapy*. London: Penguin.
Krasner, L. (1978). The future and the past in the behaviorism-humanism dialogue. *American Psychologist, 33*: 799–804.
Kuhn, T. S. (1977). *The Essential Tension: Selected studies in scientific tradition and change*. Chicago: The University of Chicago Press.
Lambert, M. J. & Ogles, B. M. (2004). The efficacy and effectiveness of psychotherapy. In: M. Lambert (Ed.), *The Bergin and Garfield Handbook of Psychotherapy and Behavior Change* (5th ed.) (pp. 139–193). New York: John Wiley.
Lane, R. D. & Garfield, D. S. (2005). Becoming aware of feelings: Integration of cognitive-developmental, neuroscientific and psychoanalytic perspectives. *Neuro-Psychoanalysis, 7*: 5–30.
Langs, R. (1976). Therapeutic Misalliances. *International Journal of Psychoanalytic Psychotherapy, 4*: 77–105.
Langs, R. (1976). *The Bipersonal Field*. New York: Jason Aronson.
Laplanche, J. & Pontalis, J. B. (1988): *The Language of Psychoanalysis*. London: Karnac.
Lecomte, C. (2007). Pour une pratique de la psychothérapie éclairée par des principes validés empiriquement. Conférence présentée lors de la Journée de formation du 27 septembre, 2007. Ordre des Psychologues du Québec.
Lecomte, C., Savard, R., Drouin, M. -S. & Guillon, V. (2004). Qui sont les thérapeutes efficaces? Implications pour la formation en psychologie. *Revue Québécoise de psychologie, 25*: 73–102.
Lecomte, C. & Gastonguay, L. -G. (1987). *Rapprochement et intégration en psychothérapie*. Montréal: Gaëtan Morin Éditeur.
Lehky, S. R. (2000). Fine discrimination of faces can be performed rapidly. *Journal of Cognitive Neuroscience, 12*: 848–855.
Lewin, K. (1935). *A Dynamic Theory of Personality*. New York: McGraw-Hill.

Lewis, L. & Schilling, K. M. (1978). Gestalt concepts of ego boundary and responsibility. A critical review. *Psychotherapy Theory, Research and Practice, 15*: 272–276.
Lichtenstein, H. (1977). *The dilemma of Human Identity.* New York: Jason Aronson. Lieberz, K. (1989). Children at Risk for Schizoid Disorders. *Journal of Personality Disorders, 3*: 329–337.
Loftus, E. F., Milo, E. & Paddock, J. (1995). The accidental executioner: why psychotherapy must be informed by science. *Counseling Psychologist, 23*: 300–309.
Maddi, S. R. (1989). *Personality Theories: A Comparative Analysis* (Fifth Edition). Chicago: The Dorsey Press. Mahrer, A. R. (1978a). *Experiencing: A Humanistic Theory of Psychology and Psychiatry.* New York: Brunner/Mazel.
Mahrer, A. R. (1989). *The Integration of Psychotherapies.* New York: Human Sciences Press.
Maslow, A. H. (1967). A theory of metamotivation: The biological rooting of the value-life. *Journal of Humanistic Psychology, 7*: 93–127.
Masson, J. (1989). *Against Therapy.* London: Collins.
McLaughlin, J. T. (1991). Clinical and theoretical aspects of enactment. *Journal of American Psychoanalytical Association, 39*: 595–614.
McWilliams, N. (1994). *Psychoanalytic Diagnosis: Understanding Personality Structure in the Clinical Process.* New York: The Guilford Press.
Messer, S. B. & Winnokur, M. (1980). Some limits to the integration of psychoanalytic and behavior therapy. *American Psychologist, 35*: 421–435.
Messer, S. B. & Winnokur, M. (1984). Ways of knowing and visions of reality in psychoanalytic therapy and behavior therapy. In: *Psychoanalytic Therapy and Behavior Therapy, Is Integration Possible?* New York & London: Plenum Press.
Meyer, L. M. (1991). Using Gestalt therapy in the treatment of anorexia nervosa. *British Review of Bulimia and Anorexia Nervosa, 5*: 7–16.
Migone, P. (1995). Expressed emotion and projective identification: A bridge between psychiatric and psychoanalytic concepts? *Contemporary Psychoanalysis, 31*: 617– 640.
Miller, M. V. (1985). Some historical limitations of Gestalt therapy. *Gestalt Journal, 8*: 51–54.
Miller, M. V. (1988). Panel de clôture de la 10e Gestalt Conference. Montréal.
Miller, M. V. (1991). Introduction. In: *Gestalt Therapy Verbatim.* Highland, NY: The Gestalt Journal Publications. Millon, T. & Klerman, G. L. (1986). *Contemporary Directions in Psychopathology.* New York: The Guilford Press.
Mitchell, S. A. (1994). The origin and nature of the Object in the theories of Klein and Fairbairn. In: J. S. Grotstein & D. B. Rinsley (Eds.), *Fairbairn*

and the Origins of Object Relations. New York: The Guilford Press. Money-Kyrle, R. (1956). Normal counter-transference and some of its deviations. *International Journal of Psycho-analysis, 37*: 360–366.

Moore, B. P. & Fine, B. D. (1990). *Psychoanalytic Terms and Concepts*. New Haven: The American Psychoanalytic Association, Yale University Press.

Moscovitch, M. (1992). Memory and working with memory: A component process model based on modules and central systems. *Journal of Cognitive Neuroscience, 4*: 257–267.

Mosher, D. L. (1977). The Gestalt awareness expression cycle as a model for sex therapy. *Journal of Sex and Marital Therapy, 3*: 229–242.

Mosher, D. L. (1979a). Awareness in Gestalt sex therapy. *Journal of Sex and Marital Therapy, 5*: 41–56.

Mosher, D. L. (1979b). The Gestalt experiment in sex therapy. *Journal of Sex and Marital Therapy, 5*: 117–133.

Nathan, P. E. & Gorman, J. M. (Eds.) (2002). *A Guide to Treatments That Work*. New York: Oxford University Press.

Nevis, S. M. (1985). Bringing the background into the foreground. *Gestalt Journal, 8*: 61–64.

Norcross, J. C. & Goldfried, M. R. (1992). *Handbook of Psychotherapy Integration*. New York: Basic Books.

Norcross, J. C. (1991). Prescriptive matching in psychotherapy. Psychoanalysis for simple phobias? *Psychotherapy, 28*: 439–443.

Norcross, J. C. (2002). *Psychotherapy Relationships That Work: Therapist Contributions and Responsiveness to Patients*. New York: Oxford University Press.

Norcross, J. C. & Lambert, M. J. (2006). The therapy relationship. In: J. C. Norcross, L. E. Beutler & R. L. Levant (Eds.), *Evidence-based Practices in Mental Health. Debate and Dialogue on the Fundamental Questions* (pp. 208–218). Washington, DC: American Psychological Association.

Norcross, J. C., Beutler, L. E. & Levant, R. F. (Eds.) (2006). *Evidence-based Practices in Mental Health. Debate and Dialogue on the Fundamental Questions*. Washington, DC: American Psychological Association.

Norcross, J. C. & Newman, C. F. (1992). Psychotherapy integration: Setting the context. In: J. C. Norcross & M. R. Goldfried, *Handbook of Psychotherapy Integration*. New York: Basic Books.

Norcross, J. C. & Goldfried, M. R. (1992). *Handbook of Psychotherapy Integration*. New York: Basic Books.

Ogden, T. G. (1979). On Projective Identification. *International Journal of Psychoanalysis, 60*: 357–373.

Ogden, T. G. (1982). *Projective Identification and Psychotherapeutic Technique*. New York: Jason Aronson.

Ogden, T. G. (1994). The concept of internal Object Relations. In: J. S. Grotstein & D. B. Rinsley (Eds.), *Fairbairn and the Origins of Object Relations*. New York: The Guilford Press. Oldham, J. M. & Morris, L. B. (1989). *The Personality Self-Portrait*. New York: Bantam Books.

Olinick, S., Poland, W. S., Grigg, K. A. & Granatir, W. L. (1973). The psychoanalytic work ego: Process and interpretation. *International Journal of Psycho-Analysis, 34*: 313–324.

Olivier, C. (1994). *Les fils d'Oreste ou la place du père*. Paris: Flammarion.

Panksepp, J. (1998). *Affective Neuroscience: the Foundations of Human and Animal Emotions*. New York: Oxford University Press.

Paris, J., Frank, H., Buonvino, M. & Bond, M. (1991). Recollection of Prental Behavior in Axis II Cluster Diagnosis. *Journal of Personality Disorders, 5*: 102–106.

Park, L. C. & Park, T. (1997). Personal Intelligence. In: M. McCallum & W. E. Piper, *Psychological Mindedness: A Contemporary Understanding* (pp. 133–167). Mahwah, NJ: Erlbaum.

Pearce, M. (1988). Eclecticism & hypnosis in the treatment of weight control. A case study. *Australian Journal of Clinical Hypnotherapy and Hypnosis, 9*: 9–11.

Perls, F. S. (1942, 1947, 1969). *Ego, Hunger, and Agression*. New York: Vintage Books.

Perls, F. S. (1969, 1978). *Gestalt Therapy Verbatim*. Gouldsboro, ME, The Gestalt Journal Press.

Perls, F. S. (1969a). *In and Out of the Garbage Pail*. Lafayette: Real People Press.

Perls, F. S., Hefferline, R. & Goodman, P. (1951). *Gestalt Therapy. Excitement and Growth in the Human Personality*. New York: Julian Press. Perls, F. S., Hefferline, R. & Goodman, P. (1979). *Gestalt Thérapie. Vers une théorie du Self. Nouveauté excitation et croissance*. Montréal: Stanké.

Perls, F. S. (1979). Planned Psychotherapy. *Gestalt Journal, 2*: 5–23. (Communication au William Alanson White Institute, New York, 1946.)

Perls, L. (1993). *Vivre à la frontière*. Montréal: Les Éditions du Reflet.

Pervin, L. (1990). *Personality: Theory, Assessment and Research*. New York: John Wiley.

Peterson, R. L. (1977). Choice, responsibility, causality, and psychotherapy. *Psychotherapy Theory, Research and Practice, 14*: 106–119.

Petit, M. (1984). *La Gestalt: thérapie de l'Ici et Maintenant*. Paris: ESF.

Pine, F. (1988). The four psychologies of psychoanalysis and their place in clinical work. *JAPA, 36*: 571–596.

Pollak, S. D. & Kistler, D. J. (2002). Early experience is associated with the development of categorical representations for facial expressions of emotion. *Proceedings of the National Academy of Science of the United States of America, 99*: 9072–9076.

Polster, E. & Polster, M. (1973). *Gestalt Therapy Integrated*. New York: Brunner/Mazel.

Polster, E. & Polster, M. (1983). *La Gestalt, nouvelles perspectives théoriques et choix personnels et éducatifs*. Montréal: Le Jour.

Polster, E. (1985). Imprisoned in the present. *The Gestalt Journal, 8*: 5–22.

Polster, E. (1987). *Every Person's Life is Worth a Novel*. New York: Norton.

Polster, E. (1988). Panel de clôture de la Gestalt Conference. Montréal.

Polster, E. (1995). *A Population of Selves: A Therapeutic Exploration of Personal Diversity*. San Francisco: Josey-Bass. Polster, M. (1987). An Interview with Erving and Miriam Polster, by R. Hycner. *Gestalt Journal, 10*: 27–66.

Pray, M. (1993). Analyzing defense: Two different methods. *Journal of Clinical Psycho-Analysis, 3*: 87–126.

Reichenbach, H. (1953). *The Rise of Scientific Philosophy*. Berkeley: University of California Press. Rennie, D. L., Phillips, J. R. & Quartaro, G. K. (1988). Grounded theory: A promising approach to conceptualization in psychology. *Canadian Psychology, 29*: 139–149.

Resnick, R. (1995). Gestalt Therapy: Principles, prisms and perspectives. *British Gestalt Journal, 4*: 3–13.

Ricoeur, P. (1965). *De l'interprétation. Essai sur Freud*. Paris: Seuil.

Robbins, M. (1980). Current controversy in object relations theory as outgrowth of a schism between Klein and Fairbairn. *International Journal of Psycho-Analysis, 61*: 477–492.

Robbins, M. (1996). The mental organization of primitive personalities and its treatment implications. *Journal of the American Psychoanalytical Association, 3*: 755–784.

Robine, J. M. (1991). Revue des livres. *Gestalt*, SFG, 2.

Robine, J. M. (1994). *La Gestalt thérapie*. Paris: Éditions Morisset. Rosenblatt, D. (1995). In opposition to "neo-Gestalt": Critical reflections on present day trends in Gestalt Therapy. *British Gestalt Journal, 4*: 47–49.

Rotenberg, V. S. (1995). Right hemisphere insufficiency and illness in the context of search activity concept. *Dynamic Psychiatry*, 150/151.

Rubens, R. L. (1984). The meaning of structure in Fairbairn. *International Review of Psycho-Analysis, 11*: 429–440.

Rubens, R. L. (1994). Fairbairn's structural theory. In: J. S. Grotstein & D. B. Rinsley, *Fairbairn and the Origins of Object Relations*. New York: The Guilford Press. Rychlak, J. F. (1977). *The Psychology of Rigorous Humanism*. New York: John Wiley.

Rychlak, J. F. (1988). The Psychology of Rigorous Humanism (2nd edition). New York: John Wiley and Sons.

Rychlak, J. F. (1993). A suggested principle of complementarity for psychology: In theory, not method. *American Psychologist, 48*: 933–942.

Saner, R. (1984). Culture bias of Gestalt therapy made in USA. *Gestalt Theory, 6*: 158–170.
Schacht, T. E. (1984). The varieties of integrative experience. In: H. Arkowitz & S. B. Messer (Eds.), *Psychoanalytic Therapy and Behavior Therapy: Is Integration Possible?* New York: Plenum. Schore, A. N. (1997). Early organization of the nonlinear right brain and development of a predisposition to psychiatric disorders. *Development and Psychopathology, 9*: 595–631.
Schore, A. N. (2003). *Affect Regulation and the Disorders of the Self.* New York:Norton.
Schore, A. N. (2003a). *Affect Regulation and the Repair of the Self.* New York: Norton.
Secord, P. (1982). *Explaining Human Behavior.* Beverley Hills: Sage. Serok, S. & Zemet, R. M. (1983). An experiment of Gestalt group therapy with hospitalized schizophrenics. *Psychotherapy Theory, Research and Practice, 20*: 417–424.
Shear, M. K., Fyer, A. J. & Ball, G. (1991). Vulnerability to sodium lactate in panic disorder patients given cognitive-behavioral therapy. *American Journal of Psychiatry, 148*: 795–797.
Shterenshis, M. V. (1999). The position of nervous diseases between internal and psychiatry in the XIXth Century. *Vesalius, 5*: (1999).
Siegel, J. (1999). *The Developing Mind.* New York: Guilford.
Solms, M. & Turnbull, O. (2002). *The Brain and the Inner World.* New York: Other Press.
Silverman, D. K. (1981). Some proposed modifications of psychoanalytic theories of early childhood development. In: J. Masling (Ed.), *Empirical Studies of Psychoanalytic Theory.* Hillsdale, NJ: The Analytic Press (1986).
Silverman, D. K. (1984). New perspectives on development and their implications for psychoanalytic treatment. *Psychoanalytic Psychology, 1*: 257–267.
Silverman, D. K. (1986). A multi model approach. Looking at clinical data from three theoretical perspectives. *Psychoanalytic Psychology, 3*: 121–132.
Simkin, J. S. (1978). Gestalt therapy and the psychological abstracts. *American Psychologist, 33*: 705–706.
Skolnik, T. (1987). What do we call survival? Re-Structuring the Gestalt therapy position in your mind. *The Gestalt Journal, 10*: 5–27.
Staemmler, F. M. (1993). Projective identification in Gestalt therapy with severely disturbed patients. *British Gestalt Journal, 2*: 104–110.
Stark, M. (1999). *Modes of Therapeutic Action: Enhancement of Knowledge, Provision of Experience, and Engagement in Relationship.* New York: Jason Aronson. Stenberg, G., Wiking, S. & Dahl, M. (1998). Judging words at

face value: Interference in word processing reveals automatic processing of affective facial simuli. *Cognition and Emotion*, 12: 755–782.

Stern, D. (1985). *The Interpersonal World of the Infant: A View from Psychoanalysis and Development Psychology*. New York: Basic Books.

Stoehr, T. (1992). Introduction aux essais psychologiques de Paul Goodman. *Gestalt, 3*.

Stoehr, T. (1994). *Here, Now, Next. Paul Goodman and the Origins of Gestalt Therapy*. San Francisco: Josey-Bass. Sullivan, H. S. (1950a). The illusion of personal individuality. In: *The Fusion of Psychiatry and Social Science*. New York: Norton, 1964. Sutherland, J. D. (1994). Fairbairn's achievement. In: J. S. Grotstein & R. B. Rinsley (Eds.), *Fairbairn and the Origins of Object Relations*. New York: The Guilford Press. Sykes-Picot, M. & Simon, R. (2004). Discoveries from the Black Box. How the neuroscience revolution can change your practice. *Psychotherapy Networker*, Sept-Oct.

Tansey, M. J. & Burke, W. F. (1989). *Understanding Countertransference*. Hillsdale, NJ: The Analytic Press. Thines, G. & Lempereur, A. (1975). *Dictionnaire général des sciences humaines*. Paris: Éditions Universitaires.

Tobin, S. A. (1982). Self-disorders, Gestalt therapy and Self psychology. *Gestalt Journal*, 5: 3–44.

Tobin, S. A. (1983). Gestalt therapy and the Self: Reply to Yontef. *Gestalt Journal*, 6: 71–90.

Tobin, S. A. (1985). Lacks and shortcomings in Gestalt therapy. *Gestalt Journal*, 8: 65–71.

Tobin, S. A. (1990). Self psychology as a bridge between existential-humanistic psychology and psychoanalysis. *Journal of Humanistic Psychology*, 30: 14–63.

Tyrer, P. (1995). Are personality disorders well classified in DSM-IV? In: W. J. Livesley (Ed.), *The DSM-IV Personality Disorders* (pp. 29–44). New York: The Guilford Press. Tzeng, O. C. S. & Jackson, J. W. (1990). Common methodological framework for theory construction and evaluation in the social and behavioral sciences. *Genetic, Social and General Psychology Monographs*, 51–76.

Viinamäki, H., Kuikka, J., Tiihonen, J., et al. (1998). Change in monoamine transporter density related to clinical recovery: a case—control study. *Nordic Journal of Psychiatry*, 52: 39–44.

Vurpillot, E. (1992). *Grand Dictionnaire de la Psychologie* (Bloch et al. Eds.). Paris: Larousse. Wachtel, P. L. (1977). *Psychoanalysis and Behavior Therapy: Toward an Integration*. New York: Basic Books.

Wachtel, P. L. (1984). On theory, practice and the nature of integration. In: H. Arkowitz & S. P. Messer (Eds.), *Psychoanalytic Therapy and Behavior*

Therapy: Is Integration Possible? New York & London: Plenum Press.
Wachtel, P. L. (1987). *Action and Insight.* New York: Guilford.
Wagner, A. W. & Linehan, M. M. (1994). Relationship between childhood sexual abuse and topography of parasuicide among women with borderline personality disorder. *Journal of Personality Disorders, 8*: 1–10.
Walters, C. E. (1976). *Mother/infant interaction.* New York: Human Sciences Press.
Wampold, B. E. (2001). *The Great Ppsychotherapy Ddebate: Models, Methods and Findings.* Mahwah, NJ: Erlbaum.
Wampold, B. E. (2006). The psychotherapist. In: J. C. Norcross, L. E. Beutler & R. L. Levant (Eds.), *Evidence-based Practices in Mental Health. Debate and Dialogue on the Fundamental Questions* (pp. 200–208). Washington, DC: American Psychological Association.
Welt, S. R. & Herron, W. G. (1990). *Narcissism and the Psychotherapist.* New York: The Guilford Press. Welwood, J. (1982). The unfolding of experience: Psychotherapy and beyond. *Journal of Humanistic Psychology, 22*: 91–104.
Wertheimer, M. (1925). Gestalt theory. In: W. Ellis (Ed.), *A Source Book of Gestalt Psychology.* London: Kegan Paul, 1938.
Westeon, D. I. (2006). Transporting laboratory-validated treatment to the community will not necessarily produce better outcomes. In: J. C. Norcross, L. E. Beutler & R. L. Levant (Eds.), *Evidence-based Practices in Mental Health. Debate and Dialogue on the Fundamental Questions* (pp. 383–392). Washington, DC: American Psychological Association.
Wheeler, G. (1991). *Gestalt Reconsidered.* Cleveland: Gestalt Institute of Cleveland Press
Wheeler, G. (1998). Towards a Gestalt developmental model. *British Gestalt Journal, 7*: 115–125.
Winnicott, D. W. (1942). Review of the nursing couple». *International Journal of Psychoanalysis, 23*: 179–181.
Wysong, J. (1992). Communication personnelle, dans le cadre de la traduction et de la publication de l'ouvrage de Laura Perls: *Living at the Boundary.*
Wysong, J. & Rosenfeld, E. (1982). *An Oral History of Gestalt Therapy. Interviews with Laura Perls, Isadore From, Erving Polster, Miriam Polster.* Highland, NY: The Gestalt Journal Publications. Yontef, G. (1983). The Self in Gestalt therapy: Reply to Tobin. *Gestalt Journal, 6*: 55–70.
Yontef, G. M. (1988). Assimilating diagnostic and psychoanalytic perspectives into Gestalt therapy. *Gestalt Journal, 11*: 5–32.
Yontef, G. M. (1988b). Panel de clôture de la 10e Gestalt Conference. Montréal.

Yontef, G. M. (1993). *Awareness, dialogue and process*. Highland, NY: The Gestalt Journal Publications. Zarcone, V. (1984). Gestalt techniques in a therapeutic community for the treatment of addicts. *Journal of Psychoactive Drugs, 16*: 43–46.

Zazzo, R. (1988). *Où en est la psychologie de l'enfant?* Paris: Gallimard. Zinker, J. (1977). *Creative Process in Gestalt Therapy*. New York: Random House.

INDEX

affective
    abilities 158
    contagion 141
    neurosciences 135
affect-reflexive interaction 144
affect regulation 135–137, 146–147
    critical developmental process 135–136
    reparatory function 139–141
    therapeutic relationship 136–139
alcoholism 4
ambivalence and anxiety 43
American conformity, social-political critique 6
American Gestalt therapists 5
American Psychiatric Association 90
anamnesis 93, 211–219
anthropomorphic reflex 57
antilibidinal ego 45, 48, 82
anxiety disorder 219

attention deficit disorder (ADD) 180–181
avoidance mechanisms 63
awareness-contact functions 196
awareness of immediate somatic experience 120–121

Benjamin, L. S. 157
Beutler, Larry, E. 150, 156–157, 162
Binge eating disorder 216, 219
borderline personalities 7
Bouchard, M. A. xiv, 5, 7–8, 15, 27–28, 36, 41, 43–44, 46–47, 49, 68, 71, 77–80, 116, 119, 121
Bracke, P. E. 19
brain in third milennium 127–128
Brentano sense 21
Brian
    acting-out behaviour 196
    adulthood 194
    antidepressant medication 206

capacity 196
cold turkey 206
intrapsychic dynamic 209
matrix of field representation (MFR) 199–200
narcissistic extensions 204
narcissistic personality disorder 194, 200
perception of a potential manipulativeness 209
self 204
traumatic events 201
Bruner, J. S. 132
Buberian existentialism 27
Bugental, J. F. T. 19
Burke, W. F. 85, 122, 137

Canadian Foundation of Health Service Research 152
Canadian Gestalt therapists 5
case studies
  Bob 167
  Brian 189
  Dandeneau, Michel 167
  Jade 211
  Scicluna, Dorothy 211
Cashdan, S.
  synthesis 5
Castonguay, Louis-Georges xiii, 150, 156–157, 162
central ego 44–45, 82
character neuroses 91
client-related therapeutic principles 157
client's
  disorganisation 138
  negative affect 142
cognitive neuroscience 131
cognitive-behavioural
  therapy 154
  treatments 153
coherent emotional expression 160
coherent global theory 5

co-morbidity 154, 156
conceptual convergence 126
confluence 7, 55, 62, 83–87, 139, 171, 226, 241
  reformulation 85
consciousness xiv, 4, 6, 9, 21, 50–51, 55–56, 63, 65–67, 69–72, 74–76, 78–80, 88, 90, 95, 97–100, 104, 107, 110–112, 116–117, 120, 123, 131–135, 141, 148, 191, 196
  continuum of 120
  embryonic 67
  ordinary 98
  theory of 71
contact 70
  between emotions and cognition 130
  boundary and therapeutic relationship 134–142
  boundary regulatory strategy 138
  cycles 113, 118
  dilemma 97–99, 133, 137, 174, 176, 196, 198
  full contact 118
  healing 230
  impasses 235
  Jade's functions 221
  post-contact 70, 118
  pre-contact 118
  reactivation of dilemma 205–206
  regulation modalities 208
  regulation modes 84
contagious affect 137
contemporary neurocognitive science 134
contemporary psychopathology xiv, 93, 109
convergence neuropsychotherapy 127
counter schizoid withdrawal 4
counter-transference effect 200
counter-transferential/corporal process 144
Cozolino, L. xv, 129, 145

creative indifference 108, 117, 119
Critchfield, K. L. 157
critical developmental process 135–136
cyclical psychodynamics 23

Damasio, A. R. 128, 135
Dandenault, Michel 165, 167
Dandeneau, Michel 167, 186
defensive functions 87–88, 198
deflection reformulation 87–88
Delisle, G. xiii, 7, 63, 84, 93, 109, 137–138, 140, 147, 149, 157–159, 161, 170, 175, 221, 223, 226, 235, 241–242
dependent personality disorder 170
depression and personality disorders 151
depressive personality disorder 170
Derome, G. xiv–xv, 5, 7–8, 15, 28, 44, 46–47, 49, 68, 71, 121
Dollard, J. 16
dream-discussion 121
Driessen, M. 132
Drouin, Marc-Simon 149–150, 154, 159
DSM classification, trans-theoretical 108
dual motivations and processes 67

eating disorder 4, 216, 219, 230, 239
eclecticism, simple-minded 8, 16
ego 3, 6, 8, 17, 22, 28, 30, 33, 36, 38, 40–45, 47–48, 51, 56, 62–63, 68, 71, 73, 76–85, 88–89, 94–97, 99, 106, 110–111, 120–122, 128, 171, 173–174, 182–183, 186, 198, 201, 208
  action of 80, 106
  at contact boundary 84
  defensive operations 79
  formation 89
  ideal 182
ego functions 63, 68, 77, 83, 85, 99, 111, 121, 171, 198, 201, 223–227, 241–242

neurotic mechanisms 83
  reformulation 78–79
  self 76
egotism 62, 83–84
electrophysiological activity 138
Elliot, R. 154
  meta-analysis of the effectiveness 151
Ellman, S. J. 139
emotional maturity 38
emotions
  facially-expressed 140
  negative 140
  psychophysiological communication 140
empathic attunement 145–146, 177
empathic-developmental response 144
empirically validated relational variables 155
empirically validated therapeutic principles 155–156
empirically validated treatments (EVT) 152–153
empty-chair technique 4
endo-psychic structure theory 18, 47
epistemological foundation 98
exciting object 44–45, 82
existential-humanist theory 56
experiential fields 96, 101, 112–116, 118, 197, 221, 234–235
  from here and now to there and then 235–239
external field 82, 86–87, 103, 111, 114–115, 118
eyewitnesses 12
Eysenck, H. J. 69, 151

Fairbairn, W. R. D.
  antilibidinal ego 82, 89
  central self 77
  clinical experience 73
  comparison with Perls 51

concept of structure 70
defensive technique 91
development of pathology 35
ego 43
ego-splitting 48
endopsychic structure theory xiv, 24, 27, 74
expel the demons 123
forgive sins 123
infantile dependency to maturity 36
internalisation in theory of 46
intra-psychic theory 20
Lamarckianism 30
libidinal ego 45, 89
motivation theory 33
object relation model of development 36
position 29–31, 33–38, 43, 73
position on dreams 49
psychoanalytical epistemology 73
sense 48
Socius 21
theory of internalised objects 40
theory of object relations xiv
theory of personality 5
thinking on structure 50
"tragic-realist" vision of 17
trilogy Central Ego-Antilibidinal Ego-Libidinal Ego 43
universal-existential generalisation 73
Federal Drug Administration (FDA) 150
Fensterheim, H. 16
Feyerabend, P. K. 11
field dynamics 34, 42, 98
field theory 6, 31, 41, 46, 49, 66–67, 83, 104, 114
configuration 81
metapsychological view 68
modes of regulation and interaction 82–88
Fine, B. D. 29, 44–45, 68–70, 73
First, M. B. 127
flesh-and-blood interlocutor 123
fluoxetine 129
Freud, S. 17, 27, 30, 32–33, 36, 41, 45, 71, 126, 128, 134, 182, 187, 208
concept of mourning 208
free-floating attention 134
notion of the superego 36
superego 45
Freudian
"death instinct" 45
connotations 41
model 62
notion of "libido" 33
sense 40
superego 182, 187
theory of consciousness 6
thinking 6
trilogy of Id-Ego-Superego 43
view of the psyche 6
Fries, P. 129–130
From, Isadore xiii–xiv, 4, 7–8, 15, 24–25, 121
functional-deductive
epistemology 12, 18
sense 12

Garfield, S. L. 3, 133, 135
generalized anxiety disorder 219
Gergen, K. 11
Gergen, K. J. 21
Gestalt conception of internalisation 68
Gestalt conceptual structure 28
Gestalt dream 4, 121
analysis techniques 4
Gestalt object relations psychotherapy, theory xiv
Gestalt practice 22–23
Gestalt Prayer 39

INDEX   267

Gestalt psychoanalysis 19
Gestalt psychology 9, 72, 129
   mother-infant relationships 72
Gestalt psychotherapy xv, 58, 103–104, 112–113, 136
   conception of 112
   from object relations to hermeneutic dialogue 103
   global objective 58
   memories 136
Gestalt theorizing 68
   internalisation and representation 68–76
   Kleinians 68
Gestalt theory 5, 7–9, 17, 20, 24–25, 28, 50, 55–56, 58, 65, 75, 85, 89–91, 103, 109, 166
   of development 20
Gestalt therapeutic interventions 119, 161
Gestalt therapy
   classical 89
   contemporary 94
   development in 89–91
   elaboration of 7
   integration of psychoanalytic concepts 57–59
   language 134
   mother-infant relationships 72
   neurotic interruption of contact 70
   "Perlsian" version 39
   personality disorder 91–97
   psychotherapy of introjected field 103
   specific concrete procedures 120–124
   techniques 4, 123
   theoretical foundations of 15
   theoretical structures 4
   theory of self 49, 61, 89
Gestalt therapy and contemporary psychoanalysis 5

Gestalt therapy theory 49
   motivation 32
   self 37, 39
Gestalt therapy's theory of human nature 33, 56
Gestalt thinking 19, 46, 55, 76
Gilbertson, M. W. 132
Ginger, S. 4, 63, 76
Goldstein, W. N. 86
Goodman, Paul xiv
   hedonistic picture of self 39
   linear-sequential vision of self 61
   self and object relations 65
   theory of the self 3, 15, 27, 41
Granger, L. 11
Greenberg, L. S. 24, 27, 33–34, 49, 55
Grotstein, J. S. 19
group psychotherapy programme 216, 230

Hefferline, R. xiv, 5, 15, 32, 55, 65, 97
   linear-sequential vision of self 61
   self and object relations 65
   theory of the self 3, 15, 27, 41
here-and-now 108, 113, 147
   experience 4, 113–116, 236–239
   micro-perspective 31
   relationship 4
here and then 113–115, 235–236, 238
   experience 115
hermeneutic and reparatory function 144
hermeneutic dialogue 103, 112–113, 116–119, 133, 138, 147–149, 155, 159, 179–181, 204
   cognitive-affective-behavioural schemas 133
   neurotherapeutic functions 133–134
hermeneutic interaction 117
hermeneutic relationship 117

human nature theory 18
  Gestalt vision of 19
hyperactivation 136–137, 209
hyperactivation/despair 137
hyperactivation/dissociation 137
hypoactive sexual desire disorder 219

Id function 41, 51, 77, 79, 91, 106, 196–198
infantile dependency 36, 51, 55, 89, 92
interactive co-regulation 140
internal saboteur (IS) 45
International Congress of Psychoanalysis 33
International Neuropsychoanalysis Society 126
interpersonal life of reciprocity 39
inter-psychic communications and influences 130
intimate relationships 178, 180
intra-psychic conflicts 7
introjected field (IF) 58, 74–75, 77–79, 83, 86, 88, 94–97, 99–101, 103, 113–114, 116, 120–124, 196–198, 221, 227, 229, 235
  inferences concerning 173, 227–229
  psychotherapy 124
introjected micro-fields (IM) 74–75, 77–79, 81–82, 88, 96–97, 99–100, 107, 110–111, 114, 123, 132–133, 180, 184–185, 197, 201, 221, 223, 225, 229, 233–234, 236, 239
  dangerous nature of 123

Kandel, Eric 126, 128
Kernberg, O. F. 20, 33, 177
Kleinian concept of projective identification 134, 141
Klein, Melanie 20, 29, 33, 36, 69, 90, 136
  paranoid-schizoid 208
  projective identification 136
Kohut, H. 46–47, 120, 177, 208
  insights 90
  treatment of narcissistic disorders 208
Kuhn, T. S. 89
  human nature theory 24
Kupfer, D. J. 127

Lamarckianism 30
Lane, R. D. 133, 135
Langs, R. 85, 137
Laplanche, J. 68
Lewin, K. 6, 27
  dynamic field psychology 27
libidinal ego 43–45, 48, 82
Lichtenstein, H. 43
limbic conversation 144

Maddi, S. R. 3, 17, 19–20, 35
Mahrer, A. R. xiii, 18–19, 23, 56, 103–105, 110–112, 118, 124, 149
  coherent psychotherapeutic models 149
  components of a psychotherapeutic system 105
  model 18, 23
  sense 56, 103, 124
masochistic (self-defeating) personality disorder 170
matrix of field representations (MFR) 79, 81, 83, 85–86, 91, 94, 96–97, 100, 106, 110, 181, 186, 199–201, 208, 225, 227, 229, 236, 242
  Bob's 17, 23
  configurations 96, 172, 229, 232, 241
  covert 227
  general configuration 81
  Jade's 227, 238–239
  overt 227
maturation 67, 69–70, 101, 129, 143

mature cerebral cortex 135
memory
　autobiographical 146
　essential structures 132
　explicit 132
　implicit 131–132
　implicit procedural 138–139
　in psychopathology and
　　psychotherapy 130–133
　long-term 131, 133
　plasticity 132–133
　procedural 131
mental function profile 195
mental illness 90–91, 127, 156
　biologically-based 90
Messer, S. B. 23
meta-psychology 6
microcosms of field 74
Mitchell, S. A. 24, 27, 33–35, 49, 55
Money-Kyrle, R. 86
mood disorder 156, 169
Moore, B. P. 68–69
mother/infant interactions 135
mother-child interactions 67
multi-axial diagnosis 108, 165, 192–193, 219
multi-axial DSM diagnosis 169
　major depressive episode 169
　personality disorder, NOS 169–170

narcissistic
　injury 4
　personalities 7
　personality disorder 170, 192, 194
native anglophones 165
nature/nurture dichotomy 127
neo-psychanalytic theories 27
neuro-affective development 135
neuronal
　coherence 129–130
　connections 143, 145
　integrations 143
　plasticity 132, 143
neuro-psychoanalysis 128
neurotic defences 19, 92
neurotic splitting 68
newborn to adult life 35–49
Newtonian and pre-Newtonian thinking 57–58
non-verbal and unconscious interactions 141
non-verbal species-specific signals 138
Norcross, John C. xiii, 16, 18, 23, 155

objective-based treatment plan 161
object relational gestalt therapy (ORGT) 131, 140, 147–149, 151, 154–162, 227
　evidence-based practice 149
　experience and mastery 165
　fundamental goals of 133
　fundamental principles of 150
　model 149, 158
　optimal utilisation 160
　perspective of 134
obsessive compulsive personality disorder 219
OCPD 220, 224
oedipal dynamics 137
Ogden, T. G. 85, 137
optimal cortical processing 145
optimal neural functioning 146
optimal therapeutic interventions 144
optimal therapy 108
organism-environment field 27–28, 55
original ego 44–45

Panksepp, J. 128, 135
parasympathetic nervous system 137
passive-aggressive version 170
pathodynamic elements 125
pathological personality 106, 135

Perls, F. xiv
comparison with Fairbairn 51
conceptual systems relevant to 62
Ego, Humor and Aggression 3, 33
Gestalt therapy of 20
Gestalt Therapy Verbatim 3, 187
In and Out of the Garbage Pail 3
linear-sequential vision of self 61
Oral resistances 33
psychopathology 40
self and object relations 65
theory of self 3, 15, 27, 41–42
transmitting the theory 24
Pérodeau, Guilhème 165, 167, 189, 209
personality disorders xiv, 5, 80, 91, 94, 96, 104, 112–113, 141, 151, 156–157, 161–162, 192, 221–222
of contemporary psychology 93
psychotherapy of 132, 139
specific context of 157
thorny problems of xiii
through experiential dialogue 230–231
treatment 111
personality function of self 70, 81, 85, 89, 100
matrix of field representations (MFR) 81, 89
reformulation of personality function 80–82
personal psychotherapy 161
personal responsibility 58
personality
conceptualization 28
disorders and mental retardation 219
disturbance 47, 108, 110, 132, 154, 156, 162
function 40, 70, 79–81, 85, 89, 95, 97, 99–100, 111, 141, 172, 199, 241
pathologies 159, 162
patterns and disorders 194

therapy 123
Phillips, J. 11
Physikos-Bios 22
polarities 112, 120, 122–124, 187
Polster, E. 57, 67, 76, 81, 84
Pontalis. J. B. 68
positive perception of client 159
post-Newtonian scientific thinking 30
post-traumatic stress 4
pre-conscious and unconscious internal world 44
projective identification 85–86, 134, 136–137, 141, 144, 147, 174, 176–177, 194–195, 209
prosodic communication 139, 144
prosodic rhythm 139
psychic defences 139
psychic energy 140
psychic experience 147
psychoanalytic concepts 57–59, 86
psychoanalytic theory of object relations xiv, 81
psychoanalytical
object relations theorists 15
thinkers 69
psychobiological response 136
Psychodynamic Diagnostic Manual (PDM) 169–170, 187, 194, 209
as hypervigilant narcissist 194
paranoid traits 194
psychodynamic therapy 129
psychodynamic tradition 4
psycho-immunitary protection 76
psychological-mindedness 196
psychology, theorising and knowledge 11
psycho-nutritive elements 76
psychopathology xiv, 7, 30–31, 38, 40, 47, 83, 91, 93, 101, 109, 130, 145
memory in 130–133
psychopharmacologic intervention works 126

psychophysiological self 69
psycho-social conflict 20
psychotherapeutic level 19
psychotherapeutic system, 150
    Mahrer's components 105
psychotherapy
    contextual model of 155
    effectiveness of 151
    functional mechanisms of 125
    hermeneutic dialogue 119
    hermeneutic success in 119
    ingredients of 152
    integration 15–17
    manual 105
    neuropsychotherapeutic
        overview 145
    optimal neuronal growth and
        integration 145–146
    permanent effects on brain 128
    symptom reproduction 166
    theory 18
psychotherapy and socio-political
    criticism 6
psychotic disorders, treatment 4

Quartaro, G. K. 11

rage and paranoia 203–204
randomized clinical trials (RCT) 153
reality of a choice 58
Regier, D. A. 127
regulatory response 142
rejecting object 44–45, 122
relational psychotherapy 132, 134
Rennie, D. L. 11
reparation 239
    neurodynamic aspects 142–145
reproduction-recognition-repair 113
reproduction-recognition-reparation
    117, 158
Resnick, R. 104, 114
result of a choice 58
retroflection reformulation 86–87

Ricoeur, P. 116
Robine, J. M. 28, 61, 63, 80, 109
Rosenblatt, D. 109
Rotenberg, V. S. 143
Rubens, R. L. 17, 33, 46–47, 70–72
Rychlak, J. F. 11, 21, 56

Schleprock, Badluck 171, 175, 187
Schore, Allan, N. xv, 136, 139, 141,
    143–144, 147, 208
    *Affect Regulation and the Repair of
    the Self* 147
    regulation of self 208
Scicluna, Dorothy 165, 211, 239
second world war 5
self and contact cycles 88–89
self and process of internalization
    development of 65–68
    non-structuring internalisations
        70–71
self-bounding processes 30
self-defeating behaviour 172, 181
self-environment differentiation 7
self, function/structure 170
self functioning 32
self healing 207
self identify 68
self in therapeutic dialogue,
    neurodynamics 125
self-objects
    differentiation 69
    embryonic representations 69
self-psychology 9
self-regulation 30
self structure of self 221–222
self theory xiv
sensory-motor capacities 65
serotonin metabolism 129
sexual behaviour 218, 228, 230
sexual disorders 4
sexual dysfunction 219
Silverman, D. K. 90
social phobia 219, 232

Société de l'Assurance Automobile du Québec (SAAQ) 197–198, 200, 202–206
  employees 195
  employees and professionals 200
  evaluation process 194
  financial settlement 205
space-time combinations 114
spatial-temporal "event" 6, 41, 66
spatio-temporal fields 106, 115
species-specific neurophysiological development 142
structuring internalisations 47, 75–76, 78–79, 95
subjective existential individualism 19
superego 17, 36–37, 43, 45, 182, 187
superiority 150–151, 153

Tansey, M. J. 85, 122
targeting change principles 161
therapeutic
  alliance 139, 141, 158, 201–202
  effectiveness and evidence 151–155
  goals 231–235
  programs 112
  relationship 106, 112–119, 122, 134, 136–140, 145, 158, 173, 231, 236–237, 242
  strategies, general 105, 112–119
  techniques, principles associated 157, 160
  universe, multi-dimensional 116
therapeutic change 105
  principles 111–112
therapist transparency principles 160–161
there and now experience 114–115, 238
there-and-then experience 113–116, 236–239

transference and countertransference
  dimension 138
  dynamics 5
transference relationship 117
traumatic relational field 137

unconscious emission, conceptualisation of 134
unconscious processes in pathology 5, 73, 140
unconscious psychic structure 75, 78, 99
unfinished developmental business 131, 197
unfinished situation (US) 29, 42, 71, 74–75, 77, 80, 82, 88–89, 97, 99–101, 112–113, 117–118, 120, 176, 196, 198, 205, 221, 229
unfolding of therapeutic process 175–177, 200–207
un-nuanced intensity 139
unusual conversation 138
usually-vigilant border guard 139

viscero-somatic experience 144

Wampold, B. E. 151, 154–156
Wertheimer, M. 72
Wheeler, G. 5, 15, 223
Winnicott, D. W. 135, 142
Winnokur, M. 18, 23
Wolf, E. S. 120

Yontef, G. M. 4, 7, 9, 15, 19, 31, 56–58, 91, 94–96
  formulation as vague 7
  integration of psychoanalytic concepts in gestalt therapy 57–59

Zinker, J. 76, 84